CAPTURING ★ ★ ★
HISTORY

BRIEF READINGS ON AMERICA
FROM DISCOVERY TO 1877

FIRST EDITION

By Ryan Jordan
University of San Diego

D1385351

 cognella® | ACADEMIC PUBLISHING

Bassim Hamadeh, CEO and Publisher
Kassie Graves, Director of Acquisitions and Sales
Jamie Giganti, Senior Managing Editor
Miguel Macias, Senior Graphic Designer
Seidy Cruz, Acquisitions Editor
Natalie Lakosil, Licensing Manager
Kaela Martin, Associate Editor
Berenice Quirino, Associate Production Editor

Printed in the United States of America

ISBN: 978-1-5165-2294-1 (pbk) / 978-1-5165-2295-8 (br)

★ CONTENTS
★
★

PREFACE   IX

CHAPTER 1: THE WORLD THE EUROPEANS ENCOUNTERED   1

Documents: 6

    1. Spanish Letter of Christopher Columbus to Luis de Sant' Angel ... (1493)

    2. Declaration Concerning the Indies from King Ferdinand of Spain (1510)

    3. Fray Bernardino de Sahagun, *General History of Things in New Spain* (1582)

    4. Bartolome de las Casas, *Very Brief Account of the Devastation of the Indies (1542)*

    5. From *The Conquest of New Spain, by Bernal Díaz,* in reference to Malinche (native American mistress to Cortés) (circa 1570)

    6. John Heckewelder, *Indian Tradition of the First Arrival of the Dutch on Manhattan Island in 1610* (1841)

    7. Richard Hakluyt, *A Discourse Concerning Western Planting* (1584)

Questions to Consider: 10

Credits   11

CHAPTER 2: THE RISE OF ENGLAND AND THE
COLONIZATION OF NORTH AMERICA   13

Documents: 18

    1. Excerpts from *Lawes Divine, Morall, and Martial* (1612, Jamestown, Virginia)

    2. Richard Frethorne, to His Mother and Father (March–April 1623), Jamestown, Virginia.

    3. George Alsop, *A Character of the Province of Maryland* (1666)

    4. The Mayflower Compact (1620)

    5. William Bradford, History of Plymouth Plantation (1642)

    6. John Winthrop, "A Model of Christian Charity" (1630)

    7. Excerpts of the Trial of Anne Hutchinson at Newton, Massachusetts (1637)

    8. Richard Ligon, *A True and Exact History of the Island of Barbadoes* (1657)

Questions to Consider: 24

Credits   24

CHAPTER 3: BRITISH NORTH AMERICA AND AN ATLANTIC ECONOMIC EMPIRE
25

Documents:
31

1. William Penn, *Some Account of the Province of Pennsylvania* (1681)
2. Declaration of Nathaniel Bacon in the Name of the People of Virginia (July 30, 1676)
3. John Easton, *A Relation of the Indian War ... 1675*
4. "Letter of Edward Randolph to the Board of Trade, discussing the colony of Carolina (1699)"
5. Thomas Mun, *England's Treasure by Foreign Trade* (1664)
6. John Locke, *Two Treatises of Government* (1689)
7. Alexander Falconbridge, *An Account of the Slave Trade on the Coast of Africa* (1788)
8. James Oglethorpe, Persons Reduced to Poverty May be Happy in Georgia (1732)
9. "Virginia Governor Alexander Spotswood Addresses the House of Burgesses (ca. 1715)"

Questions to Consider:
36

Credits
36

CHAPTER 4: ANGLICIZATION OR AMERICANIZATION? THE EIGHTEENTH-CENTURY COLONIES
37

Documents:
42

1. Gottlieb Mittelberger, "Journey to Pennsylvania in the Year 1750" (1898)
2. Jonathan Mayhew, "Discourse Concerning Unlimited Submission" (1750)
3. From Benjamin Franklin's autobiography (describing events between 1733 and 1750)
4. From Benjamin Franklin's autobiography (describing George Whitfield's preaching in 1739)
5. Benjamin Franklin, "Observations Concerning the Increase of Mankind" (1755)
6. Excerpts from the *Hamilton's Itinerarium: Being a Narrative of a Journey* (1744)
7. William Bull, "Report on the Stono Rebellion" (1739)
8. North Carolina Regulator Advertisement (January 1768)

Questions to Consider:
47

Credits
47

CHAPTER 5: TOWARD THE AMERICAN REVOLUTION, 1754–1775
49

Documents:
54

1. "The Commission of the Board of Trade" (1696)
2. Benjamin Franklin, *The Albany Plan of Union* (1754)
3. Reverend Thomas Barnard, "A Sermon Preached Before his Excellency Francis Bernard" (1763)
4. "From the Acts of the Privy Council (King's Advisers), regarding the Customs Service for the American Colonies" (1763)
5. Declarations of the Stamp Act Congress (1765), held in New York to protest the Stamp Act
6. John Dickinson, *Letters from a Farmer in Pennsylvania* (1768)
7. Charleston Merchants Propose a Plan of Nonimportation (1769)
8. John Adams, excerpts from his diary (December 17, 1773)
9. Parliament Debates the Coercive Acts" (1774)
10. Declaration and Resolves of the First Continental Congress (1774)

Questions to Consider:
60

Credits
61

Chapter 6: The American Revolution, 1775–1783 63

Documents: 68

    1. Thomas Paine, *Common Sense* (1776)

    2. Abigail Adams, from the *Adams Family Correspondence* (March, 1776)

    3. The Declaration of Independence (1776)

    4. "George Washington Asks the Continental Congress for an Effective Army" (1776)

    5. Oneida Indians Declare Neutrality (1775)

    6. Joseph Brant of the Mohawk Tribe to the British Secretary of State Lord Germain (1776)

    7. Lord Dunmore (John Murray) Promises Freedom to Slaves (1775)

    8. Lemuel Haynes, New England Mulatto, Attacks Slavery (1776)

    9. Benjamin Rush Contrasts Loyalists and Patriots (1777)

    10. Anonymous letter from Loyalists to the King (1782), printed in Hezekiah Niles's *Principles and Acts of the Revolution in America* (1822)

    11. Recollections of an Army Cook and Washerwoman (Sarah Osborn) of the Battle of Yorktown, Virginia (October 1781)

Questions to Consider: 75

Credits 75

Chapter 7: Forming a Government and Securing the Republic, 1783–1789 77

Documents: 82

    1. Congressman Charles Pinckney to the New Jersey Legislature (1786)

    2. Petition from the Town of Greenwich, Massachusetts, to the State Senate and House of Representatives (January 1786)

    3. Thomas Grover Petitions the Printer of the Hampshire Herald, on Behalf of the Massachusetts Regulators (1786)

    4. James Madison to George Washington, New York City (February 1787)

    5. James Madison to Edmund Pendleton, New York City (February 1787)

    6. *The Federalist Papers*, Number 10, Factions and Their Remedy, James Madison

    7. *The Federalist Papers*, Number 51, The System of Checks and Balances, James Madison and Alexander Hamilton

    8. *The Federalist Papers*, Number 69, A Defense of the Presidency, Alexander Hamilton

    9. Patrick Henry, Speech to the Virginia Ratifying Convention (1788)

    10. Amos Singletary, Speech before the Massachusetts Ratifying Convention (1788)

    11. Petition of North Carolina Blacks to Congress, from the Annals of Congress (January, 1797).

    12. Chickasaw Message to Congress (July 1783)

    13. Naturalization Act of 1790

Questions to Consider: 88

Credits 88

Chapter 8: The Ascendancy of the Federalists and the Crises of the 1790s 91

Documents: 95

    1. Alexander Hamilton on the Public Credit (1790)

    2. Alexander Hamilton, *Report on Manufacturers* (1791)

3. Thomas Jefferson *Notes on the State of Virginia* (1785)

4. From the Minutes of the Democratic Society of Pennsylvania, Civic Festival (May 1, 1794)

5. A Pennsylvania Democrat, Regarding the Whiskey Rebellion (1796)

6. George Washington, By the President of the United States of America, a Proclamation (1794)

7. Thomas Jefferson's Letter to Philip Mazzei (April 1796)

8. George Washington, Farewell Address (1796)

9. Thomas Jefferson, The Kentucky Resolutions (1798)

10. Joseph Brant, "Article in the American Museum" (1789)

Questions to Consider: 101
Credits   101

CHAPTER 9: JEFFERSONIAN AMERICA AND THE WAR OF 1812   103

Documents: 108

1. Thomas Jefferson's Inaugural Address (1801)

2. Thomas Jefferson, Annual Message to Congress (1808)

3. Resolutions of the Town of Beverly, Massachusetts (1809)

4. Tecumseh Confronts Governor William Henry Harrison (1810)

5. Felix Grundy, Speech in Congress (1811)

6. "The Congressional War Report" (1812)

7. Daniel Webster, Speech Before Congress Against the War (1812)

8. Resolutions of the Hartford Convention (1814)

9. Francis Scott Key, "The Star-Spangled Banner" (The Defense of Fort McHenry) (September 20, 1814)

10. Anonymous, The Hunters of Kentucky; or the Battle of New Orleans (undated, ca. 1816).

11. Nathaniel Appleton, *Introduction of the Power Loom; and Origin of Lowell* (1858)

12. James Monroe, First Inaugural Address (March 1817)

13. James Monroe, The Monroe Doctrine (1823)

Questions to Consider: 117
Credits   118

CHAPTER 10: THE RISE OF THE COTTON SOUTH, 1815–1860   119

Documents: 125

1. Andrew Jackson, Second Annual Message to Congress (1830)

2. Memorial of the Cherokee Nation (1830)

3. Solomon Northup Recalls Life Under Slavery (1853)

4. Harriet Jacobs, The Trials of Girlhood (1861)

5. David Walker, Appeal to the Colored Citizens of the World (1829)

6. From *The Confessions of Nat Turner, The Leader of the Late Insurrection in Southampton, VA* (1831)

7. A North Carolina Law Forbidding the Teaching of Slaves to Read and Write (1831)

8. James Henry Hammond Defends Slavery (1836)

9. George Fitzhugh, *Sociology for the South* (1854)

10. Mary Chestnut, Excerpts from Her Diary (1861)

11. General Manuel Mier y Terán, "Reports to His Superiors Regarding American Emigration in Texas" (1830)

Questions to Consider: 131
Credits   131

CHAPTER 11: THE MARKET REVOLUTION AND INDUSTRIALIZATION IN THE FREE STATES, 1815–1865   133

Documents: 137

1. "John Jacob Astor to Albert Gallatin" (March 14, 1818)
2. James Flint, "Letters from America," Indiana (May 4, 1820)
3. Thomas Skidmore, *The Rights of Man to Property* (1829)
4. Harriet Hanson Robinson, excerpts from *Loom and Spindle: Or, Life Among the Early Mill Girls (1890)*
5. Alonzo Potter, *The Political Economy: Its Objects, Uses, and Principles* (1841)
6. Catharine Beecher, *A Treatise on Domestic Economy ...* (1846)
7. Orestes Brownson, *The Laboring Classes* (1840)
8. British Cabinetmaker Describes Life in New York City *(1846)*
9. Gustaf Unonius, Letters from a Swedish Man (1841–1842)
10. George Templeton Strong (from New York City), Excerpts from his Diary (1838; 1857)
11. George Lawrence, *An Oration on the Abolition of the Slave Trade* (1813)

Questions to Consider: 144
Credits   144

CHAPTER 12: THE AGE OF JACKSON   145

Documents: 150

1. John C. Calhoun on the Tariff and Sectional Interests (1828)
2. Martin Van Buren to Thomas Ritchie (January 13, 1827)
3. Andrew Jackson's "Veto of the Maysville Road" (May 27, 1830)
4. Henry Clay's Speech in Support of the Maysville Road (1830)
5. Andrew Jackson's Veto Message Regarding the Bank, July 10, 1832.
6. Calvin Colton, Labour and Capital (1844)
7. Charles Grandison Finney on Sin and Redemption (1835)
8. Horace Mann, Report of the Massachusetts Board of Education (1848)
9. Anti-Slavery Convention of American Women—Proceedings (May 1837)
10. Women Declare Equality with Men at Seneca Falls (1848)
11. Walt Whitman, *Leaves of Grass* (1855)

Questions to Consider: 158
Credits   158

CHAPTER 13   159

HURTLING TOWARD CIVIL WAR, 1844–1860   159

Documents: 165

1. "John L. O'Sullivan on Texas Annexation and Manifest Destiny" (1845)
2. Henry David Thoreau, *Civil Disobedience* (1846)
3. Senator John C. Calhoun, "Proposal to Preserve the Union" (1850)
4. Frederick Douglass, Fourth of July Oration (1852)
5. Harriet Beecher Stowe, *Uncle Tom's Cabin* (1852)
6. Senator Stephen Douglas Explains the Objectives of His Bill (February 1854)
7. Letter from Axalla John Hoole, Kansas resident, to his sister (1857)

8. Senator Charles Sumner, Speech in the U.S. Senate on the "Crime Against Kansas," (May 1856)

9. Roger Taney, Dred Scott v. Sanford (1857)

10. Excerpts from "The Lincoln–Douglas Debates" (1858)

11. John Brown, "Last Statement to the Virginia Court" (1859)

12. "Prospects of Slavery Expansion," the *Charleston Mercury* (February 1860)

    Questions to Consider: 173

    Credits   173

CHAPTER 14: THE "SECOND AMERICAN REVOLUTION": THE CIVIL WAR, 1861–1865   175

    Documents: 180

1. Senator Robert Toombs of Georgia, Speech Before Constituents (November 1860)

2. George McClellan, Letter to Abraham Lincoln (July 7, 1862)

3. "General Robert E. Lee Takes the Offensive" (September 1862)

4. Clara Barton, Memoirs (1862)

5. "Abraham Lincoln Explains His Paramount Object of Saving the Union," August (1862)

6. Abraham Lincoln, The Gettysburg Address (November 19, 1863)

7. James Henry Gooding to Abraham Lincoln (September 1863)

8. Clement Vallandigham, Speech before the U.S. House (January 14, 1863)

9. William Tecumseh Sherman to James M. Calhoun (September 1864)

10. Abraham Lincoln, Second Inaugural Address (1865)

11. Sidney Andrews, *The South Since the War: As Shown by Fourteen Weeks of Travel and Observation in Georgia and the Carolinas* (1866)

    Questions to Consider: 185

    Credits   186

CHAPTER 15: AMERICA'S UNFINISHED REVOLUTION: RECONSTRUCTION IN THE SOUTH, 1865–1877   187

    Documents: 192

1. "Richard Henry Dana Presents His Grasp of War Theory" (June 1865)

2. Thaddeus Stevens, Speech before the House *(January 1867)

3. Andrew Johnson, Third Annual Message (December 1867)

4. Elizabeth Cady Stanton, "Who Are Our Friends?" (1868)

5. Testimony of Elias Hill Before Congress Regarding Ku Klux Klan Violence (1871)

6. Carl Schurz, Speech in the Senate (January 1872)

7. James Sheppard Pike Offers a Liberal Republican View of Reconstruction (1873)

8. Representative Lucius Q. C. Lamar of Mississippi, Speech Before the House,1(874)

    Questions to Consider: 196

    Credits   196

APPENDIX   199

★ PREFACE

This textbook is a narrative with primary sources covering American history before 1877. The following account of early American history seeks to incorporate various methods of writing about the past, ranging from politics and foreign policy, to economics and demography, to the concerns of scholars of race and gender. This textbook is fairly unique, because normally one set of scholars will write a narrative of the period and another set of scholars will put together an anthology of documents for this era; rarely does the same scholar who constructs a narrative also include a document anthology as a part of his or her textbook. By using roughly 150 small document excerpts with my narrative, I intend to show students the kinds of documents a historian uses to construct a story about the past (even though the number used here is only a small sample of relevant primary source material).

Ideally, students should question some or all of the conclusions drawn from the assigned documents, and debate for themselves how representative these documents are for the varied and conflicting interests present among different historical actors. My hope also is that after reading these documents, students will become curious enough to seek out longer excerpts of the writings of the authors selected here in order to further an engagement with the source material. Students may even be inspired to seek out other sources not excerpted here, in order to gain a greater or varied perspective on the events from different writers or thinkers who nonetheless described similar issues or events in the past.

One of the most challenging aspects of teaching history arises from trying to convince students that the subject of history is a constant argument, and that conceptions regarding history are directly relevant to the contested political, economic, and social debates of the present. Hopefully the story and primary documents presented here allow for teachers and students to assess one event—such as the American Revolution—from the multiple vantage points of wealthier patriots, poorer slaves, frontier whites, women, or others. What historians constantly refer to as "critical thinking," then, arises from an understanding among students that the past is debatable, and that representations made about it often come from different social, economic, gendered, or racial experiences (or prejudices). Every teacher and historian hopes that his or her students will learn to question all received forms of wisdom, and develop a healthy skepticism for ideas dictated to them by figures of authority, regardless of political orientation.

Even though I have only been teaching students for just shy of ten years (and therefore cannot claim that this book represents decades of experience), the ideas and arguments contained herein have been greatly shaped by the constant challenge of making the past relevant to those who sit in my classroom. While I am solely responsible for the quality and accuracy of what follows, this textbook would have not been brought to press without the work of University Readers, Seidy Cruz, and her production team, to whom I am very grateful.

Ryan P. Jordan
University of San Diego
June 2010

CHAPTER 1

THE WORLD THE EUROPEANS ENCOUNTERED

The roughly fifty million people in the fifteenth century, estimated to have lived from modern-day Alaska south to Chile, represented a diverse group of human beings. They are known to English-speakers as "native Americans," but that label is artificial, and masks the significant diversity of tribes, family arrangements, languages, and economic structures possessed by these people. Literally thousands of tribal groups once existed throughout the Americas, some consisting of nothing larger than extended families of only a few hundred members, while other groups, such the Incans, included thousands of people. Because history is written by the victors—in addition to the more important fact that 99 percent of these "natives" did not possess or leave behind systems of writing intelligible to Europeans—a picture of the Americas when the natives outnumbered Europeans can never fully be told. In spite of this, however, scholars are able to recover some aspects of the social, economic, and political life of these diverse peoples with the aid both of archaeology and oral traditions handed down by natives and recorded later by their descendants who spoke European languages. One should not forget that European explorers themselves wrote and said much regarding these people, but of course those sources are not the same as if the natives themselves left behind written documents.

Historians generally group native tribes into four groups, based on their mode of economic production (how they made a living): hunter-gathering, fishing, hunting, and sedentary farming. Among the first three categories of economic organization, life was lived on a much smaller, simpler scale than among those natives who practiced sedentary farming. Often the non-farming tribes combined elements of hunting, fishing, and gathering, though some tribes clearly spent more time doing one activity over the others. For example, many of the coastal natives in what is now California lived in small thatched huts; they fished and picked berries for their survival, as well as occasionally hunted small animals. These tribal bands were not large and could be easily conquered or controlled by other rival tribes (or later Europeans). Many of the natives in what became the American Plains and Prairies, such as the Apache or Navajo, were more focused on hunting bison and other larger land animals; with the help of dog-pulled sleds, these natives generally lived a more nomadic (or wandering) existence than the gathering and hunting groups in California. Later on, these hunters would adopt the horse and become fierce warriors against European expansion. All of these groups that lived so close to the land generally exhibited a much more egalitarian social structure: There were not any large landowners, bureaucrats, or kings among them, and the men did not necessarily treat women as badly as the Europeans did. This last aspect—that of gender equality—has often been noted with admiration by recent scholars, as it was with some early explorers and European thinkers who cast the "noble savage" in a light representing a simplicity, kindness, and gentleness that had long been lost in the much more developed and militarized European world.

The sedentary farming mode of production necessarily led to the most developed, largest, and strongest native American tribes. These might be thought of more correctly in European terms as "empires." This is because having a surplus of crops derives from more advanced farming techniques, enabling a society to devote time to craft making for trade, and intellectual and military training for the domination of other, weaker tribes. Such "empires" are no longer living "hand to mouth," as it were. There were many smaller groups of sedentary farmers in North America, such as the Powhatans in modern-day Virginia, the Pueblo in present-day New Mexico, and the Iroquois in what is now New York State. In what became the United States, there were large settlements of cliff dwellers in the Southwest, as well as the mound dwellers in the area around present-day St. Louis. The mound dwellers even constructed a large city, Cahokia, in the period between 600 and 1400, but such groups eventually succumbed to climate changes or attacks from invaders, and were no longer extant by the time of the arrival of Columbus in the 1490s. At the time of the Europeans' arrival in the new world, therefore, there were really only two groups of natives that most resembled a European "empire," as recognized by men like Columbus. These two groups were the Aztecs of central Mexico and the Incas of the Northern Andean region in South America.

By 1325, the Aztecs had established a large city named Tenochtitlan, the site of Mexico City today, with an alliance of other tribes in the valley. From this urban center, the Aztecs dominated trade in the region, and established relations with various tributary tribes, or bands, who owed the Aztecs labor or materials (or both), in return for various exotic items, most notably bronze jewelry and tools. In the Aztec empire, great social inequalities developed, where the local landowning gentry, priests, or chiefs could live off of the wealth generated by the lower orders, supposedly in exchange for protection from outside threats or from internal lawlessness and crime. In this way, the social structure of the Aztecs most resembled that of the Europeans, with their feudal hierarchies and priestly classes. The Aztecs believed that the "war god" needed to be appeased frequently; in 1502, thousands of people were sacrificed by having their still-beating hearts ripped from their chests at the coronation of their new ruler, Motecuhzoma (known as Montezuma in Spanish). But other, more positive signs of Aztec power can be seen in their development of a largely pictorial writing system (known as the Aztec codices) and in their study of astronomy. Their urban capital, Tenochtitlan, may have been home to as many people as some contemporary European cities, and it was replete with garbage collectors, latrines, and forms of mass transit. (The Spaniards also noted prostitutes and beggars among the urban populace). Further south, in the Andes of South America, lived the Incas. Under the reign of Pachacutec in 1438, these natives began to move out from the town of Cuzco (in modern-day Peru) to build an empire with a well-disciplined fighting force using wooden, stone, and bronze weapons. At its height, the Incan empire stretched from what is now Colombia over a thousand miles south to present-day Argentina. Although they lacked a formal writing system, they did maintain a census using ceramics, which they also used for other communication as well (such ceramics are impossible for Westerners to decipher, however). In addition, Incan engineers built roads and fortifications throughout the Andean region, and which still exist today. As with the Aztecs, the Incans supervised or controlled numerous subordinate tribes for tributary purposes and maintained a constant stream of recruits for their military.

For all of their innovations and power, however, the most advanced groups of natives such as the Aztecs or the Incans suffered from two serious disadvantages from the Europeans, or indeed even from other Eurasians and East Asians: They were highly susceptible to viruses derived from distant travel and contact with livestock, and they had not developed the use of iron and steel. Regarding diseases, scientists and scholars posit that not only the relative isolation of various tribes (even the most advanced did not travel as widely as the average Eurasian) but also their lack of contact with livestock such as the cow, rabbit, and horse made the natives highly susceptible to a whole range of Eurasian diseases, such as smallpox, influenza, and yellow fever. The biological disadvantage of the native peoples may have been responsible for a devastating collapse in their population by as much as a 90 percent decline. Such a demographic collapse significantly weakened the ability of natives to fight back against the European military and demographic onslaught initiated by Columbus.

The story of native contact with Europeans is not merely a simple story of biological extermination and military conquest, however. First of all, without some degree of native support, Europeans such as Cortés or the English settlers in Jamestown could not have survived in this strange new world. And for centuries after their initial contact with the natives, English settlers lived in near constant fear of native American reprisals and attacks, thus testifying to the enduring military and economic power of some tribes. As we will see, certain North American tribes, such as the Iroquois, maintained an ability to play off different European powers against each other into the eighteenth century, particularly once it was clear that Europeans wanted native consumer items such as beaver fur or deer peltry. Other tribes learned to use European tactics of warfare to their advantage: for example, Apache warriors in the American Plains mastered the use of the European horse, and for a time fought back against white expansion into the North American West. Elsewhere in the Americas, Europeans and natives produced racially mixed offspring who developed a taste for native customs and commodities such as drinking hot chocolate, and the existence of this new mestizo race testifies to the fact that native culture was hardly eradicated in Latin America. The nature and pace of European domination of the natives was uneven, therefore, and as late the nineteenth century, it would be possible for thousands of natives to avoid direct contact with the deleterious consequences of European invasion.

But the invasion was real, and the man who instigated the European assault on native Americans, Christopher Columbus, personally embodied many of the disparate economic, social, and political forces of the 1400s, which pushed Europeans out into the Atlantic Ocean in search of wealth. Western Europe in the 1400s was suffering from the effects of too many mouths to feed as population growth resumed after the Black Death; its appetite had also been whetted by various spices, silks, and other rare luxury items from Asia, brought to them via the Middle East and Italy. In the most basic sense, then, Europeans were hungry for more stuff, as it were, but they also possessed a militaristic society (which some would trace back to the Romans) that empowered various knights to take risks or commit violent depredations on foreign powers and peoples. So Europeans possessed the power to act on their desire for foreign goods. This power can be seen in the success Isabella and Ferdinand of Castile and Aragon, respectively, who oversaw the Christian reconquest of Muslim-controlled Granada by an army of dedicated Christian warriors in 1492. Elsewhere on the Iberian peninsula, the Portuguese had been honing their skills as sailors in the Eastern Atlantic and extreme northwest Africa since the 1400s, laying the foundations for the maritime daring and experimentation so pivotal for European success. And so the Western European world of Christopher Columbus was one of militarism, navigational enterprise, and a deep desire to find new trade goods to consume or land to conquer. Columbus, as a sailor possessing an amazing degree of self-confidence, somehow managed to convince Isabella to take a chance on his bold belief that the world was in fact smaller than generally thought (meaning Asia was only 3,000 miles west of Spain, and not 7,000 miles). He claimed that he knew how to sail west to Asia, and win for the Spanish crown far more wealth than even the Portuguese had managed to bring home in their expeditions to Africa. Willing to take a chance (the Portuguese rejected Columbus' ideas), the Spanish monarchs agreed to finance the famous voyage of the *Niña*, the *Pinta*, and the *Santa Maria*, all of which set sail on August 3, 1492.

Columbus' main discovery was that by sailing into the Atlantic Ocean, south-southwest, he would eventually find prevailing trade winds which would literally kick his ship across the Atlantic Ocean. Similarly, when leaving from the Caribbean, if one tacked north-northeast, one would find prevailing winds to take a ship back to Europe. Columbus was a daring and self-confident sailor, but nothing more. He never really knew where he was going, constantly asking Caribbean natives where was the Emperor of China, and he died never knowing where he had been. He did not bring back much in the way of material or bullion wealth from the Caribbean islands he encountered. Columbus and the men he left behind did manage to kill and oppress the natives, but without much financial success, and for this Columbus was severely reprimanded. He died in 1506 not having produced much immediate success, though he laid the foundation for a dramatic transfer of wealth, peoples, plants, and diseases referred to as the Columbian exchange. Columbus unleashed a demographic and economic revolution which, while dramatic, was also heavily one-sided in terms of winners and losers. The native population never recovered from the aforementioned smallpox, typhoid, yellow fever, and other European diseases, in addition to succumbing to European military technology. The natives did learn to use the horse or even cattle from Europeans, but only sporadically. On the other hand, Europeans gained amazing new sources of commodity and crop wealth. This can be seen in the introduction of new staple crops such as corn and the potato to Europe, while Europeans were also able to grow old-world crops—such as sugar and tobacco—in amounts previously unknown to them since disease had cleared the natives from the land. In many ways, Europeans after Columbus discovered more wealth from the Americas than they ever could have hoped to receive from Asia.

Within forty years of Columbus' voyages, the Spanish moved into the mainland of what is now Latin America with the help of Hernán Cortés and Francisco Pizarro. Cortés, using divide-and-conquer methods among subordinate, oppressed tribes of the Aztecs, moved from the Mexican seacoast up to the mountains and seized the Aztec capital of Tenochtitlan in 1521. As noted above, Cortés was helped immeasurably not just with native soldiers, but also with European steel weapons and European diseases. Grafting themselves onto the existing empire, the Spaniards often took native mistresses and did to some extent create a new race of "Americans" of mixed native and Spanish ancestry. Yet those New World subjects with the largest amount of white blood (or who appeared to have the largest amount) were still held in the highest esteem, especially if they were born in Spain and not in Mexico. A similar story of conquest would play out in Peru, led by Francisco Pizarro, who more or less repeated Cortés' tactics in the defeat of the Incan empire by the 1540s. The successes of both men brought about the beginning of the tremendous extraction of silver and gold (primarily silver) from Mexico and Peru, which was the basis of the astounding growth of the Spanish Empire. Ultimately, this reliance upon bullion extraction proved precarious for the empire (they had all their eggs in one basket, so to speak) as well as deleterious to domestic industry (it became cheaper to rely on bullion flows to buy consumer goods from foreigners than to produce manufactured goods in Spain). As a result, Spain would fall into decline by the 1700s. Their meteoric rise also led other Western European powers to try to move in on Spanish America. This often led Spanish kings to arrogantly threaten war with Spanish enemies, in particular with Protestant England.

The English had, by the late 1500s, begun to attempt to compete with the Spaniards, and would eventually succeed in their attempts to carve out a New World empire. As the sixteenth century drew to a close, numerous English "seadogs" or pirates, such as John Hawkins and Francis Drake, had taken great pleasure in raiding Spanish treasure fleets laden with gold, silver, or slaves from the New World. As time wore on, the Spanish king Philip also wanted to wage war against the English because they were now dominated by Protestant "heretics." The 1500s had seen tens of thousands of Protestants reject the dominant Roman church over issues of papal authority, as well as over the need for sacraments in Christian ceremonies. Philip of Spain saw himself as the defender of the Catholic faith in his crusade against the English, in addition to fearing the economic competition from this rising power to the northwest. But Philip overstretched in his attempted naval invasion of England in 1588—an event known simply as "the Armada." In this battle, daring English sailors sent burning fire ships into the Spanish fleet, while a stiff, northern "Protestant wind" literally dashed Philip's naval flotilla (in addition to his dreams of conquering the English) along the rocky coast of Ireland. For the English, the year 1588 represented a major shot in the arm for nationalists, such as Richard Hakluyt, who were convinced their island nation could now take on the greatest empire in the world. And Hakluyt believed this battle against Spain would be waged not only in Europe, but in the Americas as well. Slowly, various Englishmen began to dream not merely of an empire derived from the extraction of bullion, but also from the planting of colonies which would produce all of the necessary goods to make England self-sufficient, to make England the market to the rest of Europe. These ideas, later associated with mercantilist thinkers, were not widespread in 1588, but they would gain currency among the English in the next century and helped to chart the course for English, and later British, dominance, in what historians refer to as an Atlantic world of commerce. England's first attempt at building a new world colony, Roanoke in present-day North Carolina, failed miserably due to lack of preparation and squabbling with the natives. The colonists simply vanished into the woods when Walter Raleigh returned for them in 1587. But that defeat could not stop the desire for other Englishmen to make good on their dreams of North American empire.

Documents:

1. Spanish Letter of Christopher Columbus to Luis de Sant' Angel ... (1493)

The following excerpt comes from the first letter sent by Columbus to the Spanish crown, indicating he had "discovered" what he thought was part of Asia. The letter is addressed to the finance minister to King Ferdinand, Luis Sant'Angel, an early supporter of Columbus. In this letter, Columbus describes the docility of the natives he encountered on small islands that now comprise the Bahamas, in addition to extolling the potential wealth Spain might take from these islands.

I write to you so that you may know that in thirty three days I passed over to the Indies (Caribbean) with the fleet which the most illustrious King and Queen, our Lords, gave me. I have found many islands peopled with inhabitants beyond number. And, of them all, I have taken possession for their Highnesses ... In the island of [Hispaniola] there are many spiceries and great mines of gold and other metals. The people of this island, and of all the others that I have found and seen, or not seen, all go naked, men and women, just as their mothers bring them forth. ... They have no iron or steel, nor any weapons; nor are they fit thereunto; not because they be not well-formed people and of fair stature, but that they are most wondrously humble and simple. They have no other weapons than the stems of reeds in their seedling state, on the end of which they fix little sharpened stakes. Even these, they dare not use. ... Of anything they have, if it be asked for, they never say no, but do rather invite the person to accept it, and show as much lovingness as though they would give their hearts. And whether it be a thing of value, or one of little worth, they are straightaway content with whatever may be given them in return. I forbade that anything so worthless as fragments of broken platters, and pieces of broken glass, and strap-buckles, should be given them; although when they were able to get such things, they seemed to think they had the best jewel in the world. For it was amazing for those sailors to get in exchange for a strap, gold to the weight of two and a half ounces. ... And in conclusion, to your Highnesses I shall give them as much gold as they may need, with very little aid which their Highnesses will give me; spices and cotton at once, as much as their Highnesses will order to be shipped, and as much as they shall order to be shipped of mastic ... and aloe-wood ... and slaves as many as they shall order to be shipped. ...

2. Declaration Concerning the Indies from King Ferdinand of Spain (1510)

After the death of his wife, Isabella, and after both monarchs' involvement in Columbus' expeditions, Ferdinand composed several justifications for Spanish imperialism in the Americas, such as the one below. This document reveals how the man who helped to reconquer and unify various parts of the Iberian peninsula in the name of Catholicism also justified New World expansion in similar terms.

Of all these nations [including the Americas], God our Lord gave charge to one man, called St. Peter, that he should be Lord and Superior of all the men in the world, that all should obey him, and that he should be head of the whole human race, wherever men should live. ... And he commanded him to place his seat in Rome, as the spot most fitting to rule the world from. ...

So their Highnesses, Kings, and Lords of these islands and land of Tierra-firme by virtue of this donation: and some islands and indeed almost all of those whom this has been notified, have received and served their Highnesses, as lords and kings, in the way that subjects out to do—with good will, without any resistance ... when they were informed of the aforesaid facts [regarding the rule of the Pope]. ... And also they [the native] received and obeyed the priests whom their Highnesses have joyfully and benignantly received them, and also have commanded then to be treated as their subjects and vassals. ... [We ask other tribes] to take the time to consider what we have said to you and acknowledge the Church as your ruler. ... If you do so, you will do well ... if you do not do this, and maliciously make delay in it, I certify to you that, with the help of God, we shall powerfully enter into your country, and shall make war against you in all ways and manners that we can. ... We shall take you and your wives and your children, and shall make slaves of them, and as such shall sell and dispose of them as their Highnesses may command. ...

3. Fray Bernardino de Sahagun, *General History of Things in New Spain* (1582)

De Sahagun was an early Spanish missionary to the Aztec people of Mexico and one of the leading scholars of the language of the Aztecs, Nahuatl. In this account he recounts the brutality of the Spanish conquistadors, and relates material he learned from the perspective of the native peoples of Mexico, with whom he conducted extensive interviews.

In 1519 ... at the town of Cholula [in Mexico], there arose from the Spaniards a cry summoning all the [native American] noblemen, lords, war leaders, warriors, and common folk; and when they had crowded into the temple courtyard, then all the Spaniards and their allies blocked the entrances and every exit. There followed a butchery of stabbing, beating, killing of the unsuspecting Cholulans armed with no bows and arrows, protected by no shields ... with no warning, they were treacherously, deceitfully slain ...

Later ... in Tenochtitlan ... the people of the city rose in tumult, alarmed as if by an earthquake, as if there were a constant reeling of the face of the earth. Shocked, terrified, Moctezuma himself wept in the distress he felt for his city. Everyone was in terror; everyone was astounded, afflicted. Many huddled in groups, wept in foreboding for their own fates and those of their friends. Others, dejected, hung their heads. Some groups exchanged tearful greetings; others tried mutual encouragement. ... Eventually, the Spaniards took Moctezuma hostage, and finally strangled him. Then the Spanish charged the crowd with their iron lances and hacked us with their iron swords. ... The blood of the young warriors ran like water; it gathered in pools ... [but the Spanish did not win and had to flee].

But at about the same time that the Spanish had fled from Mexico ... there came a great sickness, a pestilence, the smallpox. It spread over the people with great destruction of men ... It was after all this happened that the Spanish came back [in 1521] ... Tenochtitlan held out against their siege for 75 days. Finally the Spanish took the city, destroying it and killing hundreds of thousands of Aztec citizens. Many of them were already sick and starving ... There was hunger. Many died of famine. ...The enemy pressed about us like a wall ... they herded us ... the brave warriors were still hopelessly resisting [but to no avail.]

4. Bartolome de las Casas, *Very Brief Account of the Devastation of the Indies (1542)*

As a young man, de las Casas had witnessed the brutality of Columbus on the island of Hispaniola; in later years, de las Casas tried to right the wrongs done to natives by establishing a kind of commune in Venezuela, where natives might receive fair treatment as well as pay for their work. But this experiment failed when some of the whites instigated fights with other tribes over access to slave labor. De las Casas then devoted his life to the Church by becoming a member of the Dominican order. He would continue to be an advocate for native rights throughout the 1500s, until his death in 1566.

God has created all these numberless people [the natives of the New Word] to be quite the simplest, without malice or duplicity ... free from hate and revenge as any in the world ... Among these gentle sheep, gifted by their Maker with the above qualities, the Spaniards entered as soon as they knew them, like wolves, tiger, and lions which had been starving for many days ... they [have for forty years] afflicted, tormented, and destroyed [the natives] with strange and new, and divers kinds of cruelty, never before seen, nor heard of, nor read of ... The Christians, with their horses and swords and lances, began to slaughter and practice strange cruelty among the natives. [These Christians] penetrated into the country and spared neither children nor the aged, nor pregnant women, nor those in child labour, all of whom they ran through the body and lacerated, as they were assaulting so many lambs herded in their sheepfold ...

5. From *The Conquest of New Spain, by Bernal Díaz,* in reference to Malinche (native American mistress to Cortés) (circa 1570)

Taken from the famous chronicle of Cortés' conquest of Mexico by Díaz, this account of Cortés' onetime native mistress (who also gave birth to a son by him) reveals how some natives were able to survive and even prosper under Spanish rule, if they went along with the desires of the conquistadors. Malinche is considered by many to be the mother of the "mestizo" race in Mexico, even if she is viewed as an opportunist by others.

I should like to give an account of Doña Marina (Malinche) who had been a great lady and leader [of the native people] since her childhood ... The Indians of Xicalango gave the child [Malinche] to the people of Tabasco, and the Tabascans gave her to Cortez. ... After the conquest of Mexico I passed through various places with Cortez and Doña Marina. Cortes always took her with him, as she proved such an excellent person, and good interpreter in all the wars against the natives in New Spain. ... And while Cortes was in the town of Coatzacoalcos, he summoned all of the leaders ... and Doña Marina's mother and her half brother were among them ... but the woman and her son were very much afraid of Doña Marina, thinking that she had come to put them to death, and they wept. When Doña Marina saw her mother and her half-brother in tears, she comforted them, saying that they need have no fear ... she then gave them many golden jewels and some clothes. Then she sent them back to their town, saying that God had been very gracious to her [Malinche] in freeing her from the worship of idols and making her a Christian, and giving her a son by her lord and master Cortes, also in marrying her to such a gentleman as her husband Juan Jaramillo ... she would rather serve her husband and Cortes than anything else in the world, ... This was the great beginning of our

[Spanish] conquests, and thus, praise be to God, all things prospered with us. I have made a point of telling this story, because without Doña Marina we could not have understood the language of New Spain and Mexico.

6. John Heckewelder, *Indian Tradition of the First Arrival of the Dutch on Manhattan Island in 1610* (1841)

Heckewelder, the native American missionary active during the late eighteenth and early nineteenth centuries, was most familiar with the Delaware and Mohegan tribes of the mid-Atlantic and Ohio Valley regions. In the early 1600s, he recorded this oral tradition of the first contact between Europeans and natives in what became New York City. It was often European missionaries who preserved such accounts, and it is important to note the native relationship to European technology and trade goods described by missionaries like Heckewelder.

A great many years ago ... some Indians who were out fishing saw at a great distance something remarkable floating on the water, and such as they had never seen before. ... At length the spectators concluded that this wonderful object was moving towards the land, and that it must be an animal or something else that had life in it; it would therefore be proper to inform all the Indians on the inhabited islands of what they had seen, and put them on their guard. Accordingly they sent off a number of runners and watermen to carry the news to their scattered chief that they might send off in every direction for the warriors, with a message that they should come on immediately. These arriving in numbers, and having themselves viewed the strange appearance, and observing that it was actually moving towards the entrance of the river or bay; concluded it to be a remarkably large house in which the Mannitto (Supreme Being) was present, and that he probably was coming to visit them. By this time the chiefs were assembled at York island, and deliberating in what manner in which they should receive their Mannitto on his arrival... All the idols or images were put in place, and a grand dance was supposed not only to be an agreeable entertainment for the Great Being, but it was believed that it might, with the addition of a sacrifice, contribute to appease him if he was angry with them. ... Other runners ... after arriving declare that it is positively a house full of human beings, of quite a different color from that of the Indians, and dressed differently from them; that in particular one of them was dressed entirely in red, who must be the Mannitto himself. ...The house ... at last stops, and a canoe of smaller size comes on shore with the red man, and some others in it ... The chiefs and wise men, assembled in council, form themselves into a large circle, towards which the man in red clothes approaches with two others. He salutes them with a friendly countenance, and they return the salute after their manner. The natives are lost in admiration ... A large jug is brought out by one of the Mannitto's servants, from which an unknown substance is poured out into a small cup or glass ... he hands it to the native chief standing next to him. The chief receives it, but only smells the contents and passes it on to the next chief, who does the same. The glass or cup thus passes through the circle, without the liquor being tasted by any one, and is upon the point of being returned to the Manitto, when one of the Indians, a brave man a great warrior suddenly jumps up and harangues the assembly for returning the cup. ... He then took the glass, and bidding the assembly a solemn farewell, at once drank up its contents ... He soon began to stagger, and at last fell prostrate on the ground. His companions began to bemoan his fate ... and they think he has expired. He wakes again, jumps up and declared, that he has enjoyed the most delicious sensations, and that he never before felt himself so happier as after he had drunk the cup. He asks for more, his wish is granted; the whole assembly then imitate him, and all become intoxicated.

7.   Richard Hakluyt, *A Discourse Concerning Western Planting* (1584)

Hakluyt, an English minister, was fascinated with the prospects of New World trade and exploration and did all he could to be a propagandist for English overseas empire when many in that country questioned its profitability. This excerpt also demonstrates the Protestant worldview that Catholic Spain should be stopped in her efforts to use wealth from the New World to dominate European politics and pervert "true" religion.

A brief collection of certain reasons to induce her majesty [Queen Elizabeth I] to take in hand the Western voyage and the planting there:

1. The soil yieldeth all the several commodities of Europe and of all kingdoms [England might bypass foreign sources of goods] ...

4. The passage is to be performed at all times of the year. ...

6. This enterprise may stay the Spanish King from flowing all over the face of the earth of America, if we seat and plant there in time. ...

11. At the first traffic with the people of those parts, the subjects of this realm will change many cheap commodities of these parts for commodities easily produced over there. ...

21. Many soldiers and servitors, in the end of wars ... may there be unladen, to the common profit and quiet of this realm. ...

It remains to be considered by what means and by whom this great work may be performed of enlarging the glorious gospel of Christ, and reducing infinite multitudes of these simple people that are in error into the right and perfect way of their salvation ... Now the Kings and Queens of England have the name of defenders of the faith, by which title I think they are not only charged to maintain and patronize the faith of Christ, but to enlarge it [among the natives].

It is also true that many thousands of our idle people within the realm, which, having no way to be on work [could be employed in Western plantations]. Whereas if this voyage could be set in execution ... many could be employed in planting of sugar canes, as the Portuguese have done in Madeira; in maintenance and increasing of silk worms for silk; ... in gathering of cotton whereof there is plenty ... in dressing of vines whereof there is great abundance of wine ... in fishing, salting, and drying of ling, cod, salmon, herring ...

And entering into consideration of the way this King Philip [of Spain] may be abased, I mean first to being with the West Indies, as there to lay a chief foundation for his overthrow. With the removal of this strongest hold [in the Caribbean] the mightiest and strongest walls fall flat to earth; so this prince, spoiled or intercepted for a while of his treasure ... and the people revolt in every foreign territory of his, and cut the throats of the proud, hateful Spaniards ...

Questions to Consider:

1.   Explain the social, economic, technological, political, and religious motives behind the European conquest of the Americas.

2. Name at least five important factors in the European defeat of native tribes in the New World.
3. How well did native Americans adapt to European power? Were natives always easily conquered by Europeans?
4. What was the "Columbian exchange," and how did it alter the course of world history?
5. Why did the English begin to consider overseas colonization in the late 1500s, and with what results?

Credits

- Christopher Columbus; trans. Quaritch, The Spanish Letter of Columbus. 1893. Copyright in the Public Domain.
- Copyright © King Ferdinand of Spain (CC BY-SA 3.0) at https://en.wikipedia.org/wiki/Requerimiento.
- Fray Bernardino de Sahagun, *General History of Things in New Spain*. Copyright © 1950.
- Excerpt from Bartolomé de las Casas; trans. Francis Augustus MacNutt, "Short Report of the Destruction of the Indies," *Bartholomew de Las Casas; His life, Apostolate, and Writings*. Copyright in the Public Domain.
- Excerpt from Bernal Díaz; trans. J. M. Cohen, *The Conquest of New Spain*. Copyright © 1963.
- John Heckewelder, "Indian Tradition of the First Arrival of the Dutch on Manhattan Island in 1610," *Transactions of the Historical and Literary Committee of the American Philosophical Society at Philadelphia*, vol. 1, pp. 347. 1819. Copyright in the Public Domain.
- Excerpt from Richard Hakluyt, *A Discourse Concerning Western Planting*. 1877. Copyright in the Public Domain.

★ CHAPTER 2
★ THE RISE OF ENGLAND AND THE
★ COLONIZATION OF NORTH AMERICA

The rise of England as an imperial power may have seemed unlikely in the late 1500s, but in hindsight there were several aspects of English society and politics that enabled it to compete on a global scale with the other seafaring nations of western Europe. Compared to countries such as France and Spain, the English middling classes were larger, and there had long been experimentation in producing consumer articles for sale at market through the woolen industry. In civic terms, the English gentry had wrested numerous Parliamentary privileges from their king, which meant that large segments of society were politically enfranchised and felt that they could contain the tyrannical designs of a king. As with all stereotypes, then, the idea that the English had developed an especially liberty-loving society based on private property and political freedom (at least when compared to their French, Austrian, or Spanish counterparts) had some basis in reality. When Europe experienced a large influx of bullion from the New World in the late 1500s, the English woolen industry met the now wealthier consumers' demand for textiles, thus enriching many English merchants. In turn, the monarch allowed these now wealthier merchants to keep their profits and put them into other ventures, such as overseas colonization in areas ranging from the Levant to North American fisheries. Among the English, one could say their corporations rivaled the economic power of the English monarchy itself by the end of the 1600s. This fact demonstrates the ability of various segments of English society apart from the Crown to mobilize people, wealth, and resources for the benefit of the entire country.

Thus, the individual initiative of the joint stock company greatly aided the establishment of England's first successful colony, Virginia, based at Jamestown on the James River, some 600 miles north of Spanish Florida, in 1607. Of course, the company would eventually need a royal bailout (the first of many in the history of England's rise to power) but the profit motive remained among the colonists. This was important, since the colony seemed constantly teetering on the brink of collapse during its first decade, and it looked as though Jamestown might go the way of that other English fort in North America, Roanoke, which had fallen apart and vanished from sight in the late 1580s. But with the help of martial law laid down by men like John Smith, the colonists would be required to plant crops, stop fighting with or fraternizing with natives, and otherwise make productive use of their time and money. Though the threat of starvation and native attacks constantly lurked and the reality of disease demoralized the settlers, this tiny fort built in a swamp near a river slowly began to turn a profit, due to the discovery of tobacco. It has been said that the Virginia colony was built on smoke. The luxury item of tobacco was one of those old-world items that grew in much larger amounts in the New

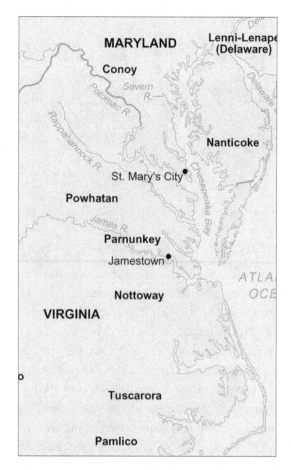

Map of the colonies of Virginia and Maryland around 1640.

World soil, and exemplified the wealth-making power of the Columbian exchange mentioned in the last chapter. Supplying a bad habit in Europe eventually produced the great Virginian fortunes of the eighteenth century.

But most settlers who came to Virginia in the period from 1607–1680 came as indentured servants—a condition not much better than slavery—except that if you survived your 5–7 year term of service (most did not) you did receive free land, tools, and seed. While some servants managed to take advantage of the opportunities of freedom, most died, and many more were permanently scarred from the disease, labor abuse, and other exploitative practices of the tobacco planters. There was also a large gender imbalance in the colony, which might allow for the few women brought over to quickly marry, but could also lead to all kinds of sexual misconduct and violence in this settlement that was at times quite wild and uncivilized. The landowners in Virginia ruled the society, at times with an iron fist. On the other hand, Virginia landowners did establish the seeds of American democracy with the House of Burgesses, and in keeping with the decentralized nature of the English empire, the monarch had little involvement in the day-to-day affairs of this colony. With the help of the local planter elite, who also oversaw militia duty, the whites were able to overcome a near-successful native attack from the local Powhatan tribe in 1622. It should be remembered that the Jamestown colony infringed upon a rather large native confederation of sedentary farmers, headed by the chief Powhatan, when the English landed in 1607. Powhatan envisioned the two groups living in harmony, or possibly felt that the English should assimilate to native ways. This is the most likely interpretation of the ceremony described by John Smith where Powhatan's daughter, Pocahontas, threw herself on Smith, protecting him from other natives symbolically threatening to kill him (this occurred after Smith had been taken hostage by the Powhatans and brought to Powhatan). But Pocahontas would later be taken captive herself by the English, who had no intention of assimilating with the natives, thus symbolizing the deterioration in native/English relations (she would later die in England). After Powhatan's death, his nephew, Opechancanough rose to power and he saw the writing on the wall: Virginia was not big enough for both the Powhatans and the English. Opechancanough correctly surmised that there were many more Englishmen coming and that they wanted to take the land for the production of tobacco, much to the detriment of native farming and hunting. Therefore, in March 1622, Opechancenough helped launch a surprise attack on Jamestown; in some cases the natives pretended to want to share a meal with the English before drawing knives to kill them. Fortunately for the English, there were many men away from Jamestown and they managed to fight back against the warriors, but the damage was substantial—nearly 400 settlers were killed. Yet, the natives would never again come so close to dislodging the English in Virginia, who were there to stay.

Along with Virginia, other English pirates and adventurers began establishing toeholds in the Caribbean in the spirit of the quest for Spanish treasure by the "seadogs." Beginning in 1623, several small islands in the Lesser Antilles came under the control of English pirates, and small tobacco plantations could be found on the Jamestown model in islands such as Barbados and Montserrat by the 1630s. However, most of these settlements remained quite precarious until the English found a marriage of convenience with Dutch sugar refiners looking for additional supplies of sugar from the Americas. By the 1640s, various Dutch entrepreneurs helped English settlers in the Caribbean develop the sugar plantation, which changed the Caribbean islands forever by opening up untold riches to those few whites who managed to successfully manage this premodern factory. Making sugar was not easy. The cane needed to be quickly cut and carried to large stone crushers, and then finally put in vats of oil for boiling. Body parts were often caught in the crushers, and serious burns also frequently occurred. Few English servants wanted this work, so a more easily exploitable group of laborers had to be found. Such a group existed in the form of African slaves. Since sugar was so profitable—it remained an expensive luxury in Europe—thousands of sailors enlisted to make the dangerous, deadly voyage to Western Africa to enslave untold thousands of Africans for work on these plantations. Thus, by the 1660s, the slave trade was born, along with a system of heritable enslavement for blacks. The Caribbean islands quickly filled up with these slaves, who would outnumber the whites eight to one, and would be strictly supervised with a new and strenuous "black code." Such codes forbade movement, restricted emancipation, and otherwise tried to outlaw slave revolts. White planters lived in constant fear of slave revolt, and presided over a decidedly violent and dangerous labor system, but it was extremely profitable both for the slave owners as well as for the mother country. In time, large-scale slavery of blacks would spread from the English Caribbean and north to the Virginia mainland colony, via the new colony of Carolina (see Chapter 3).

Meanwhile, another important group of English people, broadly known as "Puritans," began looking to the Americas as a place to establish a special "city upon a hill." Here they hoped to start English society anew. Dating from at least the early 1500s, dissident members within the Church of England felt that King Henry's reforms of Roman Catholic hierarchy and theology hardly went far enough (Henry simply left the Catholic church so that he could divorce Catherine of Aragon, after all, and he did not intend to dramatically alter Catholic theology). On the other hand, the "Puritans"—either in theory or practice—emphasized several ideas regarding the nature of church and society that were at once democratic but also highly exclusionary. They believed that only those who had experienced a spiritual rebirth—who could demonstrate that they took Christian precepts seriously—should belong to the established church. All other unregenerate people would only exist as a polluting influence on the "elect." (The Puritans also believed that only a finite number of people would ever be able to get into heaven.) Furthermore, unholy practices, ranging from cockfighting to the theater, and even to pagan aspects of Christmas celebrations, were all to be rooted out in the Puritans' ideal church and society. The Puritans also implied that they wanted to do away with the special rule of bishops, the monopoly of the church over much land in England, as well as any vestige of Catholic "sacraments" which conferred "grace" on believers simply by attendance at mass or by the confessional. Puritans, like other Calvinists, instead emphasized salvation by the inward faith of the believer. In short, the Bible existed as the sole source authority for Puritans, and not the traditions of a man made church. Since the Puritans were so skeptical of the established English church headed by the king, they were understandably accused of being traitors or revolutionaries against the state. (This more or less came to pass as the Puritans helped to execute King Charles I in 1649 over issues of clerical governance and taxation within England.) In other words, religious radicalism and political radicalism were one and the same in seventeenth-century England.

In 1620, after it was clear that the Virginia Company was not going to fall apart, a group of Puritan separatists (individuals who did not simply intend to reform the English church, but who wanted to leave it altogether) left from Holland, where they had been essentially hiding out from English authorities, to sail to the Americas. These separatists thought they wanted to start a society from scratch in or near Virginia. Instead of reaching Virginia, however, these separatists onboard a ship called the *Mayflower*, got blown off course and landed in what is now Massachusetts, where they established the colony of Plymouth. The colony's founding document, known as the Mayflower Compact, provides another example of the individual initiative and democratic governance that would characterize this colony of believers. They would share nearly equally in the suffering, but also in the successes of this new colony dedicated to the rigorous principles of Puritanism. As with the Virginia settlers, the Plymouth settlers would not have survived long without the hospitality of the local Wampanoag tribe and a curious former European-native American slave named Squanto, who surprisingly spoke English. These natives thought that the English would be useful allies and trading partners against other more powerful tribes, and the Thanksgiving story comes from this initial harmony extant between the two groups.

Ten years later another more powerful, better financed group of Puritans direct from England settled north of Plymouth and founded the port town of Boston. Their colony would be the Massachusetts Bay Colony, most closely associated with John Winthrop, a fairly wealthy Puritan landowner who wanted to provide personal leadership for his "city upon a hill." Winthrop had high hopes for his colony: he believed that it would be an example for old England regarding how to build a society in accordance with correct Bible principles. Winthrop restricted holding office to church members (though ministers could not hold public office), and he established a General Court. Not unlike the House of Burgesses in Virginia, this court supervised colonial affairs from the local level, away from the king. Since the majority of initial settlers possessed similar theological views as Winthrop, this basically meant that a far greater degree of popular involvement in the day-to-day affairs of the colony existed in Massachusetts than within conventional English civil society. However, intellectual and theological dissension was hardly unknown in the New England colonies—indeed, such arguments may have been augmented because of the highly literate, articulate (and some would say self-righteous) nature of the settlers. In the first few decades of settlement, several settlers both in Massachusetts Bay and Plymouth ran afoul of the conventional authorities, usually over questions of church governance and theology. Roger Williams, for example, was essentially a separatist who did not believe the Massachusetts government should demand loyalty from unbelievers. He ended up leaving Massachusetts to establish the new colony of Rhode Island in 1635. Anne Hutchinson also felt that church leaders relied too little upon faith in their sermons and teachings, and when she tried to organize opposition to such leaders (besides claiming that God spoke directly to her, which is heretical in traditional Christian thinking), she found herself banished to the colony of Rhode Island as well.

But wherever these New England dissidents went, they tended to establish organized, inward-oriented towns built around churches. Unlike Virginia and the Caribbean, then, New England exhibited an organized, coherent appearance that more successfully reproduced the social and cultural stability of the mother country. This can also be seen in

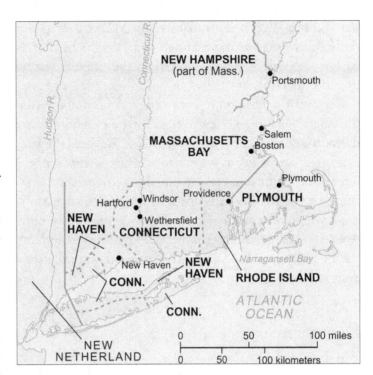

Map of the New England Colonies around 1650.

demographic terms. Whereas Virginia and the Caribbean suffered from high mortality rates and gender imbalances, New England families were strong from the beginning. Because the migrants did not come to New England for economic so much as ideological reasons, they came as well-established families with at least some capital. It was not uncommon for cousins, aunts, uncles, and grandparents to migrate to New England, nor was it unheard of for families to exist with over ten children. Also unlike more Southern regions, New England, though cold, was also spared the awful tropical diseases which wrought such havoc on English people in the Chesapeake and in the Caribbean. Therefore, New England possessed a degree of demographic health and stability, which matched the general theological cohesion and sense of purpose in the region. This region also did not attract that much additional migration (apart from necessary sailors and fishermen) after the initial waves of Puritan migration. The lack of further emigration to New England also had to do with the longer-term, relative tolerance afforded religious dissenters in England, after a century of bloodshed and strife over the issue.

With expansion to the south and east, the New Englanders soon encroached on land belonging to the Dutch East India Company and their colony of New Amsterdam in today's Long Island, New York. The Dutch settlers of New Amsterdam shared much in common with the English Puritans—a deep hatred of Roman ritual and an interest in business enterprise, in their case the fur trade with the natives. As mentioned earlier, the Dutch also eyed American exploration and settlement, and those in New Amsterdam hoped to co-opt the English Puritans living in their territory into supporting Dutch interests. But the English Puritans proved to be more English than Puritan, and when King Charles II decided to kick the Dutch out of the Hudson River area to make room for expanding English settlements, the Puritans aided the English in two Anglo-Dutch wars fought in the 1660s. Although they were a wealthy nation, the Dutch were smaller than the English and also proved to have a greater interest in more lucrative endeavors in South America and the Far East. Therefore, official Dutch power over the Hudson regions ended in 1667. However, many Dutch landholders stayed in the English colony of New York as a type of landed aristocracy, and the ethnic and linguistic diversity encouraged by the Dutch (New Amsterdam was said to be home to eighteen different European languages, as well as to the first Jewish synagogue in North America) would be an interesting point of contrast with the homogeneity of New England. The English success at colonizing parts of North America from present-day Maine to the Caribbean, and their success at growing crops themselves which were previously only purchased from Middle Eastern or Asian sources, demonstrated that the English were in North America to stay. By the late 1600s, the English turned their attention to solidifying that power with even more settlements and even more emigration.

Documents:

1. Excerpts from *Lawes Divine, Morall, and Martial* (1612, Jamestown, Virginia)

These laws were part of the reforms of the Jamestown colony instituted by Governor Thomas Dale after several setbacks for the colony (such as starvation, lack of discipline, and disease) had nearly destroyed Jamestown. These laws were part of the process whereby the colony began to right its course in order to survive in the New World.

No manner of person whatsoever, shall dare to detract, slaunder, calumniate, or utter unseemely, and unfitting speeches, either against his Majesties Honourable Councell for this Colony, resident in England, or against the Committies, Assistants unto the said Councell, or against the zealous indeavors, & intentions of the whole body of Adventurers for this pious and Christian Plantation, or against any publique booke, or bookes, which by their mature advise, and grave wisedomes, shall be thought fit, to be set foorth and publisht, for the advancement of the good of this Colony, and the felicity thereof, upon paine for the first time so offending, to bee whipt three severall times, and upon his knees to acknowledge his offence and to aske forgivenesse upon the Saboth day in the assembly of the congregation, and for the second time so offending to be condemned to the Galley for three yeares, and for the third time so offending to be punished with death. No man of what condition soever shall barter, trucke, or trade with the Indians, except he be thereunto appointed by lawful authority, upon paine of death. ...

No man shall rifle or dispoile, by force or violence, take away any thing from any Indian comming to trade, or otherwise, upon paine of death. Every tradsman in their severall occupation, trade and function, shall duly and daily attend his worke upon his said trade or occupation, upon perill for his first fault, and negligence therin, to have his entertainment checkt for one moneth, for his second fault three moneth, for his third one yeare, and if he continue still unfaithfull and negligent therein, to be condemned to the Gally for three yeare.

All overseers of workmen, shall be careful in seeing that performed, which is given them in charge, upon paine of such punishment as shall be inflicted upon him by a martial Court. No souldier or tradesman, but shall be ready, both in the morning, & in the afternoon, upon the beating of the Drum, to goe out unto his worke, nor shall hee return home, or from his worke, before the Drum beate againe, and the officer appointed for that business, bring him of, upon perill for the first fault to lie upon the Guard head and heels together all night, for the second time so faulting to be whipt, and for the third time so offending to be condemned to the Gallies for a year.

No man or woman, (upon paine of death) shall runne away from the Colonie, to Powhathan, or any Savage leader whatsoever. ...

2. Richard Frethorne, to His Mother and Father (March–April 1623), Jamestown, Virginia.

Not much is known about this early indentured servant, but his letter is one of the first to document the perspective of a white indentured servant in the first 20 years of the Jamestown settlement. It is important to note how his perspective differs from those who tried to promote emigration to the colony of Virginia.

Loving and kind father and mother ... this is to let you understand that I your child am in a most heavy Case by reason of the nature of the Country. It is such that it causes great sickness, as the scurry and divers other diseases, which maketh the body very poor, and Weak, and when we are sick there is nothing to comfort us; for since I came out of the ship, I never ate any thing but peas and water gruel ... Several men and boys cry out day and night, Oh that they were in England without their limbs and would not care to lost any limb to be in England again. Though they beg from door to door, we live in fear of the Enemy every hour, yet we have had a combat with them on the Sunday before Shrovetide, and we took two alive, and make slaves of them ... We are fain to get other men to plant with us, and yet we are but 32 to fight against 3000 if they [natives] should come ... How then shall we doe for life as we live even in their teeth, they may easily take us but that God is merciful. ... I have nothing at all, no not a shirt to my backe, but two Rags nor no Clothes, but one poor suit, nor but one pair of shoes, but one pair of stockings ... I am not half a quarter so strong as I was in England, and all is for want of victuals, for I do protest unto you, that I have eaten more in a day at home than I have allowed me here for a Week. ... Good father do not forget me, but have mercy and pity my poor miserable case. I know if you did but see me you would weep to see me, for I have but one suit, but it is a strange one. ...

3. George Alsop, *A Character of the Province of Maryland* (1666)

It is worth comparing Alsop's views below with those of Frethorne. It may also be important to consider that Alsop returned to England after his successful stint as a servant in Maryland, and that his life was cut short by diseases he contracted while in the Chesapeake region.

There is no truer Emblem of Confusion either in Monarch or Domestic Governments, then when either the Subject, or the Servant, strives for the upper hand of his Prince, or

Master, and to be equal with him, from whom he received his present subsistence ... Why then, if Servitude be so necessary that no place can be governed in order, nor people live without it, this may serve to tell those which prick up their ears and bray against it, That they are none but Asses, and deserve the Bridle of a strict commanding power to rein them in ... Let such where Providence hath ordained to life as Servants, either in England or beyond the Sea, endure the pre-fixed yoak of their limited time with patience, and then in a small computation of years, by an industrious endeavor, they may become Masters or Mistresses of Families themselves. And let this be spoke to the deserved praise of Maryland. That the four years I served there were not to me so slavish, as a two years Servitude of Handicraft Apprenticeship was here in London.

They whose abilities cannot extend to purchase their own transportation over into Maryland, (and surely he that cannot command so small a sum for so great a matter, his life must needs be mighty low and dejected) I say they may for the debarment of a four years sordid libety, go over into this Province and there live plenteously well ...

If the Servant dwells not with the Merchant they made their first agreement with, they may choose whom they will serve under ... and the two make an agreement as one would do in England ... Let those chaps who are always breathing forth those filthy dregs of abusive exclamations [regarding indentured servitude] be identified as professing a damnable untruth. ... For know, that the servants here in Maryland of all Colonies, distant or remote Plantations, have the least cause to complain, either for strictness of Servitude, want of Provisions, or need of Apparel: Five days and a half in the Summer weeks is the allotted time tha the work in; and for two months, when the Sun predominates in the highest pitch of his heat, they claim an ancient and customary Privilege to repose themselves three times a day. ...

The women that go over into this Province as Servants, have the best luck here as in any place of the world besides; for they are no sooner on shore, but they are courted into a Copulative Matrimony, which some of them ... had they not come to such a Market with their Virginity might have kept it by them until had been mouldy. ...

4. The Mayflower Compact (1620)

Because the colonists onboard the Mayflower were blown off course and ended up settling some thousand miles away from Virginia, the leaders of the voyage decided to enter into a social compact, essentially mandating self-government away from royal authority. This document is often seen as an early example of the democratic possibilities of the New England settlement, even though the government was dominated by radical Puritan believers.

IN THE NAME OF GOD, AMEN. We, whose names are underwritten, the Loyal Subjects of our dread Sovereign Lord King *James*, by the Grace of God, of *Great Britain*, *France*, and *Ireland*, King, *Defender of the Faith*, &c. Having undertaken for the Glory of God, and Advancement of the Christian Faith, and the Honour of our King and Country, a Voyage to plant the first Colony in the Northern Parts of *Virginia*; Do by these Presents, solemnly and mutually, in the Presence of God and one another, covenant and combine ourselves together into a civil Body Politick, for our better Ordering and Preservation, and Furtherance of the Ends aforesaid: And by Virtue hereof do enact, constitute, and frame, such just and equal

Laws, Ordinances, Acts, Constitutions, and Officers, from time to time, as shall be thought most meet and convenient for the general Good of the Colony; unto which we promise all due Submission and Obedience. **IN WITNESS** whereof we have hereunto subscribed our names at *Cape-Cod* the eleventh of November, in the Reign of our Sovereign Lord King *James*, of *England*, *France*, and *Ireland*, the eighteenth, and of *Scotland* the fifty-fourth, *Anno Domini*; 1620.

5.   William Bradford, History of Plymouth Plantation (1642)

Although Plymouth was in some ways more democratic than "old" England, the theocratic tendencies of its leadership can be seen in the vicious treatment afforded those who dared to transgress against Puritan standards of morality. The following excerpt reveals how the colony was based on the rule of the Old Testament, no matter how brutal that rule might have seemed to people in England.

Marvilous it may be to see and consider how some kind of wickedness did grow and break forth here, in a land where sin was no witnessed against ... and severely punished when it was known ... And yet all this could not suppress the breaking out of sundrie notorious sins ... But that which is worse, even sodomie and bugarie...have broke forth in this land, oftener than once, I say it may be justly marveled at, and cause us to fear and tremble at the consideration of our corrupt natures, which are so hardly bridled, subdued, and mortified. ... There was a youth whose name was Thomas Granger; he was servant to an honest man of Duxbery, being about 16 or 17 years of age ... He was this year detected of buggery (and indicted for the same) with a mare, a cowe, [two] goats, five sheep, [two] calves, and a turkey ... And accordingly he was cast by the jury, and condemned, and after executed about the 8 of September 1642. A very sad spectacle it was; for the first mare, and then the cowe, and the rest of the lesser cattle, were killed before his face, according to the law of Leviticus: 20 15. And then Granger himself was executed. The cattle were all cast into a great and large pit that was dug for purposes of them, and no use made of any part of them. ... It may be asked how so many wicked persons and profane people should so quickly come over into this land, and mix themselves amongst them, seeing it was religious men that began this work, and they came for religion's sake.

6.   John Winthrop, "A Model of Christian Charity" (1630)

As the main founder and governor of Massachusetts Bay Colony, Winthrop laid out the idealistic hope that his society in the wilderness would in fact be a model for England, a country he feared was beyond saving from within. This excerpt reveals the extreme self-confidence of the Puritans, who saw themselves as fighting on the right side of a cosmic battle with the forces of Satan in conventional English society.

Thus stands the cause between God and us. We are entered into covenant with Him for this work. We have taken out a commission. The Lord hath given us leave to draw our own articles. We have professed to enterprise these and those accounts, upon these and those ends. We have hereupon besought Him of favor and blessing. Now if the Lord shall please to hear us, and bring us in peace to the place we desire, then hath He ratified this covenant and sealed our commission, and will expect a strict performance of the articles contained in it; but if we shall neglect the observation of these articles which are the ends we have propounded, and, dissembling with our God, shall fall to embrace this present world and prosecute our carnal intentions, seeking great things for ourselves and our posterity, the Lord will surely break out in wrath against us, and be revenged of such a people, and make us know the price of the breach of such a covenant.

Now the only way to avoid this shipwreck, and to provide for our posterity, is to follow the counsel of Micah, to do justly, to love mercy, to walk humbly with our God. For this end, we must be knit together, in this work, as one man. We must entertain each other in brotherly affection. We must be willing to abridge ourselves of our superfluities, for the supply of others' necessities. We must uphold a familiar commerce together in all meekness, gentleness, patience and liberality. We must delight in each other; make others' conditions our own; rejoice together, mourn together, labor and suffer together, always having before our eyes our commission and community in the work, as members of the same body. So shall we keep the unity of the spirit in the bond of peace. The Lord will be our God, and delight to dwell among us, as His own people, and will command a blessing upon us in all our ways, so that we shall see much more of His wisdom, power, goodness and truth, than formerly we have been acquainted with. We shall find that the God of Israel is among us, when ten of us shall be able to resist a thousand of our enemies; when He shall make us a praise and glory that men shall say of succeeding plantations, "may the Lord make it like that of New England." For we must consider that we shall be as a city upon a hill. The eyes of all people are upon us. So that if we shall deal falsely with our God in this work we have undertaken, and so cause Him to withdraw His present help from us, we shall be made a story and a by-word through the world. We shall open the mouths of enemies to speak evil of the ways of God, and all professors for God's sake. We shall shame the faces of many of God's worthy servants, and cause their prayers to be turned into curses upon us till we be consumed out of the good land whither we are going.

And to shut this discourse with that exhortation of Moses, that faithful servant of the Lord, in his last farewell to Israel, Deut. 30. "Beloved, there is now set before us life and death, good and evil," in that we are commanded this day to love the Lord our God, and to love one another, to walk in his ways and to keep his Commandments and his ordinance and his laws, and the articles of our Covenant with Him, that we may live and be multiplied, and that the Lord our God may bless us in the land whither we go to possess it. But if our hearts shall turn away, so that we will not obey, but shall be seduced, and worship other Gods, our pleasure and profits, and serve them; it is propounded unto us this day, we shall surely perish out of the good land whither we pass over this vast sea to possess it.

7. Excerpts of the Trial of Anne Hutchinson at Newton, Massachusetts (1637)

The New England culture of reflection and examination regarding all things spiritual even encouraged women to experiment with preaching and exhorting within a society dedicated to purging itself of the "unregenerate" (the unsaved). But the case of Hutchinson also reveals the difficulty Puritan leaders had at establishing boundaries for believers in order to prevent the possible chaos of every person interpreting the Bible in his or her own fashion.

Governor: Mrs. Hutchinson, the court you see hath laboured to bring you to acknowledge the error of your way that so you might be reduced, the time grows late, we shall therefore give you a little more time to consider of it and therefore desire that you attend the court again in the morning … [The next morning]

Governor: We proceeded … as far as we could … There were divers things laid to her charge: her ordinary meetings about religious exercises, her speeches in derogation of the ministers among us, and the weakening of the hands and hearts of the people towards them. Here was sufficient proof made of that which she was accused of, in that point concerning the ministers and their ministry, as that they did preach a covenant of works when others did preach a covenant of grace, and that they were not able ministers of the New Testament, and that they had not the seal of the spirit, and this was spoken not as was pretended out of private conference, but out of conscience and warrant from scripture alleged the fear of man is a snare and seeing God had given her a calling to it she would freely speak. Some other speeches she used, as that the letter of the scripture held forth a covenant of works, and this is offered to be proved by probable grounds. …

Controversy—should the witnesses should be recalled and made swear an oath, as Mrs. Hutchinson desired, is resolved against doing so

Governor: I see no necessity of an oath in this thing seeing it is true and the substance of the matter confirmed by divers, yet that all may be satisfied, if the elders will take an oath they shall have it given them. …

Mrs. Hutchinson: After that they have taken an oath I will make good what I say.

Governor: Let us state the case, and then we may know what to do. That which is laid to Mrs. Hutchinson charge is that, that she hath traduced the magistrates and ministers of this jurisdiction, that she hath said the ministers preached a covenant of works and Mr. Cotton a covenant of grace, and that they were not able ministers of the gospel, and she excuses it that she made it a private conference and with a promise of secrecy, &c. Now this is charged upon her, and they therefore sent for her seeing she made it her table talk, and then she said the fear of man was a snare and therefore she would not be affeared of them. …

Dep. Governor: Let her witnesses be called.

8.   Richard Ligon, *A True and Exact History of the Island of Barbadoes* (1657)

Ligon was a hapless merchant who took the risk of going to Barbados to try to regain his fortune lost in business difficulties in England in the 1640s. Unfortunately, all that he acquired in the Caribbean was bad health from fevers, and this forced Ligon to return to England in the 1650s. He was soon in jail for his debts, and, though released, died not long thereafter in 1662. It is not clear if he wrote this account while in jail, but it was first published during his lifetime, in 1657.

I can name a planter here that feeds daily two hundred mouths [meaning black slaves], and keeps them in such order, as there are no mutinies among them; and yet of several nations from Africa. The first work to be considered is weeding … after which comes the planting [of the sugar cane] … The next thing he is to consider is his factory … [consisting] of the Boiling-house … the filling room, the Still house, and Curing House; and in all these there are great casualties [among the slaves] … by, for example, the violence of the heat from the Furnaces. … Now to recruit these Cattle, Horse, Camels, and Negroes … Merchants must be consulted, supts provided, and competent Cargo of goods adventured [in Africa] ... A Master of a ship, and a man accounted both able, stout, and honest, having transported goods of several kinds from England to a part of Africa ... and there exchanged his Commodities for Negroes ... and did not, as the manner is, shackle one to another, and them secure, but thinking them honest and faithful ... and the slaves being double the number of those on the ship, found their advantage, got weapons in their hands, and fell upon the sailors ... cutting their throats so fast, that all were lost ... before they even got out of the river [Gambra in Africa]. ...

But ... I will let you see how much the land here hath been advanced with profit [between 1647–1654] ... I have a seen a plantation of five hundred acres, which could have been purchased for four hundred pounds sterling; and now half of this Plantation ... was sold for seven thousand pounds sterling ... with time I believe that two thirds of the island will be fit for Plantations of Sugar, which will make it one of richest Spots of earth under the Sun. ...

Questions to Consider:

1. Why is the Jamestown colony considered by some to be a lottery? Why would young English men and women take a chance on being indentured servants in that colony? Why might they think twice before emigrating?
2. What was the Puritan movement? Which reforms advocated by them do you find admirable, if any, and which ones do you not find so attractive?
3. Compare and contrast the society, economy, political structures, and religious values of the Chesapeake, New England, and Caribbean English colonies.
4. What role did Caribbean colonies play in the economic and racial development of the English empire in the New World?

Credits

★ CHAPTER 3
★ BRITISH NORTH AMERICA AND
★ AN ATLANTIC ECONOMIC EMPIRE

By 1700, with the development of productive economies in Virginia, New England, the Caribbean, and with the annexation of New York, the English colonies possessed increasing importance within the empire. For the English, these colonies began to represent stable societies—and not mere frontier outposts—that demonstrated the rising power of the English (later British) nation as a whole. As further evidence for this trend, the English founded two new major colonies on the Eastern seaboard of North America by 1700, Pennsylvania and Carolina (later divided into separate North and South colonies), and each played an important role in the economic, political, and social development of the mainland thirteen colonies. In their own distinct ways, the two colonies symbolized the growing power of the commodity-export model so essential to the success of the British empire in the Atlantic. Pennsylvania, founded by the Quaker proprietor William Penn, established religious toleration coupled with large amounts of German and Scottish emigration. His colony therefore represented an important infusion of diversity into the colonies. Based in large part on wheat farming, Pennsylvania was often referred to as "the best poor man's country in the world," and many grew rich off of the production of grains for export. On the frontier to the south of Virginia, the colony of Carolina represented the extension of the Caribbean model of plantation slavery to the colonial mainland. Instead of sugar, though, the planters grew rice, and in so doing amassed the largest fortunes on the mainland. Carolina was the first mainland colony with an enslaved, subservient black majority, and this new racial hierarchy set an ugly tone for the development of white man's democracy in the eighteenth century, even as it dramatically enriched the British empire as a whole.

The colony of Pennsylvania was founded in 1680 by William Penn, a member of another radical Protestant group, the Quakers, produced by the social and political upheavals caused by the "Puritan Revolution" of the mid-seventeenth century. The Quakers did not pay church taxes, did not recognize the authority of priests and bishops, and they emphasized the "inner light" within all human beings that could be superior to human laws and institutions. Most Puritans felt that the Quakers went too far in their emphasis on direct human encounters with the divine; they also disliked the Quakers' pacifism, which seemed to deny the authority of human governments. But this persecuted group among English society found a home in North America with the help of Penn, who was actually a descendent of the English aristocracy and who was owed a debt by the king. The king essentially gave Penn the land which became Pennsylvania, and this fortuitously meant that an unpopular religious group might leave the English realm. Penn saw his colony as a "New Jerusalem" (note the similarity to Winthrop's ideas about Massachusetts Bay as a "city upon a hill"), but unlike Massachusetts, Pennsylvania would be a place far more open to religious diversity—with Penn's guarantee of religious toleration—and would also be a place where Quaker pacifism would be a guiding philosophy of government. Quaker pacifism therefore set an important, welcoming tone among the natives, since Penn was determined to buy native land, and to mandate that white settlers not otherwise encroach upon tribal grounds. In response, other native tribes throughout the colonies sought to come live in Penn's "peaceable kingdom."

Carolina, another colony established with royal land grants in 1680, was quite different from Pennsylvania. Although there was an initial attempt made by various aristocratic proprietors to control the emigrant populace, power quickly devolved to former Caribbean planters who found the climate of Carolina an ideal place to expand the slave plantation economy first pioneered in islands such as Barbados and Jamaica. Instead of sugar, the white Carolina planters grew rice and indigo (a type of clothing dye). The main, planned city, Charleston, eventually grew to rival many of the other seaport towns, and symbolized the wealth and power of the planter elite. Slavery was now present on the mainland, and it would eventually prove too tempting for other white colonists to resist as a source of cheap labor. But by taking the lead in bringing plantation slavery to the mainland, Carolina also established a dangerously unstable racial hierarchy, which threatened slave revolts.

The Carolina colony also embraced another characteristic of white colonial expansion, namely, taking a hard line with the natives. This was in stark contrast to the peaceful posture adopted by Pennsylvania toward its resident tribes. By the late seventeenth century, white planters in Carolina began selling guns to local native tribes in exchange for human beings. This meant that another slave trade came into existence in North America to provide even more cheap labor than that supplied by Africa. But the other cynical reason that Carolinian whites embraced this native American slave trade was to supposedly weaken and destroy various tribes in the southeast. Eventually, of course, there was blowback in the Yamassee Rebellion of 1715—which ended the Indian slave trade—but in the long term, violence against natives would generally succeed at pushing back the coastal tribes. Such was the case at the other geographic end of the mainland colonies, in New England. There, in the 1670s, a leading Wampanoag chieftain, Metacom, had had enough of white land encroachment, resource depletion, as well as with Puritan efforts at cultural domination through the so-called "praying Indian" settlements where natives were the subjects of attempted conversions to Western values. Metacom, known to the English as "King Philip," organized a successful coalition of several New England native tribes and launched a powerful assault on the white colonists in New England in 1676. Armed with guns they had traded from the whites, the natives spread terror and death, destroying over a dozen villages. Most of the 4,000 deaths were natives, but this constituted a huge percentage of the population of both races in New England. Eventually, the English managed to overcome the natives because of two repeated weaknesses in native societies. One, the natives eventually ran out of ammunition, since they did not make it themselves, and more importantly, the English employed the divide-and-conquer strategy of bribing the Mohawk natives in New York to help stamp out the revolt. By 1677, the New Englanders effectively destroyed the integrity and viability of native coastal tribes like the Wampanoags. They would exist in small enclaves, but coastal native tribes would never again threaten the dominance of the English.

At the same time that the English crushed native resistance in New England, white Virginian servants also revolted over what they saw as a lack of assistance from wealthier Virginians regarding putting down native attacks from the Doeg tribe. Elite Virginians soon learned to fear the power of their former indentured servants who now had guns and who would use them in a broad tax revolt against the Virginian government, headed by Governor William Berkeley. The poorer

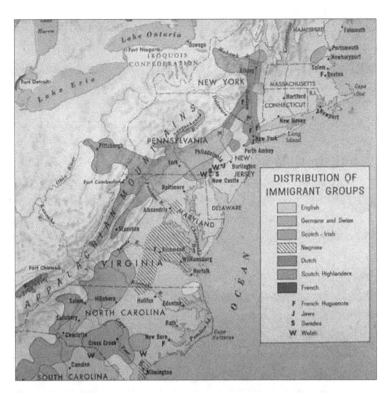

Map of areas to which certain ethnic groups migrated in the 1600s and 1700s.

whites, led by Nathaniel Bacon, eventually burned Jamestown to the ground when their demands for greater defense against natives and lower taxes went ignored. Only when Bacon died, and with the threat of royal military intervention, did Bacon's revolt run its course, leaving the elites more or less in charge. But the colony was changed forever: there would be a new capital at Williamsburg, and perhaps of more importance, black slaves would increasingly be used instead of white servants who, frankly, demanded too much of their social betters. So along with the growing English wealth from sugar and with the growing slave presence in Carolina, the rebellion of white servants helped convince white elites to transform the tobacco colony of Virginia into a society with slaves.

The African slave trade, well entrenched as the 1700s dawned, epitomized the Atlantic economy, which was the focus of the British Empire of the eighteenth century. Ships and shipping, of course, were indispensable in this empire; increasingly the English state enacted numerous laws, known as the Navigation Acts, to encourage the English colonists to trade only with other English people, and to require that only English ships—manned only with English sailors—be used in the Atlantic trade. In this way, the Navigation System desired to make England (and later Great Britain) self-sufficient, meaning that the English would always sell more things to other powers than they would import from foreigners. Eventually, the Navigation Acts would also include strenuous duties, or taxes, on foreign items in an effort to make certain that colonists only sold and bought goods to or from Great Britain. It has been debated how well these laws were enforced, but there was no question that the system of Atlantic trade, where colonists sold raw materials to Britain and in turn used or consumed British goods, made everyone involved much, much wealthier. But as mentioned earlier, cheap labor provided the basis for this wealth, and the process of getting such labor wasn't pretty. In addition to all of the dangers facing the white slave traders, including death from tropical disease and African slave revolts, it was, of course, the slaves themselves who endured a horrendous journey which, if they were lucky, ended in death (which was against the will of their enslavers). Local tribes began the slave trade by taking prisoners from the African countryside to the great slave forts (such as El Mina in Benin). From these forts, the recently enslaved would be inspected by the whites, who rarely went too far into the African mainland. And then the worst part of the slaves' journey still lay ahead: the so-called "middle passage" (or a second passage) of a triangular trade originating in London, stopping in Africa, and leaving for the Americas once finished goods (such as guns) had been traded for the slaves. The slaves were treated as nothing better than commodities on these ships, crammed together in suffocating quarters, where many died from disease as they were stuck in excrement and other filth below deck. When slaves died, they were simply dumped unceremoniously into the ocean. For the slave traders, it was important not to buy all their slaves in the same place, so as to avoid any effort at coordinated revolt among slaves who might be able to communicate with each other.

The commoditization of human beings did not stop with the slave ships, but rather continued in the English New World with a system of force, terror, and brutality that would enable whites to maximize their profits. What has been called "New World slavery" has been depicted as far more brutal and awful than other forms of slavery in human history, because the Africans were often simply worked to death, and they and their descendents generally had little legal rights to ever gain freedom. New World slavery represented an inherited legal condition imposed by whites on a group of people who could be dehumanized because they were a foreign, supposedly "uncivilized," exotic, "other." What was unimaginably barbaric for Africans was amazingly profitable for whites, since slavery was the necessary foundation for the production of sugar, tobacco, rice, and indigo, and played a large role in the production of grains and other basic materials sent home to England from the Americas. For this reason, by 1750 black slavery spread beyond Virginia, to Philadelphia, New York City, the wheat-growing farms of the middle Atlantic, as well as to the shipping and fishing ports of New England. In the North, no large plantation slave gangs existed; instead, slaves tended to work on small farms. Northern slaves generally did more important work than their plantation counterparts to the South, through their use in artisanal shops or on ships.

The growing wealth of the colonies not only led the English to devise Navigation Acts to make sure that all of this wealth stayed within the empire (for example, the colonists were not to trade with the Dutch, Spanish, and French), but also encouraged monarchs to try to stop the colonists from doing things independent of royal authority. This tension was most pronounced in Puritan New England, but it existed throughout the colonies, particularly once the strong-handed king, James II, came to the throne in 1678. James II was privately a Catholic, someone who was accused of wanting to rule without Parliament (he believed, unlike many of his subjects, that kings had a "divine right" to govern). In the case of New England, James tried to abolish the General Court in Massachusetts and really wanted an end to all local autonomy. James nearly succeeded, but for the fact that he so antagonized the English people that they literally invited an invasion from Holland by William of Orange in 1688. When William

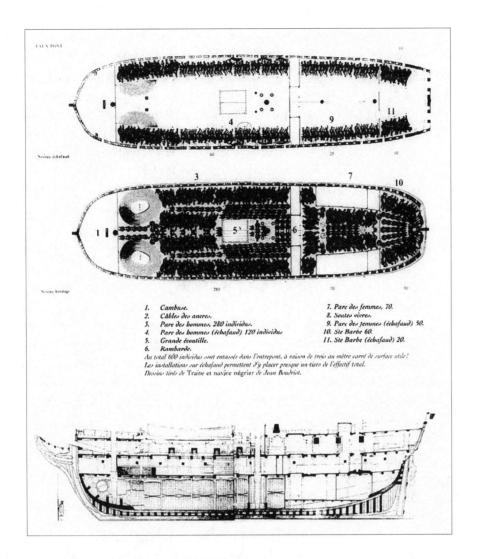

Depiction of slaves on a slave ship, circa 1700.

sailed from Holland and arrived in Torbay in Southern England in the fall of 1688, the English army simply folded; few wanted to defend James. This "Glorious Revolution," where James was sent packing to France, was reenacted in the colonies, where royal governments took it on the chin, and where the New Englanders retained most—though not all—of their local autonomy. Back in England, John Locke wrote what would become the standard justification of the ability of subjects to revolt against an unjust leader in order to defend the subjects' "life, liberty, and property." Such a strong defense for limited monarchy and the liberty of the propertied "commoners" would later help inspire colonial Americans to launch their own revolt less than a century later.

The "Glorious Revolution" of 1688–1689, however, also led to war with France. Because Louis XIV was none too pleased that the English would dare challenge the divine right of kings, in addition to his own designs on Europe, the French replaced the Spanish as the great enemy to the English nation. The new English king William did much to strengthen his kingdom—his subjects felt comfortable loaning money to the English state, and this would be an essential reason for the war-making prowess of Great Britain. William also laid the foundations for the incorporation of Scotland and Northern Ireland as constituent parts of a new "union" of Great Britain, finalized in 1707. The English nation was flexing its muscles, but the wars fought with the French certainly left their mark on the colonists, since the colonists were often on the front lines of battles with the French in the New World. Such was the case in New England, where during the first of four wars against the French, known as King William's War, further damage was done to frontier settlements, in addition to a crippling defeat of the New England militia during a failed attempt to take land in Canada. Coming less than 15 years after the traumatic experience of King Philip's (Metcaom's) War, the people of New England could be forgiven for being a bit paranoid regarding the collapse of their world. Most historians of the Salem witch trials attribute them to the social dislocation and economic stress of the late-seventeenth-century wars in New England. Originating with the accusation made by orphan girls that they had been bewitched through playing games with a West Indian slave girl named Tituba, recriminations flew around the village of Salem, Massachusetts, that several women and men had brought Satan to their once godly village. The clerical authorities were inclined to believe this as an explanation for the difficulties of the past several years, and before the mania was stopped by the colonial assembly, nineteen adults were hanged. The witch trials have fascinated numerous generations of Americans, and do speak to some of the more vicious aspects of Puritan culture. Yet the witch hysteria can also be interpreted as one of many responses to the growing pains of the mainland colonies slowly adjusting to the new and varied realities of an expanding British Empire.

As the eighteenth century dawned, therefore, several different impulses can be seen at work within the mainland English colonies. On the one hand, the stage was set for increased economic growth with a steady supply of slaves and a growing navy and merchant marine to provide the necessary transportation to bring American commodities and crops to market, as well as to import new labor. Increasingly, it would be possible for colonists to live in nicer surroundings, for cities to grow, as well for roads to be constructed, and for the establishment of a print culture. On the other hand, the English colonies might also see the downside of living under the increasing scrutiny of Great Britain, and of living in a theater for wars between European powers jealous of each other's colonial gains. Eighteenth-century Americans would therefore be subject to increasing trade restrictions, as well as to the increasing threat of military engagement, both with the French as well as with the Spanish. It should be remembered that the Spanish still held Florida, and were also trying to build more forts in modern-day Texas, Arizona, and, by the 1760s, in California. This was in addition to the increasing efforts of the French, under Canadian governor Lord Frontenac to build a string of forts from modern day Detroit, Michigan, south to New Orleans, Louisiana, ominously signaling to the British that their empire might be strangled from the west. The themes of oceanic trade and imperial war would play a great role in the eighteenth century, and both would help to influence the eventual decision made by colonial Americans to create their own nation.

Documents:

1. William Penn, *Some Account of the Province of Pennsylvania* (1681)

In this document, Penn, the Quaker founder of Pennsylvania, lays out his support for further coloni-zation on the part of England. It is important to note the similarity of Penn's views with the earlier statements of men such as Richard Hakluyt and with the early mercantilist Thomas Mun, both of whom understood how powerful England would become by establishing overseas colonies.

Colonies, then, are the seeds of nations begun and nourished by the care of wise and populous countries, as conceiving them best for the increase of human stock, and beneficial for commerce ... With justice I deny the vulgar opinion against plantations [colonies], that they weaken England. They have manifestly enriched, and so strengthened the nation, which I briefly evidence thus:

First, Those that go into a foreign plantation, their industry there is worth more than if they stayed at home, the product of their labor being in commodities of a superior nature to those of this country. ...

Second, More being produced and imported than we can spend here, we export it to other countries in Europe, which brings in money ... And this is to the advantage of the English merchants and seaman. ...

I shall now process to give some account of my own concern [in establishing Pennsylvania] ... For navigation it has two rivers ... For timber and other wood there is variety for the use of man. For fowl, fish, and wild deer, they are reported to be plentiful in those parts ... The commodities that the country is thought to be capable of are silk, flax, hemp, wine, cider, woad, madder, licorice, tobacco, pot ash, iron, hides, barrel staves, beef, pork, sheep, wool, and corn—also furs, peltry, minks, raccoon ... etc.

For the constitution of the country, the royal patent shows that the people and governor have a legislative power, so that no law can be made, nor money raised, but by the people's consent. ... That the rights and freedoms of England—the best and largest in Europe—shall be in force there. ... [and even more] ... such as the freedom of religion.

2. Declaration of Nathaniel Bacon in the Name of the People of Virginia (July 30, 1676)

This document, representing the views of the Virginian insurgent Bacon, reveals how difficult it was for colonial elites to accommodate the economic and social demands of a growing number of poorer frontier whites, many of whom had been indentured servants. It is important to note, therefore, that revolts such as the one led by Bacon helped encourage wealthy whites to turn to the use of more easily controlled African slaves in the years ahead.

[All complaints directed against Governor William Berkeley of Virginia]

For having, upon false pretenses of public works, raised great unjust taxes upon the com-moners for the advancement of his private favorites and other sinister ends ... and for not having in any measure advanced this hopeful colony either by fortifications, towns, or trade. ...

For having protected, favored, and emboldened the Indians against his Majesty's loyal subjects, never appointing any due response to their many invasions, robberies, and murders committed upon us. ...

For having ... [assumed] a monopoly of the beaver trade with the natives ... and therefore having betrayed ... the lives of his loyal subjects to the barbarous heathen.

For having ... expressly countermanded and sent back our army ... when it was on the track of those Indians who now in all places burn, spoil, [and] murder. ...

And we do further demand that the said Sir William Berkeley with all the persons [previously listed] be forthwith delivered up or surrender themselves within four days after the notice thereof ... or that [wherever] the said people ... be protected ... we declare the owners, masters, or inhabitants of the said places ... to be traitors to the people ... and bring them to Middle Plantation. ...

3.   John Easton, *A Relation of the Indian War ... 1675*

Rhode Island deputy governor Easton played an important role in trying to defend the New England colonies against the native American forces of Metacom, known as "King Philip," in the 1670s. Before the fighting began, he met with representatives from the natives, and the grievances listed below are an important indicator of how much natives lost out to white land encroachment in North America in the late 1600s.

[The representatives sent by King Philip] said that when the English first came, their king's father [Massasoit] was a great man ... and he constrained the Indians from wronging the English and he gave them corn and showed them how to plant ... but their king's brother came miserably to die by being poisoned, and another grievance was if 20 of their honest Indians testified that an Englishmen had done them wrong, it was as nothing, and if but one of the worst Indians testified against another Indian when it pleased the English, that was sufficient. Another grievance was when their kings sold land the English would claim more than was agreed to ... and other [native] kings being prone to drunkenness the English cheated them ... [also] English cattle and horses still increased so that when the natives removed from the English they still could not avoid having their crops destroyed by [English livestock].

4.   "Letter of Edward Randolph to the Board of Trade, discussing the colony of Carolina (1699)"

Randolph, an English official, was employed to inform Parliament through the Board of Trade regarding the state of the new colony of Carolina. The Board of Trade had been established as a special agency with the sole purpose of gathering and organizing data on the rapidly growing English empire. This excerpt reveals how foreign competition was often on the minds both of settlers as well as those officials representing colonial authority.

The Province has 4 Negroes to every white man, and not above 1100 white families, English and French ... Their main city is Charlestown. ... In the year 1686, one hundred Spaniards with Negroes and Indians landed 50 miles to the southwest of Charlestown, where they murdered the brother in law of the Governor of the Province ... They also fell upon a settlement of Scotchmen at Port Royal where there was not above 25 men in health to oppose them ... I find the inhabitants greatly alarmed upon the news that the French continue their resolution to make a settling on the Mississippi river, from where they may come over to the Ashley River without opposition ... The great improvement made in this province is wholly owing to the industry of the Inhabitants … they are set upon making Pitch, tar and Turpentine and planting rice and can send over great quantities yearly if they had the encouragement from England to make it, having about 5,000 Slaves to be employed in that service … but they have lost many of their vessels [by] the way war with the French and some lately by the Spaniards. …

5.   Thomas Mun, *England's Treasure by Foreign Trade* (1664)

Mun was a onetime director of England's East India Company, an early and important colonial business involved in overseas trade. In England's Treasure by Foreign Trade, Mun lays out the theory of the favorable balance of trade, whereby a nation should always export more than it imports. Mun's arguments helped to lay the foundation for the Navigation Acts, which sought to highly regulate trade between the American colonies and the mother country.

It is fit [my son] that I say something of the merchant, which I hope in due time shall be thy vocation … for the merchant is worthily called the steward of the kingdom's stock, by way of commerce with other nations, a work … which ought to be performed with great skill and conscience, so the private gain may ever accompany the public good … [Many are confused regarding] the means how to either enrich or impoverish a commonwealth, when in truth [such success or failure] is only effected by the mystery of their trade, as I shall plainly show in that which follows. …

Although a kingdom may be enriched by gifts received [such as gold or silver], or by purchase taken from other nation, yet these things are uncertain and of small consideration when they happen. The best means, therefore, to increase our wealth and treasure is by foreign trade, wherein we must ever observe this rule: to sell more to strangers yearly than we consume from them. … We may likewise diminish out imports, if we would soberly refrain from excessive consumption of foreign wares. … The value of our exports likewise may be much advanced when we perform it ourselves in our own ships, for then we get not only the price of our wares … but also the merchants gains, the charges of insurance, and of freight to carry them beyond the seas … And especially foreign wares brought in [to this nation] to be sold again should be favored [against taxation] … but the consumption of such foreign wares by people [in England] should be [more heavily taxed], which will eventually turn to the profit of the kingdom in the balance of trade. …

All the mines of gold and silver which are as yet discovered in the world are not of so great a value as those of the West Indies … in the possession of the King of Spain … and though formerly they found an incredible advantage … from both the traffic of the East [meaning Asia] and the treasure of the West Indies … now this great profit is failed, and the mischief removed by the English, Dutch, and others which partake in those East-India trades as ample as the Spanish subjects. It is further to be considered, that besides the disability of the Spaniards by their native commodities to provide foreign wares for their necessities—whereby they are forced to supply the difference with [gold and silver bullion], they have likewise the canker of war, which doth infinitely exhaust their treasure, and disperse it. … The sum of all that hath been spoken … is briefly thus … so much treasure only will be brought in or carried out of a commonwealth, as the foreign trade doth over or under balance in value. … Behold then the true form and worth of foreign trade, which is, the great revenue of the King, the honour of the kingdom, the noble profession of the merchant … the means of our treasure, the sinews of our wars, the terror of our enemies. …

6. John Locke, *Two Treatises of Government* (1689)

This treatise was published not long after the peaceful overthrow of the authoritarian King James II of England, and is a justification of the need for subjects to take back their natural rights when those rights have been infringed upon by a monarch. It is important to note the impact of such natural rights ideology on the later American Revolution in the 1770s. But it is also worth considering that Locke's definition of "natural" rights was restricted to white Englishmen, and did not necessarily refer to a broader defense of human rights.

If man in the state of nature be so free, as has been said, if he be the absolute lord of his own person and possessions … why will he part with his freedom? … To which it is obvious to answer, that though in the state of nature he has a right to freedom, yet the enjoyment of it is very uncertain and constantly exposed to the invasion of others. … This makes him willing to quit a condition which however free is full of fears and continual dangers; and it is not without reason that he seeks out others … [with which] to join into society … for the mutual preservation of their lives, liberties, and estates, which I call by the general name, property. … Government has no other end but the preservation of property. …

[Speaking of unjust confiscation of private property] … What is my remedy for a robber that so broke into my house? Appeal to the law for justice. But perhaps justice is denied, or I am crippled and cannot … If God has taken away all means of seeking remedy, there is nothing left but patience … [But often] the conquered have no court or arbitrator on earth to appeal to … the unjust use of force … puts a man into a state of war with another … for by using force, the way of beasts, he become liable to be destroyed by him he uses force against. …

7. Alexander Falconbridge, *An Account of the Slave Trade on the Coast of Africa* (1788)

Falconbridge was a former ship's surgeon on several British slave-trading voyages before being converted to the antislavery movement by British abolitionists such as Thomas Clarkson in the late 1700s. His accounts of the slave trade form an important, candid account of the viciousness of the eighteenth-century slave trade, and along with the account of former slaves such as Olaudah Equiano helped the antislavery movement wage a propaganda campaign against the slave trade.

As soon as the wretched Africans, purchased at the fairs, fall into the hands of the black traders, they experience an earnest of those dreadful sufferings which they are doomed in the future to undergo … great numbers perish from cruel usage, want of food … etc. …

Nor do these unhappy beings, after they become the property of the Europeans (from whom as a more civilized people, more humanity might be expected), find their situation in the least made better. Their treatment is no less rigorous. …they are frequently stored so close [on the slave ships], as to admit of no other posture than lying on their sides … They are placed nearly midway between the decks, at the distance of two or three feet from each deck. … About eight in the morning, the Negroes are generally brought upon deck. Their irons being examined, a long chain … is run through the rings of the shackles of the men, and then locked to another ring bolt, fixed also in the deck. … Upon the Negroes refusing to eat, I have seen coals of fire, glowing hot, put on a shovel, and placed so near their lips, as to scorch and burn them … I have also been credibly informed that a certain captain in the slave trade poured melted lead on such of the Negroes as obstinately refused their food. … On board the ships, the common sailors are allowed to have intercourse with such of the black women whose consent they can procure ... The officers are permitted to indulge their passions among them at pleasure, and sometimes are guilty of such brutal excesses as to disgrace human nature. ... It sometimes becomes necessary to shut every conveyance by which air is admitted [below decks]. The confined air, rendered noxious by the effluvia exhaled from their bodies ... soon produces fevers and fluxes, which generally carried off great numbers of them. ...

8. James Oglethorpe, Persons Reduced to Poverty May be Happy in Georgia (1732)

The colony of Georgia was idealistically established as a kind of rehabilitation camp for debtors. It was further assumed that those former debtors would not own slaves, so that they would have more time to defend planters in the neighboring colony of South Carolina against slave revolts, native incursions, or against foreign powers. Oglethorpe, a British military officer and member of Parliament, was the main leader of this business enterprise. However, within a decade, plantation agriculture, and not antislavery yeoman farming, came to typify the colony of Georgia.

Having thus described ... the pitiable Condition of the better sort of the Indigent, an Objection arises against their Removal ... It may be asked, if they can't get Bread here [in England] for their Labour, how will their Condition be mended in Georgia? The Answer is easy: They have Land there for nothing; and that Land [in Georgia] is so fertile that ... they receive an Hundred fold increase for taking very little Pains [of improving a wilderness] ...

The Legislature is only able to take a proper Course for the Transportation of small offenders, if it shall seem best ... The manners and Habits of very young Offenders would meliorate in a Country not populous enough to encourage a profligate Course of Life, but a Country where Discipline will easily be preserv'd. These [whites] might supply the Place of Negroes, and yet (because their servitude is only to be temporary) they might upon Occasion be found useful against the French, or Spaniards; indeed as the Proportion of Negroes now stands, that Country would be in great Danger of being lost, in Case of a War with either of those Powers. The present Wealth of the Planters in their slaves too probably threatens their future Ruin, if proper Measures be not taken to strengthen their Neighborhood with larges Supplies of Free-men.

9. "Virginia Governor Alexander Spotswood Addresses the House of Burgesses (ca. 1715)"

Spotswood was a successful governor of Virginia, in part because he understood the need to properly defend frontiers, as well as pay off, or otherwise entice, subordinate native tribes to be supportive of his colony. His views reveal the growing importance of backcountry settlers as a necessary buffer against natives and foreign powers in the early 1700s.

The next Matter I shall Recommend to you is the providing more effectually for the Security of your Frontiers against foreign Indians, who notwithstanding the many parties of Rangers have been on foot killed and carried off at least Twenty of our outward Inhabitants and Tributary Indians ... I am persuaded that the settling of free Protestants among our Inhabitants (on the frontier) would be a better and cheaper Safe guard to the Country than the old Method of Rangers. ... [Also] our tributary Indians will accompany white settlers, with the hope of converting many natives in the faith of our Church. ... And thus averting war. ...

[In addition] our tributary Indians, whom I am settling out with a few white men to accompany them in their Ranges, and to observe their Actions or Correspondence with foreign Indians, will need no longer Such a Guard, when by the blessing of God they become Christians, according to a Treaty I have this year made with them, for Educating all of their Children in the faith of the Church. ...

Since your last Session, I have received a large quantity of Ammunition with a Number of very good arms and other necessaries of Warr, given by her late Majesty for the Service of this country. [Nonetheless] I remark to you the naked State both of your harbors and frontiers, the disarmed Condition of your Militia, the Inconvient length of many Counties ... and I leave to your consideration whether the giving Encouragement for Extending your out settlements to the high ridge of the Mountains ... to secure the colony from the Incursions of the Indians and more dangerous encroachments of the French. ...

Questions to Consider:

1. Compare and contrast the economic, political, and racial aspects of the two English colonies of Carolina and Pennsylvania.
2. What was the process by which English colonists were able to defeat insurgent native tribes in the coastal areas of North America in the late 1600s and early 1700s?
3. Explain the economic theories associated with mercantilism and the Navigation Acts. Were they necessary for Britain's success, in your opinion?
4. Explain how domestic politics in England, as well as England foreign policy, impacted the North American colonies between 1660 and 1715.
5. What was the middle passage? Describe its effects on both black and white people.

Credits

CHAPTER 4
ANGLICIZATION OR AMERICANIZATION?
THE EIGHTEENTH-CENTURY COLONIES

In many ways, eighteenth-century mainland American colonists embraced the culture of their mother country: they were overwhelmingly Protestant, and they all shared in a common heritage of "liberty" against arbitrary monarchical government. And on a more mundane, material level, eighteenth-century white colonists benefited greatly from the economic connection to Great Britain, even if some did not like the trade restrictions practiced by the mother country against foreign imports. As the eighteenth century wore on, at least up until 1763, colonial Americans continued to imbibe elements of British intellectual and political culture and could be said to be growing more attached to Great Britain, not less so. On the other hand, over the course of the early and mid eighteenth century, significant differences emerged between the colonies and the mother country, differences that speak to the origins of a particularly "American" way of life. These differences can also be said to be the root causes for Revolution in 1775. For one thing, there was a far greater degree of religious and ethnic diversity in the mainland colonies (by the standards of the day, meaning that other Northern European languages and dissenting Protestants possessed pockets of real power in certain areas), and white Americans did not tolerate the kind of overbearing aristocracies or church authorities to which most Englishmen and Europeans had long become accustomed. The structure of American society also differed greatly from the mainland, in that the average white male colonist possessed much more land than a comparable Englishman, and every white man, it seemed, owned a gun and could vote. Of course this relative equality among white men masked the viciousness of American racial hierarchies, but this element of racial polarization too, made the colonies unique from the mother country. Finally, the white majority had experienced a far greater degree of self-government than was enjoyed even in Britain, and one could say that the forces culminating in the American Revolution began when Great Britain allowed colonists the right to elect and sit in their own legislative bodies in the 1600s.

There are several examples of how the connection between colonists and mother country enriched both in the eighteenth century, however. For one, the colonists benefited greatly from being able to sell their tobacco, rice, or lumber in England, with the support of British military assistance, and with the insurance provided by companies such as Lloyd's of London. Another beneficial relationship (for whites) can be seen with the African slave trade; with the English government helping to provide support for the Royal African Company (a slave-trading concern established in the late seventeenth century), one wonders if it would have been as easy for colonists to gain access to slaves in the early 1700s. Still another example of the partnership of the mother country with the colonists can be seen with foreign immigration: Queen Anne went

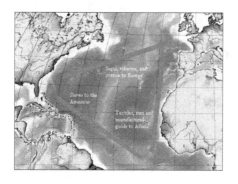

This is the customary trade route preferred by the Crown between the mainland colonies, Africa, and the mother country.

so far as to actually sponsor the emigration of Germans from various points in central Europe in the early 1700s. These intrepid foreign colonists assisted in the overall colonial effort of carving out a living in the wilderness of North America (often by violently taking land from the natives). The Rotterdam emigrants supported by either Queen Anne, William Penn, or by other Dutch merchants also speak to the role of entrepreneurship in the settling of the American colonies. Men like Penn and his merchant investors hoped to turn a profit by lending emigrants money for the voyage. Such a credit scheme was just another example of the role individual investors played in the construction of the British colonies in the Americas (as opposed to the direct royal control epitomized by the Spaniards.) As a symbol of the strength, durability, and power of this emerging British Atlantic Empire, most of the immigrants to the Americas (including slaves) were not from England, and as for the brutality of this system, the largest single group of emigrants were, in fact, African slaves. At least 250,000 of them came to the colonies over the course of the 1700s.

The growth in the economy and in the society of the mainland colonies could be seen everywhere. Several of the old seaport cities, such as Boston, New York, and Philadelphia, now boasted large brick mansions, newer taverns, mercantile firms, and wider streets to handle all of the traffic. Indeed, what is thought of as colonial architecture on the east coast of the United States (brick or stone buildings) dates from the period after 1700, as people could finally afford to leave behind the cheaper wood construction of the prior century. Material life, therefore, improved dramatically for many—if not for most—white colonists. But new clothing, new silverware, china, carriages, rugs all address what has been termed "the refinement" of the colonies. The dramatic growth of newspapers also signaled the growing wealth and sophistication of Americans. In this regard, the life story of Benjamin Franklin is crucial, as he was something of a media magnate in the eighteenth century, understanding the need for reading material which not only entertained, but which linked colonists to each other and to the mother country. The growth of this print culture, of course, could mean that the colonists might become increasingly aware of their political rights, and that these newspapers could be a dangerous breeding ground for sedition against established authority.

Such was the case with Peter Zenger in 1735, who dared to print material criticizing Governor Cosby of New York's patronage schemes as corrupt. Under British law, the language used in Zenger's piece qualified as seditious libel, but the jury hearing the case effectively nullified this law, because they believed the charges were true. The jury therefore rejected British law that criminalized all personal criticism of public figures. The not guilty verdict fired the imagination of radicals on both sides of the Atlantic, and was an early warning shot across the bow of British authority regarding the willingness of Americans to respect the privileges and prerogatives of British government. The trial also exemplified the questioning of tradition throughout the eighteenth-century Western world normally associated with the Enlightenment. A diverse movement that included mathematicians, philosophers, but also monarchs, the Enlightenment revealed a growing belief in the ability of human reason to unlock the natural laws of the universe. Those who viewed themselves as enlightened hoped that humanity would no longer be slaves to mysterious superstitions and should question everything, and learn for themselves through observation and experimentation. We have seen how this impulse not only impacted the sciences, but also played a role in the political thinking of someone like John Locke, who posited that people were essentially good and could be trusted to rise up against tyrannical leaders in order to govern themselves.

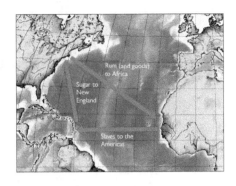

This is the route used at times by smugglers who sought to circumvent royal supervision of American trade.

Among the colonists, many individuals epitomized the Enlightenment outlook; again, the biography of Benjamin Franklin is instructive because he also took part in numerous scientific experiments, most famously regarding electrical charge. Such science, conducted in colonies largely unpopulated by Europeans just a century earlier, reveals how quickly the colonies were growing in wealth and prestige. Another man involved in new scientific fields included John Bartram of Philadelphia, who established an international reputation in the emerging field of botany: Carolus Linnaeus (arguably the most important botanist of his day) himself referred to Bartram as the "greatest natural botanist in the world." Along with Franklin, Bartram helped to establish the American Philosophical Society in 1743, devoted to supporting the work of other science in the colonies. The organization exists to this day. The intellectual ferment associated with the new interest in questioning the received wisdom of the ages also permeated all of the new educational institutions, which came into existence in the colonies in the 1700s. New colleges and universities (including much of what would later be termed the "Ivy League") emerged in the 1700s, often funded by the numerous Protestant denominations vying for converts at the time, and in some cases the faculties of these colleges were imported from elite institutions in Europe. Such was the case with John Witherspoon, a Scottish parson, who became the president and head professor of the small Presbyterian College of New Jersey (later to become Princeton University) in 1768. His courses on moral philosophy represented Enlightenment ideals of reasoning and thinking regarding the nature of man, and did not simply rely upon biblical or theological texts. Witherspoon also brought new geographic instruments and other material from across the Atlantic. Witherspoon sought to train not only ministers, but also intellectuals who might question large aspects of contemporary, conventional society. It is no surprise that one of Witherspoon's pupils was James Madison, who would later play a prominent role in the drafting of the Federal Constitution of 1787.

Even among evangelical Christians—individuals who may not have appreciated the rationalist currents of the age—the eighteenth-century attack on entrenched privilege can be seen with the "Great Awakening" of the middle part of the decade, epitomized by the amazingly popular preaching of the British self-taught minister, George Whitfield. As something of a media star, Whitfield spoke to thousands of colonists in open fields or in towns, and he helped to inspire a broad movement of Protestants to leave their old churches and their college trained ministers behind, in order to better interpret the Bible for themselves. As a social phenomenon, what has been called the "Great Awakening" really meant that an already fractured religious landscape in

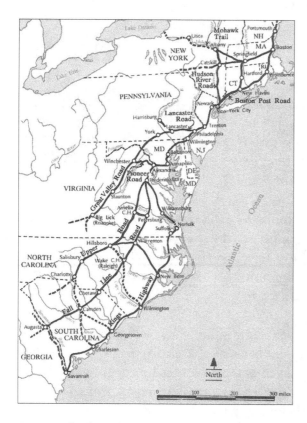

A map of colonial roads. By the mid-eighteenth century, it became possible to travel between all the mainland colonies on foot or horseback, something unimaginable just fifty years earlier.

the colonies (the Church of England was in the minority and had to compete against at least half a dozen other churches for tax support) would only grow more so. The social fragmentation—or what some would call democratization—in the world of religion could impact both genders and all races, of course. This could be dangerous business if slaves were taught to read the Bible, and such unintended consequences of literacy and mobility would lead slave owners to try to better monitor their enslaved workers.

So along with the eighteenth century's increased wealth, sophistication, and literacy came further growing pains within the mainland colonies, which in some cases were simply a continuation of the internal social and class conflicts that had plagued the colonies in the seventeenth century. First and foremost, with the huge influx of African slaves, the possibility of slave revolts dramatically increased. The largest revolt in the eighteenth-century mainland occurred in Stono, South Carolina, in 1739. In this revolt dozens of slaves managed to get their hands on weapons and butchered at least 60 whites in their homes. The roving bands of slaves were discovered almost by accident by the lieutenant governor, and there was serious retribution for those involved. But the revolt exposed the laxity of the law enforcement in South Carolina, and in response the state legislature passed an elaborate new "black code" to stop black literacy, secret meetings, and to otherwise clamp down on the autonomy of slaves in nearly every respect. Similar problems also plagued New York. In 1711, slaves reputedly started a fire along Broadway, and in 1741 an elaborate plot was uncovered consisting both of slaves and lower-class whites. These two disgruntled groups—both cheap laborers used by other colonists to build their thriving economy—intended to blow up the ammunitions depot at the end of Manhattan Island in order to burn the whole city down. These events furthered the interest in leading New Yorkers in trying to tighten restrictions both on slaves and on servants.

But the social tensions affecting colonial America did not stop at the boundaries of seaport towns and tidewater plantations; the vast unregulated stretches of land in the west toward the Appalachians also saw serious challenges to Eastern law and order. As white farmers pushed west into the mountain valleys, in some cases hundreds of miles away from the coast in colonies such as New York, Pennsylvania, or North Carolina, they grew increasingly discontent with the lack of law enforcement, lack of roads, or even with the lack of available land free to buy (a lot of land was owned by large families or speculators). These Western frontiersmen also saw little need to pay taxes to elite politicians in the east who did not generally share the proceeds with Westerners. The frontiersmen's resentments were not unlike those that fired Bacon's Rebellion in the 1670s, but now these tensions threatened many more areas. New York saw land riots occur when New England farmers moved west and disputed the heavy taxation of the old New York elite; Scottish and Scots-Irish in Pennsylvania similarly disliked Quaker and Anglican elites in Philadelphia telling them that they should not fight with natives to take land for themselves. In the case of Pennsylvania, these disputes eventually led to a group of frontiersmen, called the "Paxton Boys," marching on Philadelphia and threatening to burn it to the ground if the Easterners would not provide defense for the frontier. Elsewhere in these new, unregulated, Western regions, mobs of farmers would close down courts, intimidate law enforcement, and in the case of North Carolina "Regulators," otherwise resort to open battle with the military of the colony at the Battle of Alamance in 1771.

These internal social, economic, or racial tensions were at times made worse by the increasing proclivity of Britain to fight wars with France and Spain after 1690. In addition to King William's War, mentioned in the last chapter, the first half of the 1700s found the colonists being dragged into two more imperial wars on behalf of Great Britain: Queen Anne's War from 1702 to 1713, and King George's War from 1739 to 1748. In Queen Anne's war, New England colonists in Maine and Massachusetts were once again hit by a combined raid of French and native forces at places such as Deerfield, Massachusetts, where scores of colonist civilians died. Although the British managed to take Acadia (in Canada) from the French, the war also exacerbated frontier tensions in the south when native tribes were brought into the ambit of the European powers' battles with each other. More colonies were impacted twenty years later with renewed conflict in King George's War. During this war, widespread fear of Spanish incitement of slaves, not only in South Carolina, but even as far away as New York led to increased efforts at monitoring slaves (as mentioned earlier). The possibility of slave and servant revolts caused by Spanish forces again revealed to colonists the costs of belonging to an expanding British Empire. Meanwhile, New Englanders during King George's War helped the mother country take the important Canadian port of Louisbourg, only to find that Great Britain negotiated its return to France for other more valuable properties elsewhere in the world. The New England militia and shipping industry had paid a high price in the war, and felt snubbed by Britain's lack of interest in keeping the valuable Canadian port. This last example of conflicting interests between Great Britain and her colonies demonstrates that all was not perfect with the colonial/British relationship in the mid-1700s.

With the looming threat of internal dissension, coupled with the reality that the colonists might at times be on their own to fight Britain's enemies, many of the wealthiest colonists may have wondered whether the British government or military was going to be able to help them out if they needed aid to restore internal order or to defend against external attack. The Board of Trade—an organization based in London supposedly interested in overseeing colonial affairs—certainly hoped to settle the frontier with stable families committed to Protestantism (as opposed to the Catholicism of Britain's main enemies, France and Spain), and also hoped the new settlers would provide defense against slave insurrections. But the ability of central authorities in London to bend the colonies to their will was never great. It certainly makes sense that as the colonies "matured"—meaning that as they grew both in wealth and evolved into a more complex society in need of local leaders well equipped to manage the "lower orders"—the local elite would increasingly turn away from Great Britain for leadership, and look to themselves to take charge of a new and independent country.

Documents:

1. Gottlieb Mittelberger, "Journey to Pennsylvania in the Year 1750" (1898)

A German schoolmaster and church organist, Mittelberger traveled to Philadelphia in 1750 with the many "newlander" servants attracted to Pennsylvania for its high wages and free land. Yet Mittelberger, who returned to Germany after only three years in Pennsylvania, felt that the servants had been misled, even as thousands more continued to come to Pennsylvania in the decades following Mittelberger's journey. (Incidentally, this account was not published until long after Mittelberger's death).

The sale of human beings in the market on board the ship [when the German servants arrive] is carried out thus: Every day Englishmen, Dutchmen, and High-German people come from the city of Philadelphia ... and go on board the newly-arrived ship ... and select among the healthy persons such as they deem suitable for their business, and bargain with them how long they will serve for their passage money, which most of them are still in debt for. ... Many parents must sell and trade away their children like so many head of cattle; for if their children take the debt upon themselves ... the parents often do not know where and to what people their children are going, it often happens that such parents and children, after leaving the ship, do not see each other again for many years, perhaps no more in all their lives. ... It often happens that whole families ... are separated by being sold to different purchasers, especially when they have not paid any part of their passage money. When a husband or wife has died at sea, when the ship has made more than half of her trip, the survivor must pay or serve not only for himself or herself but also for the deceased. When both parents have died over half-way at sea, their children, especially when they are young and have nothing to pawn or pay, must stand for their own and their parents' passage, and serve till they are 21 years old. ... When a serf has an opportunity to marry in this country, he or she must pay for each year which he or she would have yet to serve, 5 or 6 pounds.

2. Jonathan Mayhew, "Discourse Concerning Unlimited Submission" (1750)

This sermon from the leading Congregationalist minister of Boston's West Church in the mid-1700s, Mayhew, reveals the religious libertarianism that could, under the right circumstances, constitute a serious challenge to the British crown. In 1750, however, colonial Americans believed the British crown would continue indefinitely its policy of "benign neglect" toward the colonies in terms of low taxes and unobtrusive government regulations. For this reason, it is likely that Mayhew sounded so positive regarding the liberty-loving nature of the British constitution.

God be thanked one may, in any part of the British dominions, speak freely (if a decent regard be paid to those in authority) both of government and religion, and even give some broad hints that he is engaged on the side of liberty, the Bible and common sense, in opposition to tyranny, priestcraft and nonsense, without being in danger either of the bastile or the inquisition; though there will always be some interested politicians, contracted bigots, and hypocritical zealots for a party, to take offense at such freedoms. ... Those nations who are now groaning under the iron scepter of tyranny, were once free. So they might, probably, have remained, by a seasonable precaution against despotic measures ... Tyranny brings ignorance and brutality along with it. It degrades men from their just rank into the class of brutes. ... This is true of tyranny in every shape. ... For which reason it becomes every friend to truth and human kind, every lover of God and the Christian religion, to bear a part in opposing this hateful monster. ...

Some have thought it warrantable and glorious to disobey the civil power in certain circumstances, and in cases of very great and general oppression, when humble remonstrances fail of having effect and when the public welfare cannot be otherwise provided for and secured, to rise unanimously even against the sovereign himself in order to redress their grievances—to vindicate their natural and legal rights, to break the yoke of tyranny and free themselves and posterity from inglorious servitude and ruin. It is upon this principle that many royal oppressors have been driven from their thrones into banishment and many slain by the hands of their subjects. It was upon this principle that Tarquin was expelled from Rome, and Julius Caesar, the conqueror of the world and the tyrant of his country, cut off in the senate house. It was upon this principle that King Charles I was beheaded before his own banqueting house. It was upon this principle that King James II was made to fly that country which he aimed at enslaving. And upon this principle was that revolution brought about, which has been so fruitful of happy consequences to Great Britain. ...

If it be our duty, for example, to obey our king merely for this reason, that he rules for the public welfare ... it follows, by a parity of reason, that when he turns tyrant, and makes his subjects his prey to devour and to destroy, instead of his charge to defend and cherish, we are bound to throw off our allegiance to him and to resist. ... [L]et us learn to be free and to be loyal both.... and while I am speaking of loyalty to our earthly prince, suffer me just to put you in mind to be loyal also to the supreme ruler of the universe, by whom kings reign and princes decree justice.

3. From Benjamin Franklin's autobiography (describing events between 1733 and 1750)

Franklin, a noted media magnate in his own day, as well as scientist and civic leader, both observed and took part in the various processes whereby the American colonies matured and became more refined in the middle of the eighteenth century. Franklin composed his autobiography between 1771 and 1790, but it remained unfinished at the time of his death.

At the time I established myself in Philadelphia there was not a good book-seller's shop in any of the colonies south of Boston ... those who loved reading were obliged to send for their books from England; the members of the Junto [philosophical club] had each a few ... I proposed that we should each bring out books [to a common room] where they would not only be ready to consult in our conferences, but become a common benefit, each of us being at liberty to borrow as he wished to read at home. ... Finding the advantage of this little collection, I proposed to render the benefit from the books more common by commencing a public subscription library. ... The institution soon manifested its utility, was imitated by other towns, and in other provinces. The libraries were augmented by donations, reading became fashionable ... and in a few years [many colonists] were observed by strangers to be better instructed and more intelligent than people of the same rank generally are in other countries. ...

4. From Benjamin Franklin's autobiography (describing George Whitfield's preaching in 1739)

Whitfield's revivals symbolized a growing democratic revolt against clerical authority in the mid eighteenth century, as well as demonstrated how a stronger, more unified American print market helped to fuel new forms of religious community.

In 1739 arrived among us from Ireland the Reverend Mr. Whitfield, who had made himself remarkable there as an itinerant preacher. He was at first permitted to preach in some of our churches; but the clergy, taking a dislike to him, soon refused him their pulpits, and he was obliged to preach in the fields. The multitudes of all sects and denominations that attended his sermons were enormous, and it was a matter of speculation to me, who was one of the multitude, to observe the extraordinary influence of his oratory on his hearers, and how much they admired him. ... It seemed as if all the world were growing religious, so that one could not walk through the town in an evening without hearing psalms sung in different families of every street.

He preached one evening from the top of the Court-House steps [in Philadelphia], which are in the middle of Market Street, [crossing Second Street]. Both streets were filled with his hearers. ... Being among the hindmost in Market Street, I had the curiosity to learn how far he could be heard, by retiring backwards ... I found his voice distinct till I came near Front Street ... [and] computed that he might well be heard by more than thirty thousand people.

5. Benjamin Franklin, "Observations Concerning the Increase of Mankind" (1755)

Franklin wrote this essay out of an interest in what we would call demography, but also as an attempt to influence British trade and tax policy. Significantly, Franklin's calculations would later be used by Thomas Malthus (1766–1834) to argue that growing populations would in fact outstrip finite resources, even though Franklin argues exactly the opposite in this essay. Franklin's views on race are also noteworthy, as they demonstrate an unfortunate tendency toward ethnic rivalry and racial prejudice among Anglo Americans dealing with new immigrants.

Land being thus plenty in America, and so cheap as that a laboring man, that understands husbandry, can in a short time save money enough to purchase a piece of new land sufficient for a plantation whereon he may subsist a family, such as not afraid to marry. For even if they look far enough forward to consider how their children, when they grow up, are to be provided for, they see that more land is to be had at rates equally easy, all circumstances considered. ...

Hence, marriages in America are more general, and more generally early than in Europe ... And if in Europe they have but four births per marriage, here we have eight. ... But notwithstanding this increase, so vast is the territory of North America, that it will require many ages to settle it fully. And till it is fully settled, labour will never be cheap here, where no man continues long a labourer for others, but gets a plantation of his own [and] no man continues long a journeyman to a trade, but goes among those new settlers, and sets up for himself. Hence labor is no cheaper now in Pennsylvania than it was thirty years ago, though so many thousands of laboring people have been imported. ...

The legislator that makes effectual laws for promoting trade, increasing employment, improving land by more or better tillage ... and the man that invents new trades, arts, or manufacturing, or new improvements in husbandry, may be properly called the father of their nation. ... Britain should not too much restrain Manufactures in her Colonies: a wise and good Mother will not do it. To distress, is to weaken, and weakening the Children weakens the whole family. ...

The importation of foreigners into a country that has as many inhabitants as at present employments and provisions for subsistence will bear, will be in the end no increase of people, unless the newcomers have more industry and frugality than the natives. And they will provide more subsistence and increase in the country, but they will generally eat the natives out. Nor it is necessary to bring in foreigners to fill up any occasional vacancy in a country, for such vacancy (if the laws are good) will soon be filled by natural generation...And since detachments of English from Britain sent to America will have their places at home so soon supplied, and increase so largely here, why should the Palatine boors [meaning poor Germans] be suffered to swarm into our settlements, and by herding together establish their language and manners to the exclusion of ours? Why should Pennsylvania, founded by the English, become a colony of aliens? ... Which leads me to one remark: that the number of purely white people in the world is proportionally very small. All Africa is black or tawny. Native Americans chiefly so. And in Europe the Spaniards, Italians, French, Russians, and Swedes are generally of what we call a swarthy complexion, as are the Germans—the Saxons only excepted, who with the English make up the principal body of white people on the face of the Earth. ... Why increase the sons of Africa by planting them in America, where we have so fair an opportunity, by excluding all blacks and tawneys, of increasing the lovely white and red? But perhaps I am partial to the complexion of my country, for such kind of partiality is natural to mankind.

6. Excerpts from the *Hamilton's Itinerarium: Being a Narrative of a Journey* (1744)

As a visitor from Scotland, Hamilton reveals in his itinerarium, or diary, a combination of wonder, amusement, and horror, which typified many European upper-class observers of the American colonies. His travel account is one of the few from a mid-eighteenth-century foreign traveler.

New York
Saturday, June 16

I found the city less in extent, but by the stir and frequency upon the streets, more populous than Philadelphia. I saw more shipping in the harbor. The houses are more compact and regular, and in general higher built, most of them after the Dutch model, with their gavel ends facing the street. There are a few built of stone; more of wood, but the greatest number of brick, and a great many covered with pantile and glazed tile with the year of God when built figured out with plates of iron, upon the fronts of several of them. The streets in general are but narrow and not regularly disposed. The best of them run parallel to the river, for the city is built all along the water, in general. This city has more of an urban appearance than Philadelphia. Their wharfs are mostly built with logs of wood piled upon a stone foundation. In the city are several large public structures. There is a spacious church, belonging to the English congregation, with a pretty high, but, heavy, clumsy steeple, built of freestone. …

New London, Connecticut …

I went home at six o'clock, and Deacon Green's son came to see me. He entertained me with the history of the behavior of one Davenport, a fanatic preacher there, who told his flock in one of his enthusiastic rhapsodies, that in order to be saved they ought to burn all their idols. They began this bon-fire with a pile of books in the public street, among which were Tillotson's *Sermons* [a rationalist preacher] … along with many other excellent authors, and [they then] sang hymns over the pile while it was burning. They did not stop there, but the women made up a lofty pile of hoop petticoats, silk gowns, short cloaks, cambrick caps, red-heeled shoes, fans, necklaces, gloves, and other such apparel, and what was merry enough, Davenport's own idol, which topped the pile, was a pair [simply] of old wore-out plush breeches. …

7. William Bull, "Report on the Stono Rebellion" (1739)

As lieutenant governor of the colony of South Carolina, Bull accidentally came across the leaders of the Stono revolt marching and celebrating as they tried to make their way to Spanish Florida. Bull was able to alert the South Carolina militia, who then put down the revolt.

My Lords, I beg leave to lay before your Lordships an account of our Affairs, first in regard to the Desertion of our Negroes. … On the 9th of September last, at Night, a great Number of Negroes arose in rebellion, broke open a store where they got guns, killed twenty-one White persons, and were marching the next morning in a Daring manner out of the Province, killing all they met and burning several Houses as they passed along the Road. I was returning from Granville County with four Gentlemen and met these Rebels at eleven o'clock in the forenoon and fortunately discerned the approaching danger time enough to avoid it, and to give notice to the Militia who on the Occasion behaved with so much expedition and bravery, as by four o'clock the same day to come up with them and killed and took so many as put a stop to any further mischief at that time, forty four of them have been killed and executed; some few yet remain concealed in the Woods expecting the same fate, seem desperate. …

It was the Opinion of His Majesty's Council with several other Gentlemen that one of the most effectual means that could be used at present to prevent such desertion of our Negroes is to encourage some Indians by a suitable reward to pursue and if possible to bring back the Deserters, and while the Indians are thus employed they would be in the way ready to intercept other that might attempt to follow and I have sent for the Chiefs of the Chickasaws living at New Windsor and the Catawba Indians for that purpose. …

8. North Carolina Regulator Advertisement (January 1768)

This is one of the earliest extant published demands from regulators in central and Western North Carolina. This document demonstrates the severe growing pains experienced by the colonies, when frontier areas felt neglected or oppressed by Eastern leaders. By 1771, the grievances listed below would lead to open warfare at the Battle of Alamance, where the regulators were finally suppressed.

We the under subscribers do voluntarily agree to form ourselves into an Association to assemble ourselves for conferences for regulating public Grievances and abuses of power in the following particulars with others of like nature that may occur:

1. That we will pay no taxes until we are satisfied they are agreeable to law and applied to the purposes therein mentioned unless we cannot help and are forced.
2. That we will pay no Officer any more fees than the Law allows unless we are obliged to it and then to shew a dislike to and bear open testimony against it.
3. That we will attend our Meetings of Conference as often as we conveniently can or is necessary in order to consult our representatives on the amendment of such Laws as may be found grievous or unnecessary and to choose more suitable men than we have heretofore done for Burgesses and Vestry men and to petition his excellency our Governor the Honorable Council and Worshipful House of Representatives His majesty in Parliament et cetra, for redress of such Grievances as in the course of this undertaking may occur and to inform one another and to learn, know, and enjoy all the Privileges and Liberties that are allowed us and were settled on us by our worthy Ancestors, the founders of the present Constitution in order to preserve it in its ancient Foundation that it may stand firm and be unshaken.
4. That we will contribute to Collections for defraying necessary expenses attending the work according to our abilities.
5. That in cases of differences in Judgment we will submit to the Majority of our Body.

To all which we do solemnly swear or being a Quaker or otherwise scrupulous in Conscience of the common Oath to do solemnly affirm that we will stand true and faithful to this cause until we bring them to a true regulation according to the true intent and meaning of it, in the judgment of the Majority.

Questions to Consider:
1. It has been said that the growing wealth of the colonies—as well as her growing attachment to the mother country—paradoxically led to a desire for mainland Americans to be free of British rule. Based upon what you have read so far, how could this be the case?
2. How were white American colonists impacted by intellectual and cultural trends in the mother country and in Europe? What effect did this have on the civic and political ideals of the colonies?
3. To what extent were the social, economic, and political conflicts of the eighteenth century caused by Great Britain, and to what extent were they caused by the American colonists themselves?

Credits

- William Dollarhide, "A map of colonial roads," *Map Guide to American Migration Routes, 1735-1815*. Copyright © 1997.
- Gottlieb Mittelberger; trans. Carl Theo. Eben, "Journey to Pennsylvania in the Year 1750," *Gottlieb Mittelberger's Journey to Pennsylvania in the Year 1754*. 1898. Copyright in the Public Domain.
- Jonathan Mayhew, "Discourse Concerning Unlimited Submission," *A Discourse Concerning Unlimited Submission and Non-Resistance to the Higher Powers*. 1818. Copyright in the Public Domain.
- Excerpts from Benjamin Franklin, *Autobiography of Benjamin Franklin*, ed. Frank Woodworth Pine. 1916. Copyright in the Public Domain.
- Benjamin Franklin, "Observations Concerning the Increase of Mankind," *Observations Concerning the Increase of Mankind, Peopling of Countries, etc. 1755*. Copyright in the Public Domain.
- Excerpts from Alexander Hamilton, *Hamilton's Itinerarium: Being a Narrative of a Journey*, ed. Albert Bushnell Hart. 1907. Copyright in the Public Domain.
- William Bull, "Report from William Bull, re. Stono Rebellion." 1739. Copyright in the Public Domain.
- Excerpt from "Regulators Advertisement No. 4," *The Colonial Records of North Carolina, vol. 7*, ed. William L. Saunders, pp. 671-672. 1768. Copyright in the Public Domain.

★ CHAPTER 5
★ TOWARD THE AMERICAN REVOLUTION,
★ 1754–1775

As mentioned in the previous chapter, colonial white Americans generally saw no alternative to British rule in the mid-1700s, if for no other reason than the colonists' material advancement depended upon their connection to an empire that was quickly becoming the greatest since Rome. By the 1750s, Great Britain also stood on the cusp of vanquishing their one great colonial competitor, France. Therefore, by 1763, the British and their colonists would be part of a triumphant victory against a foreign, Catholic foe and things should not have been better for the relationship between the American colonists and those in the homeland. But in just 12 short years, the Americans would be in all-out revolt against the mother country. So an absolutely essential question for students of the relationship between colonists and the mother country between 1763 and 1775 is: what went wrong? The simple answer is that Great Britain came away from the Seven Years' War believing that the colonists needed to pay more for the "benefits" of empire, and this desire led the British to take the dangerous step of disregarding the right of colonists to decide upon their own internal taxation through their own local assemblies, so that the Parliament might directly tax the Americans. This infringement on the customary privilege of the colonists' local government—one that had been in force for well over a century—was viewed by the American mainland colonists as an effort by their leaders to enact a conspiracy to enslave them. Furthermore, the colonists believed that the British constitution itself, defined here as a liberty-loving legal and political system, was now under assault. In order to save that British liberty, therefore, colonial Americans embarked on a revolution to establish a new republic.

The immediate trigger for the imperial crisis between mainland colonies and the mother country came from the growing tensions between the British and the French in the mid-1700s. This was in no large part due to the very success of the colonists, who were now pushing in droves toward—and in some cases over—the Appalachian mountain chain. By 1750, thousands of British settlers (who now included Scottish, Irish, and Germans) now lived in areas by the Ohio River or by the Great Lakes, which the French laid claim to largely because they wanted to take part in the lucrative fur trade with the natives. In addition, wealthy English land speculators wanted to invest in, or otherwise "open up" areas of land in what is now Western Pennsylvania, Ohio, and Kentucky. The best known groups of these land speculators formed the Ohio Company, a real estate firm which many of the best families of Virginia had bought into (including such future revolutionaries as George Washington.) By the early 1750s, the French had had enough of English land encroachment on territory they saw as under their control, and the French began to build several new forts in what is now Western New York,

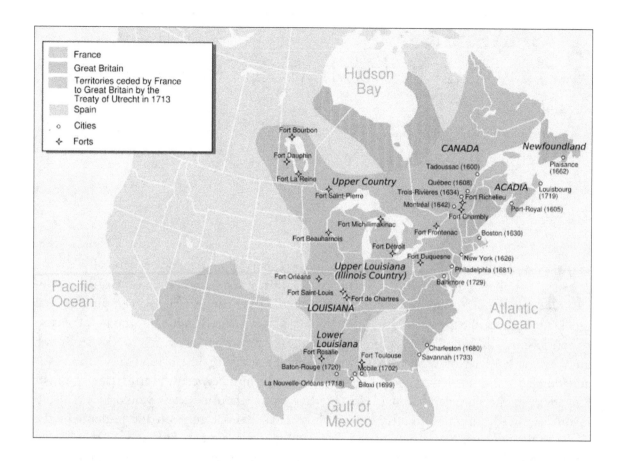

North America on the eve of the French and Indian, or Seven Years, War.

Pennsylvania, and Ohio for two purposes: one, for defense against the British, and two, to ensure that local tribes remained loyal fur traders with the French. In response, of course, the British could not just sit back, and they decided to build more forts of their own, such as Fort Necessity in Western Pennsylvania. But this fort, hastily constructed by a young militia officer named George Washington, was no match for the French, and Washington endured the embarrassing and deadly defeat at that fort in July of 1754. When another military leader, Edward Braddock, tried again a year later to eject the French from Fort Duquesne, not only were the British defeated, but Braddock was killed. For the English, something had to done, as the French with their native allies now threatened the entire backcountry tenuously inhabited by white British colonists. In response to this dire situation came British prime minister William Pitt, who believed in marshalling the resources of the British gentry–funded debt market (one of the financial tools the French did not have) to borrow heavily and to take the French on throughout the globe. In addition, the British sent more than 20,000 redcoats to the American colonies and to Canada. This tipped the scales in favor of the Americans, and with great British expense, the French were vanquished: all of Canada, the Ohio Valley, and the lower Mississippi region now existed as a vast terrain for settlement and economic production supposedly for white Americans. Or so the colonials thought.

In reality, all of the British aid came with strings attached, and since the British saw themselves as the greatest empire in the history of the modern world—and since their redcoats had so wildly outperformed the provincial militia during the Seven Years' War—the British felt they needed to remind the Americans who was boss, as it were. Of course, the British believed that they had the power and ability to do this. As we will see, throughout the 1760s and 1770s, the British constantly overestimated what they could make the colonists do, all the while accomplishing nothing more than driving the colonies out of the empire. There were three main "imperial crises" between 1763 and 1775: the first was the Stamp Tax of 1765; the second, the Townshend

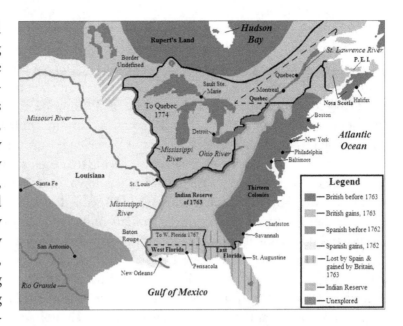

This map reveals the dramatic increase in British territory after their victory over France in 1763. All of this new territory would, of course, not be cheap to manage in the years ahead.

Revenue Program of 1767; and the third and final one being the crisis surrounding the Tea Act of 1773. Furthermore, throughout the 1760s and 1770s, the British constantly sought to increase troop deployments to the colonies, and this further inflamed the colonists' dislike of the new taxes.

In 1765 George Granville, the leader in Parliament, announced that he needed to raise a revenue to help pay off the war debts, as well as to help station more redcoats in the colonies, primarily to regulate all of the new land now acquired from France, in addition to preserving the lucrative fur trade with the natives. (These requests came on the back of increased attempts at prosecuting smuggling and otherwise tightening up the Navigation System with the Sugar Act in 1764, it should be added.) To pay for his ambitious program, Granville proposed and won passage of a Stamp Tax, which meant that every deed, will, mortgage, indenture, and newspaper in the colonies now had to have a certain number of one cent stamps on it to be legally sold or transacted. Besides the nuisance of paying the tax, what so angered the colonists about this new tax was that it was paying for matters relating to internal defense, matters that had customarily been handled by the local colonial assemblies. Of course, these assemblies were not likely going to pay this tax for redcoat soldiers in any event, but the colonists also made the argument that the prerogatives, or rights, of their local assemblies were now being infringed upon by Parliament. And in response, nearly every colonial legislature issued protests against the tax, and colonists convened a Stamp Act Congress in New York, where the colonists tried to band together to convince the Parliament of how displeased they were with these new tax measures.

But opposition to the Stamp Tax continued far beyond the halls of the representative assemblies. During the 1760s, groups of ordinary citizens such as the "Sons of Liberty" sprang into action, representing an important mobilization of common people. Eventually this sort of popular involvement became absolutely necessary to carry out the revolution from the patriot perspective. With the encouragement of the Sons of Liberty, the crowd got in on the action and terrorized and nearly killed the stamp collectors or other colonial officials when the authorities tried to land and sell the stamps. In the case of Boston, the mob got so out of hand they actually demolished the mansion of the lieutenant governor, Thomas Hutchinson, thus signaling the willingness of British subjects to seriously challenge authority and private property if they believed their liberty was being taken away. Seeing that their stamps couldn't even be landed in any of the colonial seaports, Parliament backed down. Still, Parliament continued to maintain that it had the right to tax the colonists, and issued a declaration stating so in 1766.

American colonists were not sure if Parliament had learned its lesson, but within a year they would find out definitely that Parliament not only would not change course, but wanted to try to tax and control the colonists even more. The new prime minister, Charles Townshend, was convinced the colonials were spoiled brats who needed to be put in their place, and he devised a new and trickier way to attempt to raise revenue. What made the Townshend program all the more odious was that the revenue gained would likely not be used to pay down the war debt. Instead, Townshend intended the money to be used to tighten the enforcement of smuggling violations against the Navigation System, to create a new American Board of Customs commissioners to be headed by a man named Lord Hillsborough, besides making colonial judges and governors independent of the funding of the local assemblies. So in reality, Townshend simply wanted to tighten royal control over the colonies—regardless of the cost—and he proposed new duties on paint, lead, glass, and tea to do this. He assumed that Americans would have no choice but to pay these duties, since they were all necessary imports not generally produced in America. But he, like most leaders in Parliament, had no clue regarding the earnestness of the colonists to resist taxation, even if it meant extreme hardship. Led in part by the writings of John Dickinson, colonists devised a nonimportation movement, or boycott, and threatened local merchants if they purchased these goods taxed by Townshend. Once again, the local assemblies made a coordinated effort to organize resistance with a document called the "Circular Letter." This letter reaffirmed the commitment of American politicians to the boycott. For daring to protest the king and Parliament, the new Secretary of State of the colonies, Hillsborough, dissolved every one of these assemblies (they were eventually reinstated). Although it took time, this boycott did work, and the Townshend program was repealed in a couple of years.

Still, an uneasy calm existed, especially as the increased military presence made the colonists feel as though they were being occupied by a foreign power. Beginning with the proclamation line of 1763, Americans were forbidden from taking as much land as they wanted from the natives, and more redcoat garrisons were stationed throughout the frontier and in the seaport cities to demonstrate the seriousness of the British toward enforcing various aspects of imperial policy. This desire for troops only increased once it became clear that colonial Americans sought to resist the various taxation schemes. It should also be remembered that in the 1700s, soldiers were not paid much, and were expected to be housed and employed by the local populace. In the context of American resistance, this was akin to pouring gasoline on a fire, and in the case of Boston, tensions boiled over between the citizens and redcoats in the so-called "Boston Massacre." In March of 1770, redcoats became a symbol of tyranny associated with the duty on tea, which remained in force from the Townshend scheme. After a small boy was killed

Map of the thirteen mainland British colonies on the eve of Revolution.

in an earlier scuffle with a merchant accused of trading with the British, scattered fights broke out over the city. This culminated in the redcoats being outnumbered and attacked with stones; the colonists were literally daring the redcoats to fire so as to whip up other colonies to eject the military force from Boston. The soldiers did indeed fire, killing five of the rioters. Although they were acquitted, the "Boston Massacre" was used by the patriots to increase the alarm among the colonists regarding the threat of a standing army in North America.

British ministers should have learned from this incident the lesson of dealing carefully with the colonists. But parliamentary leaders were in no position to bow down and grovel for respect from the colonists, and believed that entire communities needed to be punished with military occupation if they insisted on being insubordinate. The British adhered even more to this hard-line mentality when a ship trying to prosecute smuggling, the *Gaspee*, was attacked and burned by colonists in Rhode Island when it ran aground in June 1772. Parliament threatened to send Americans to England for trial, but, of course, no American cooperated in determining who was involved. But the die was cast: the British would begin to think about the need to use martial law to try to enforce what they saw as simple respect for the empire. As mentioned earlier, by this point, there was no hope of getting enough money to balance the books of the empire, as it were. Rather, by the early 1770s, Parliament simply wanted colonists to admit their allegiance to the empire.

And so in 1773, in an idiotic effort to bail out the British East India Company, Parliament gave the company a monopoly on the tea trade (thus cutting out Dutch competitors), in order to both lower the price, but also to force Americans to pay the Townshend duty. By having no choice but to buy East India tea (which was technically cheaper), Parliament (at this point headed by Lord North) assumed they couldn't lose. Of course, the British were wrong. Colonial Americans were not about to assent to any more regulations from Parliament, besides the fact that those colonial tea merchants who traded with other countries were now losing business with the East India monopoly. It soon became apparent that most colonial governors would not allow the tea to be landed, but Thomas Hutchinson of Massachusetts was different. Hutchinson had been under attack in the press for having denounced the "liberty men" among his subjects to the British. Hutchinson was therefore all the more determined to try to land the hated East India tea, even though other colonial governors knew better. Rather than be intimidated into having to purchase this tea, a meeting of concerned colonial subjects—led in no small part by Samuel Adams—got riled up and decided to dump the tea (worth the equivalent of several million current U.S. dollars) into Boston Harbor.

This gesture was not lost on British leaders in London, who responded with fierce measures known as the Coercive or "Intolerable" Acts. In addition to closing the port of Boston until the tea was paid for, Parliament abolished representative government in Massachusetts, placing it under the authority of General Thomas Gage in 1774. The Coercive Acts also attempted to curtail colonial land speculation in the west with the Quebec Act (in addition to recognizing the legality of Catholicism in that recently-won colony from France). The acts inflamed colonists far beyond New England, and in response the First Continental Congress was formed, with all colonies sending representatives to Philadelphia in September 1774. This congress soon endorsed new boycotts against Great Britain, both in terms of importing (which had dated back to the Townshend protests) but also exporting goods. Shutting down all trade to Great Britain represented an important effort to teach London a lesson regarding how serious Americans were in defending their liberty. In numerous locales throughout the mainland colonies, groups of concerned subjects banded together to terrorize or coerce merchants into supporting the boycott. These associations also helped lay the foundations for government separate from the monarchy and Parliament. The colonists had come a long way from the failed efforts at unity seen with the Albany Congress of 1755; now, it was at least conceivable that the individual colonies might begin to act as one to strike boldly against an empire which they believed had betrayed them.

Documents:

1. "The Commission of the Board of Trade" (1696)

King William appointed eight paid commissioners to advise him regarding the empire and trade policy, but its supervisory powers were never as great as its desire for influence. By the mid-1760s, this board had lost much of its influence and credibility with Parliament, though it would be revived in later years.

His Majesty's Commission for promoting the trade of this kingdom and for inspecting and improving his plantations in America and elsewhere. ... [we, the monarch, do] empower you ... to take an account of the state and condition of the general trade of England, and also of the several particular trades in all foreign parts ... and to inquire into and examine what trades are or may prove hurtful, or are or may be made beneficial to our kingdom of England, and by what ways and means the profitable and advantageous trades may be more improved and extended ... [and those not] rectified and discouraged. And we do hereby further require you to inform yourselves of the present condition of the respective plantations ... the administration of the government and justice in those places [as well as] the commerce. ... And we do empower you to examine such acts of the assemblies of the plantations ... as shall ... be sent hither for our approbation; and to set down ... the usefulness or mischief thereof to our Crown and to England ... and also to require an account of all moneys given for public uses by the assemblies in our plantations.

2. Benjamin Franklin, *The Albany Plan of Union* (1754)

Franklin proposed this plan at the Albany Congress, as a means of showing Great Britain the ability of colonists to work together to address frontier tensions. Although the plan is significant as an early attempt at union, it is more notable for its failure.

Plan of a Proposed Union of the Several Colonies ... that humble application be made for an Act of Parliament, by virtue of which one general Government may be formed in America ... That the said General Government be administered by a President General, to be appointed and supported by the Crown And a Grand Council to be Chosen by the Representatives of the People of the Several Colonies ... That the President General with the Advice of the Grand Council, hold or direct all Indian treaties in which the General Interest or Welfare of the Colonies may be concerned, and make peace or declare War with Indian Nations. That they make such Laws as they Judge Necessary for regulating all Indian Trade. That they make all Purchases from Indians for the Crown, of Lands now not within the Bounds of particular Colonies, or that shall not be within their Bounds when some of them are reduced to more Convenient Dimensions. ... That they raise and pay Soldiers, and Build Forts for the defence, of any of the Colonies, and Equip Vessels of Force to guard the Coasts and protect the Trade on the Ocean ...

Franklin's response:

All of the Assemblies in the colonies have, I suppose, had the Union Plan laid before them; but it is not likely, in my Opinion, that any of them will act upon it so as to agree to it, or to propose any Amendments to it. Every body cries that a Union is absolutely necessary [for the thirteen colonies], but when they come to the Manner and Form of the Union, their weak minds are presently distracted. So if ever there be an Union, it must be form'd at home by the Ministry and Parliament. I doubt not but they will make a good one, and I wish it may be done this Winter.

3. Reverend Thomas Barnard, "A Sermon Preached Before his Excellency Francis Bernard" (1763)

This sermon, from an American minister who eventually decided to side with the British during the Revolution, reveals the patriotic fervor felt by many colonists in the immediate aftermath of British victory in the Seven Years' War. Many colonists felt quite proud to be British, and yet not more than 12 years later, the colonists of Massachusetts were in revolt against the mother country.

Britain, favoured of God, has hitherto maintained her Liberty ... may she ever flourish, and 'under her Shadow we shall all be safe. ...' Intestine frauds and treasons, the Weakness and Wickedness of Princes, foreign invasions, have all in Event ... served to fix Liberty more firmly. ...

England ... for a century past [has] been constantly endangered by the insidious Arts of France, the unceasing enemy of her Tranquility. ... At length, this aspiring power rightly judged that her future efforts ... would be vain if the British Plantations on the Continent of America should flourish and extend, and derive Wealth and Strength for their Mother-Country (as they found the inhuman stimulating the Savages to their Destruction would not effect the Purpose. ... The Exaltation of Great Britain to the Summit of earthly Grandeur and Glory, was reserved in the Counsels of God for the Age and Reign of GEORGE the *Third*. ...

Now commences the Era of our quiet Enjoyment of those Liberties which our Fathers purchased with the Toil of their whole Lives, their Treasure, and their Blood ... Here shall our indulgent Mother ... be served and honoured by Growing Numbers with all Duty, Love and Gratitude.

4. "From the Acts of the Privy Council (King's Advisers), regarding the Customs Service for the American Colonies" (1763)

Distinct from the Board of Trade, the Privy Council nonetheless shared in the board's belief that the mainland American colonists needed to show more respect for British trade law. The unruly behavior of the American colonists during the Seven Years' War also fueled a desire among the British government to take a tougher stance with the colonists concerning taxes and trade.

We observe with concern that through neglect, connivance, and fraud, not only the revenue due this empire is impaired but the commerce of the colonies is diverted from its natural course [to other countries such as Spain, Holland, or France] ... Attention to objects of so great importance ... is more indispensible when the military establishment necessary for maintaining these colonies requires a large revenue to support it, and when [the colonies'] vast increase in territory and population the proper regulation of their trade of immediate necessity lest the continuance [of evasion] render all future attempts to remedy them utterly impracticable. ... We have endeavored therefore to discover and remove the causes of the deficiency of this revenue and of the contraband trade with other European nations ... we have ordered all officers belonging to the customs service to stay in the colonies, to reside there for the foreseeable future ... We have directed that all the officers of the revenue in the colonies ... by regular and constant correspondence give an account ... and inform us of any obstructions they may meet ... We are further of the opinion that ... Majesty's ships and troops ... [use] force under their respective commands as will be most serviceable in suppressing these dangerous practices, and in protecting the officer of the revenue from the violence of any desperate and lawless persons.

5. Declarations of the Stamp Act Congress (1765), held in New York to protest the Stamp Act

At the encouragement of the Massachusetts Assembly, representatives of nine colonies met in 1765 in Manhattan to protest the new tax measures being advocated by Parliament. This would not be the last time where colonial legislatures asserted a right to meet and confer in order to challenge parliamentary authority over the colonies.

The members of this congress ... with minds deeply impressed by a sense of the present and impending misfortunes of the British colonies on the continent ... make the following declarations ... respecting the most essential rights and liberties of the colonists ...

2. That his Majesty's liege subjects in these colonies are entitled to all the inherent rights and liberties of his natural born subjects within the Kingdom of Great Britain.

3. That it is inseparably essential to the freedom of a people, and the undoubted right of Englishmen, that no taxes should be imposed on them, but with their own consent, given personally, by their representatives. ...

6. That ... it is unreasonable that the people of Great Britain [should] grant to his Majesty the property of the colonists ...

7. That the late act of Parliament entitled, an act for granting and applying certain Stamp Duties ... by imposing taxes on the inhabitants of these colonies ... by extending the jurisdiction of the courts of admiralty [courts without juries] ... have a manifest tendency to subvert the rights and liberty of the colonists. ...

12. That the increase, prosperity, and happiness of these colonies, depend upon the full and free enjoyment of their rights and liberties, and an intercourse with Great Britain, mutually affectionate and advantageous. ...

Lastly ... it is the indispensable duty of these colonies to the best of sovereigns ... to procure the repeal of the Act for granting and applying certain stamp duties ... and of the other late Acts for the restriction of American commerce.

6. John Dickinson, *Letters from a Farmer in Pennsylvania* (1768)

The Pennsylvania lawyer and legislator Dickinson wrote these letters as part of a continued effort on the part of colonial leaders to unify behind opposition to renewed British attempts at taxation under Charles Townshend. Dickinson's letters were largely responsible for the growing colonial movement to boycott British goods as a way of protesting British tax policy.

The parliament unquestionably possesses a legal authority to regulate the trade of Great Britain, and all her colonies ... all [laws] before were calculated to regulate trade, and preserve or promote a mutually beneficial intercourse between the several constituent parts of the Empire ... The raising of a revenue [however] was never intended by parliament. ... Mr. Grenville first introduced this language [in the Stamp Act].

We feel to sensibly that any ministerial measures related to these colonies ... may divide the spoils torn from us in what manner he [Townshend] pleases, and we shall have no way of making him responsible ... if he should then reward the most profligate, ignorant, or needy dependents ... with places of the greatest trust [over the colonies] ... the house of common will not ... contradict a minister who shall tell them it is become necessary to lay a new tax upon the colonies. ...

How many there are who, if they can make an immediate profit to themselves, by lending assistance to those whose projects plainly tend to the injury of their country, rejoice in their dexterity and believe themselves entitled to the character of able politicians ... Miserable men! [Their] opinions are certainly as detestable as their practices are destructive. ... Our vigilance and our union are success and safety, Our negligence and our division our distress and death. ...

7. Charleston Merchants Propose a Plan of Nonimportation (1769)

This document in favor of a boycott further reveals the growing attempts at unity by colonists in different regions to oppose the Crown. What does it mean that these merchants would even seek to stop further imports of the very slaves who in large part built their colony?

Resolutions

1. That we will encourage and promote the use of North American manufactures in general, and those of this province in particular. And any of us who are vendors thereof, do engage to sell and dispose of them at the same rates as heretofore.
2. That we will upon no pretence whatsoever ... import into this province any of the manufactures of Great Britain, or any other European or East India good. ...
3. That we will us the utmost economy in our persons, houses, and furniture; particularly, that we will give no mourning, or gloves, or scarves at funerals.
4. That from and after the 1st day of January, 1770, we will not import, buy, or sell any Negroes that shall be brought into this province from Africa. ...
5. That we will not purchase from, or sell for, any masters of vessels, transient persons, or non-subscribers, any kind of European or East India goods whatever, excepting coals and salt, after the 1st day of November next.
6. That as wines are subject to a heavy duty, we agree not to import any on our account or commission, or purchase from any master of vessel, transient person, or non-subscriber, after the first day of January, next.

8. John Adams, excerpts from his diary (December 17, 1773)

The Boston lawyer and colonial legislator Adams would come to play a large role in the forming of the Continental Congress, and would become vice president and later president of the United States. His Diary provides a window on his responses to many of the seminal events of the late eighteenth and early nineteenth centuries, including the so-called Boston Tea Party.

Last night, 3 Cargoes of Bohea Tea were emptied into the Sea. This Morning a Man of War sails.

This is the most magnificent movement of all ... The people should never rise without doing something to be remembered—something notable and striking. ... This however is but an Attack upon Property. Another similar Exertion of popular power may produce the destruction of Lives. Many persons wish, that as many dead Carcasses were floating in the Harbour as there are Chests of Tea. ...

What measures will the Ministry take, in Consequence of this? ... will they punish us? How? By quartering troops upon Us?—by annulling our Charter?—by laying on more duties? By restraining our Trade? By sacrifice of Individuals or how.

The Question is whether the Destruction of this Tea was necessary? I apprehend it was absolutely and indispensably so—To let it be landed, would be giving up the Principle of Taxation by Parliamentary Authority, against which the Continent have struggled for 10 years. ...

9. "Parliament Debates the Coercive Acts" (1774)

Although the vote in Parliament's favor of the Coercive Acts was not close, it is important to understand that there were those in Parliament who saw things in a similar fashion as the Americans.

General Conway: The consequence of this bill will be very important and dangerous. Parliament cannot break into a right without hearing the parties. The question then simply, is this—Have they been heard? What! Because the papers say a murder had been committed, does it follow they have proved it? ... Gentlemen will consider, that this is not only the charter of Boston, or of any particular part, but the charter of ALL America. Are the Americans not to be heard? ... I do think, and it is my sincere opinion, that we are the Aggressors and Innovators, and not the Colonies. We have irritated and forced upon them for these six or seven years past. We have enacted such a variety of laws, with these new taxes, together with a refusal to repeal the trifling duty on tea: all these things have served no other purpose but to distress and perplex. ... Have you not a legislative right over Ireland? And yet no one will dare say we have a right to tax. These acts respecting America, will involve this country and its ministers in misfortunes, and I wish I may not add, in ruin ...

Mr. Rigby: I think this country has a right to tax America; but I do not say that I would put any new tax on at this particular crisis; but when things are returned to a peaceable state, I would then begin to exercise it. And I am free to declare my opinion, that I think we have a right to tax Ireland, if there was a necessity to do so, in order to help the mother country. If Ireland was to rebel and resist our laws, I would tax it. The mother country has an undoubted right and control over the whole of its colonies. Again, sir, a great deal has been said concerning requisition. Pray, in what manner is it to be obtained? Is the king to demand it, or are we, the legislative power of this country to send a very civil, polite gentlemen over to treat with their assemblies? ... Is he to tell the speaker that we have been extremely ill used by our neighbors the French. That they have attacked us in several quarters; that the finances of this country are in a bad state; and therefore we desire you will be kind enough to assist us, and give us some money? Is this to be the language of this country to that; and are we thus to go cap in hand?

Mr. C. Fox: I believe America is wrong in resisting against this country, with regard to legislative authority. ... But, sir, there has been a constant conduct practiced in this country, consisting of violence and weakness: I wish those measures may not continue, nor can I think that the stamp-act would have been submitted to without resistance, if the administration had not been changed; the present bill before you ... irritates the minds of the people, but does not correct the deficiencies of [our] government [in the colonies]. ...

Sir Richard Sutton read a copy of a letter, relative to the government of America, from a governor in America, to the Board of Trade, shewing that, at the most quiet of times [formerly] the dispositions to oppose the laws of this country were strongly ingrafted in them, and that all their actions conveyed a spirit and wish for independence. If you ask an American, who is his master? He will tell you he has none, nor any governor but Jesus Christ. I do believe it, and it is my firm opinion, that the opposition to the measures of the legislature of this country, is a determined prepossession of the idea of total independence.

10. Declaration and Resolves of the First Continental Congress (1774)

Influenced by the outbreak of hostilities in Massachusetts, all colonies except Georgia sent representatives to a new congress meeting in September in Philadelphia. By this time, many delegates were determined to make a stronger, unified stance against Britain, and among other things, this congress decided upon a complete cessation of all trade with the mother country, known as the non-exportation movement.

Whereas ... that the inhabitants of the English Colonies in North America, by the immutable laws of nature, the principles of the English constitution, and the several charters of compacts, have the following Rights. ... That our ancestors who first settled these colonies were at the time of their emigration ... entitled to all the rights, liberties, and immunities of free and natural-born subjects within the realm of England ... That the respective colonies are entitled to the common law of England, and more especially ... [are entitled] to the great and inestimable privilege of being tried by a jury of their peers. ... That they have the right to peaceably assemble, consider their grievances, and petition the King. ... That the keeping of a standing army in these colonies, in times of peace, without the consent of the legislature of that colony in which such army is kept, is against law. ... In the course of our inquiry, we find many infringements and violations of the foregoing rights ... and proceed to state such acts and measures as have been adopted since the last war, which demonstrate a system formed to enslave America. [Then proceeds to protest the "Coercive Acts."]

Questions to Consider:

1. It has been said that the American patriots revolted against Britain because they possessed an idealized notion of British liberty. Put another way, American patriots revolted out of a need to preserve certain British values, which were being subverted in the mother country. Is this statement true?
2. Did Great Britain chase the mainland colonies out of the empire? Why or why not?
3. Considering both the long-term (back to 1607) and short-term causes of the American Revolution, at what point did a revolution become inevitable, in your opinion?
4. Were the mainland colonists different from the mother country than even they realized in 1775? If true, did this fact make a revolt inevitable?

Credits

- Copyright © Pinpin (CC BY-SA 3.0) at https://commons.wikimedia.org/wiki/File:Nouvelle-France_map-en.svg.
- Copyright © Jon Platek (CC BY-SA 3.0) at https://commons.wikimedia.org/wiki/File:NorthAmerica1762-83.png.
- "Map of Territorial Growth 1775," *National Atlas of the United States*. 1775. Copyright in the Public Domain.
- "The Commission of the Board of Trade," *The Manuscripts of the House of Lords, 1695-1697: New Series*, vol. 2. 1903. Copyright in the Public Domain.
- Excerpts from Benjamin Franklin, "July 10, 1754," *The Albany Plan of Union*. 1754. Copyright in the Public Domain.
- Excerpt from Benjamin Franklin, *From Benjamin Franklin to Peter Collinson*. 1754. Copyright in the Public Domain.
- Reverend Thomas Barnard, "A Sermon Preached Before his Excellency Francis Bernard." 1763. Copyright in the Public Domain.
- "From the Acts of the Privy Council (King's Advisers), Regarding the Customs Service for the American Colonies."
- Excerpts from The Declaration of Rights of the Stamp Act. 1765. Copyright in the Public Domain.
- John Dickinson, *Letters from a Farmer, in Pennsylvania*. 1774. Copyright in the Public Domain.
- Excerpt from "Resolutions," *Publications of the Colonial Society of Massachusetts*, vol. 19, pp. 218-219. 1918. Copyright in the Public Domain.
- Excerpts from John Adams, "December 17, 1773," *Diary*. 1773. Copyright in the Public Domain.
- "Parliament Debates the Coercive Acts," *Principles and Acts of the Revolution in America*, pp. 195. 1882. Copyright in the Public Domain.
- Declaration and Resolves of the First Continental Congress. 1774. Copyright in the Public Domain.

★ CHAPTER 6
★ THE AMERICAN REVOLUTION, 1775–1783
★

By the spring of 1775, the colony of Massachusetts found itself under military rule, but as usual, this did nothing to stop the desire of the American colonists to continue to govern themselves and to otherwise coordinate resistance against the Crown. When military general and Massachusetts governor Thomas Gage closed down the General Court in Boston (the main colonial legislative body), men such as Samuel Adams and John Hancock simply moved west to Concord, where they could assemble and more importantly, stockpile weapons in the event of an all-out war. Seeing this, Gage, under direction from Lord North in London, in fact decided to march west toward Concord with the intent of arresting Adams and Hancock to attempt to break up the extralegal, shadow government headed by those two men. However, as Gage marched toward Concord, he was met by the local colonial militia (also known as the minutemen) at the village of Lexington. The colonials may have actually started to walk away when the "shot heard round the world" was fired (no one is quite sure by whom), and the rest, as they say, was history. Although the colonial militia retreated at Lexington, they soon regrouped and overwhelmed the redcoats, sending them fleeing back to Boston. Although many other colonists had hoped to appeal to the king, and perhaps were frightened to death of actually trying to break away from the greatest empire in the Western world, it was really only a matter of time from that fateful day in April 1775 until independence would be declared.

After Gates realized that he could not take Concord by force, he asked Parliament for more reinforcements—in fact, he asked for nearly as many redcoats as had been used to defeat the French in the Seven Years' War. This should have given pause to the British government, but as we have seen, the government was obsessed with trying to use force to simply keep the Americans in the empire. The British had embraced a military escalation and it appeared that nothing could deter the majority in the British government from continuing this policy of force, even if there were some dissenters. Meanwhile, Americans convened a Second Continental Congress for the purpose of rallying the colonists to the defense of New England. John Adams nominated George Washington of Virginia to lead a new, transcolonial Continental Army, organized with the intent of supporting the efforts in New England to eject the British from Boston. The congress also allowed John Dickinson's "Olive Branch" petition to the king, but this act likely was motivated more by desperation and fear than anything else. Many colonists tried to believe that the king was really on their side, and had been misled by Parliament. However the king soon showed his colors as a hard-liner himself by rejecting this petition. As the months progressed, two main developments would push the Second Continental Congress to declare independence. First and foremost, Washington, the Continental Army, and the New England militia proved quite effective at making life difficult for the British in Boston. At the Battle of Bunker Hill, for example, in June 1775, General Gage suffered incredible losses (something like three to one redcoat deaths for patriot deaths) while retaking the high ground overlooking Boston to prevent a patriot siege. The ability of the patriots to stand up to the British certainly represented a shot in the arm to the patriots' self-esteem: perhaps they could take on the British and win, after all. Over the course of the next several months, the patriots demonstrated that they controlled the entire countryside outside of Boston: this meant that ammunition stockpiles, citizens' militias, and local governments were all unified in their effort to eject the British from Boston. In particular, the ability of the patriots to take the artillery and gunpowder from Fort Ticonderoga played a role in the intimidation of General William Howe during the patriot fortification of Dorchester Heights. Howe determined that it was too dangerous to risk his men and ships trying to keep Boston, and he retreated in March 1776. Howe's retreat further demonstrated that the Americans could stand their ground against the supposedly better-trained, "superior" redcoats.

In conjunction with these military successes, however, came a pamphlet written by the relatively unknown radical pamphleteer, Thomas Paine, advocating independence. His treatise, *Common Sense*, further encouraged Americans to make a break once and for all with a political and economic system in Britain that was not working for the colonists. Paine challenged Americans to see their struggle as one on behalf of millions of other people, as an inspiration to all who sought to embrace "enlightened" ideals of republican government, apart from the corruptions and abuse of the entrenched privileges of monarchy and aristocracy. Paine was a believer in democracy, and advocated that the new governments put forth by Americans stay as close to the people as possible. While it is debatable what role *Common Sense* actually played in the eventual ratification of the Declaration of Independence in July of 1776, there can be little doubt that the optimism it expressed regarding the ability of these simple colonists to make the world over again represented an elegant and prophetic statement regarding the rising power of what would become the United States (even if the founding fathers were not nearly as radical as Paine).

Formal independence, however, coincided with a myriad of challenges for the Americans. For one, the British military, this time under William and John Howe, began a new, wider assault on the colonies by occupying New York City in 1776. Word had also come of the offer made by the Virginia royal governor, Lord Dunmore, to arm slaves for actions against the patriot "traitors." But in addition to these newer military challenges, the nagging concern confronted Americans about how to create and sustain an independent government, both at the level of the states as well as at the level of "Congress," which would soon be termed a "Confederation." Given the deep suspicion of the colonists toward central authority (since they were fighting a war against it), it is not hard to understand why the first state constitutions favored the lower houses, and otherwise tried to thwart any attempt to give any one man too much power in the office of governor. In addition, these states dragged their feet when it came to approving any sort of document affirming new powers to Congress or to the Confederation. And, on a related note, the states proved completely inept or unwilling to properly fund Washington's Continental Army, which was the only real example of a national institution, especially during the 1770s. In spite of these challenges, however, the patriots demonstrated a determination to prosecute a guerrilla war, especially in the areas away from the seacoasts and from redcoat control, which countered the constant threat of Washington's army falling apart.

Indeed, with the escalation of the war to the New York/New Jersey area by the autumn of 1776, Washington purposefully placed his fragile army in harm's way in order to rally patriot support. Washington was lucky that General Howe proved to be more willing to try to reestablish colonial loyalty than in pursuing Washington's army. Howe essentially let Washington retreat from Brooklyn, just east of the main city of New York on Manhattan, all the way north to Peekskill, New York, where Washington crossed the Hudson and retreated back south, parallel to New York City, and into New Jersey. There Washington mounted a surprise offensive at Trenton and at Princeton, around New Year's 1777, further revealing that he could keep the Continental Army together, as well as challenge British redcoats. This was true even as the British occupied New York City and were about to occupy the colonial capital at Philadelphia. But these facts did not matter to many Americans supportive of revolution: the important point was that Washington's army did not lose its resolve. The patriots also kept their resolve in spite of the loss of their capital, Philadelphia, in the fall of 1777. In European warfare, to capture the enemy's capital was everything. But in the sparsely populated, non-urban United States, the loss of their capital was more of an embarrassed inconvenience for the Americans. Congress simply moved to New Jersey.

Additionally, the redcoats, while succeeding at taking port cities, were no match for the deep forests of the mainland interior. In the fall of 1777, the British failed miserably under John Burgoyne to defeat American forces in upstate New York. Burgoyne, who did not coordinate his movements with Howe so that Howe might bring him necessary reinforcements, found his long supply lines cut by colonial militias under John Stark. Burgoyne also lost Hessians and natives along the way. In October of 1777, Burgoyne ended up surrendering his entire army of more than 6,000 men to the forces of Continental Army general Horatio Gates. This victory not only revealed to Americans the weakness of the British when trying to subdue areas away from the seacoasts, but proved to be the tipping point that caused the French to ally with the Americans. This was no small achievement, since in addition to men and money, the French would also mobilize their navy on behalf of the American patriots. With their navy, the French could distract the British all over the world, while cutting off supplies and reinforcements to the British in the United States (this is in fact what happened at the final battle of Yorktown in 1781). By supporting the Americans, the French hoped to win territory back from the British, or at least damage their inveterate foe; however, in hindsight, the Americans gained far more from this alliance than did the French.

Now that the war had escalated to the point of a global conflict, there was little restraining the British from trying to incite domestic insurrections within their rebellious colonies so as to destroy the resilience of the patriot cause. It was not that difficult to convince native tribes that the Americans were their enemy, since colonists had been aggressively moving in on tribal land in the Ohio valley and Kentucky since the late 1760s. Most natives—if they chose to support a side in the Revolution—chose the British, but many natives understood that there would be no winners if and when warfare came to the frontier. But the war came by 1778,

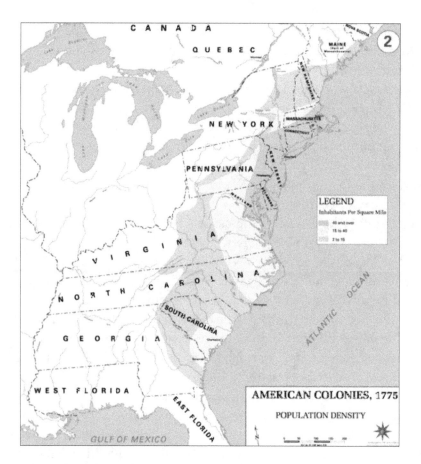

The Colonial Population in 1776. The westward thrust of white settlement can be seen in this map.

with Burgoyne's penetration into upstate New York, and the resulting mobilization of natives in support of Britain. With the help of tribal leaders such as Joseph Brant, the frontier regions of Western New York and of Pennsylvania were now subject to native attacks. The same was true in the Ohio valley, where in 1779 the patriot officer George Rogers Clark mounted a successful offensive against tribes such as the Delaware, Creek, and Shawnee (who often, though not always, acted as British agents), only to have the Americans routed by 1782. "Indian hating," as it has been termed by historians, became a normal fact of life on the frontier, as the Americans were all too happy to use native support for the British as an excuse to exterminate native peoples. Infamously, at Gnadenhutten, in the Ohio Territory, American forces outright massacred a hundred unarmed Christian native women and children, many of whom were praying as the onslaught occurred.

As the British war effort escalated and intensified, slaves were also mobilized by the British, though unlike the natives, they were not nearly as one-sided in their support for the king. But it remains the case that the British were the first to offer freedom to male slaves who joined the British military, with Lord Dunmore's offer to slaves in late 1775. Dunmore formed his "African brigade," and when he lost power, simply removed them to the British loyalist stronghold of New York City in 1777. It has been said that hundreds of blacks tried to reach Manhattan Island by ferry, and that the British had to shut it down for fear of too many "indigent" blacks. But elsewhere in the colonies, the British welcomed American slaves into their ranks: in late 1777 slaves fled to Howe's army as he took Philadelphia, and by 1781, Lord Cornwallis was in the possession of hundreds of American slaves as he made preparation for the final battle at Yorktown. But as a reminder of the pervasive racism of the eighteenth century, when supplies ran low for his troops during the patriot siege of Yorktown, Cornwallis chased his African-American troops away into the line of fire, and they were predictably mowed down by patriot shelling. Therefore, if you were an African American in the Revolutionary War, you would not automatically assume the British to really be your friends, but rather that they were opportunistically taking advantage of your labor. This may explain why several thousand former slaves fought for the patriot cause, though it should also be noted that in New England, white patriots began to support emancipation efforts during the drafting of state constitutions in the late 1770s. In any event, it has been said that both in the Continental Army as well as in the individual militias, many of the Revolutionary War units were as racially integrated as any in American history prior to World War II. As a result of fighting for either side, as well as because of the dislocations of battle which allowed for slaves to escape, it has been estimated that 10,000 slaves were freed during the war itself; this number represented approximately 6 percent of the total number of African Americans enslaved before the war. Of more importance for the patriot war effort, the British use of black slaves (which probably did not amount to more than the single thousands) did not make up for the determination of patriots to expel a foreign occupying force. Slaves—not unlike native Americans—could not be relied upon by the British to win the war.

Thousands of backcountry whites (usually recent immigrants from Scotland, Ireland, or Germany) also found themselves targets of British recruitment efforts, since these more marginal whites resented the economic and political domination of the Eastern colonial elites. But as with slaves and natives, British efforts to use the frontier whites against the patriots yielded mixed results. The strategy of mobilizing backcountry whites was most prevalent in the South, though it also occurred in areas such as New Jersey, where the British military had a strong presence during the war. Yet as the British marched or landed in the South, in the third and final phase of the war beginning around 1779, they still could not outmaneuver local patriots or the patriots' own native American or backcountry allies. The British military simply proved unable to hold enough ground long enough to permanently offset the power of the revolutionaries. Often, when the redcoats would leave, that would expose the local loyalist regiments to reprisals from the patriots, therefore causing other colonial Americans to think twice before agreeing to support British redcoats who did not have the follow-through to provide a strategy for long-term success. However, the war was not over yet, as several factors did briefly work in favor of the British in the late 1770s, giving them hope that they might be able to pull off a victory. The British in the South were effective at controlling seaport towns such as Savannah, Charlestown, or Wilmington, North Carolina. They even scored an important victory at Camden, in August 1780, a good hundred miles east from the seacoast of South Carolina. Furthermore, the British were aware of reports that food shortages, riots, and desertions from the Continental Army might mean that Americans were losing the resolve to fight. Certainly by 1780, Washington's army had seen better days—many men died of disease, and many were near starved for lack of supplies, due to the recurring problems of getting resources from the states.

On the other hand, after five years of war, the British public had also lost much confidence in their war ministers, so both sides really had to deal with a general war fatigue. In this dead-locked environment came news of the patriot victory at Cowpens in January of 1781. With a detachment of the Continental Army coupled with hardened militia fighters under Daniel Morgan, the patriots managed to outfight the British at Cowpens, a location further away from the coast than Camden in South Carolina. This backwoods defeat once again revealed how the British could not manage a frontier war away from the seaports. By the fall of 1781, Washington managed to maneuver the rest of the Continental Army from New Jersey to southeastern Virginia at a place called Yorktown, with French forces both from the north and from the sea. At this battle, French naval support proved vital, since the forces of François Comte de Grasse beat out the British to hem in General Cornwallis at his coastal encampment. When Washington arrived, he was able to besiege Yorktown and the British troops until they surrendered on October 19, 1781, in the largest defeat since Saratoga. This was a disaster for the British, and the war was now all but over (there were continued naval engagements around the world with the French and Spanish, however.) The formal Treaty of Paris ended the war in February 1783. Although the military conflict ceased, the battle to establish a viable republic was only beginning in 1783, as the thirteen disparate colonies did not possess a functioning currency or a government capable of taking its place as an equal to other European powers. Many conservatives doubted the ability of the republic to survive, and in many ways the largest crises of the Revolutionary generation still lay ahead. Although in hindsight it appears inevitable that the United States would survive the 1780s, that was not so obvious to those living at the time.

Documents:

1. Thomas Paine, *Common Sense* (1776)

Born in Britain, Paine had failed at several different careers before receiving a letter of recommendation from Benjamin Franklin to go live in Philadelphia in 1774. There, he edited the Pennsylvania Magazine, where his writing skills found appreciation. In 1776 he anonymously wrote Common Sense, which supposedly sold over 100,000 copies and helped push the colonists toward independence.

Alas, we have long been led away by ancient prejudices, and made large sacrifices to super-stition. We have boasted the protection of Great Britain, without considering, that her motive was interest not attachment; that she did not protect us from our enemies on our account, but from her enemies on her account. ... Much has been said of the united strength of Britain and the colonies, that in conjunction they might bid defiance to the world. But ... this continent would never suffer itself to be drained of inhabitants, to the support the British arms in either Asia, Africa, or Europe. Besides what have we to do with setting the world at defiance? Our plan is commerce, and that, well attended to will use the peace and friendship of all of Europe, because it is the interest of all Europe to have in America a free port. ... I challenge the warmest advocate of reconciliation to shew a single advantage ... by being connected with Great Britain. I repeat the challenge, not a single advantage is derived. ...

O ye that love mankind! Ye that dare oppose, not only the tyranny, but the tyrant, stand forth! Every spot of the old world is overrun with oppression. Freedom hath been hunted round the globe. Asia, and Africa, have long expelled her—Europe regards her like a stranger, and England hath given her warning to depart. O! receive the fugitive, and prepare in time an asylum for mankind.

2. Abigail Adams, from the *Adams Family Correspondence* (March, 1776)

In these letters, Abigail Adams tries to convince her husband John to include the rights of women in the possible document favoring independence from Britain, which was supported by many delegates such as John. John's response reveals the fundamental social conservatism typical of many—though not all—of the founding leaders of the United States.

I long to hear that you have declared an independency—and by the way in the new Code of Laws which I suppose it will be necessary for you to make I desire that you would remember the Ladies, and be more generous and favourable to them than your ancestors. Do not put such unlimited power into the hands of the Husbands. Remember all Men would be tyrants if they could. If particular care and attention is not paid to the Ladies, we are determined to have a rebellion. ... but [it is hoped that men] will willingly give up the harsh title of Master for the more tender and endearing one of Friend. Why then, not put it out of the power of the vicious and the Lawless to use us with cruelty and indignity with impunity. Men of Sense in all Ages abhor those customs which treat us only as the slaves of your Sex. Regard us then as Beings places by providence under your protection and in imitation of the Supreme Being make use of that power only for our happiness.

John Adams' response: As to your extraordinary Code of Laws, I cannot but laugh. We have been told that our Struggle has loosened the bands of Government every where. That Children and Apprentices were disobedient—that schools and Colleges were grown turbulent—that Indians slighted their Guardians and Negroes grew insolent to their Masters. But your Letter was the first Intimation that another Tribe more numerous and powerful than all the rest were grown discontented.—This is rather too coarse a Compliment but you are so saucy, I wont blot it out.

Depend upon it, We know better than to repeal our Masculine systems ... [but] we have only the Name of Masters, and rather than give up this, which would completely subject us to the despotism of the petticoat, I hope General Washington and all our brave heroes would fight. ... I begin to think the [British] ministry as deep as they are wicked. After stirring up Tories, Landjobbers [speculators], Trimmers [political opportunists], Bigots, Canadians, Indians, Negroes, Hanoverians, Hessians, Russians, Irish Roman Catholics, Scotch Renegadoes, at last they have stimulated the [missing text] to demand new Privileges and threaten to rebel.

3. The Declaration of Independence (1776)

Though drafted with the aid of John Adams, Benjamin Franklin, Robert Livingston, and Roger Sherman, most of the following document was authored by Thomas Jefferson. By July 1776, the Second Continental Congress had exhausted negotiation with the mother country, and faced an impending escalation of the war to the mid-Atlantic states by Great Britain, and thus decided to make an official break with the mother country.

When in the course of human events it becomes necessary for one people to dissolve the political bands which have connected them with another and assemble among the powers of the earth, the separate and equal station to which the Laws of Nature and Nature's God entitle them ... the opinions of mankind require that they should declare the causes which impel them to the separation.

We hold these truths to be self-evident, that all men are created equal, that they are endowed by their Creator with certain inalienable rights, that among these are Life, Liberty and the pursuit of Happiness—That to secure these rights, Governments are instituted among Men, deriving their just powers from the consent of the governed—That whenever any form of Government becomes destructive of these ends, it is the Right of the people to alter or to abolish it, and to institute new Government. ... The history of the present King of Great Britain [George III] is a history of repeated injuries and usurpations, all having in direct object the establishment of an absolute Tyranny over these States. To prove this, let Facts be submitted to a candid world.

He has refused his Assent to Laws, the most wholesome and necessary for the public good ...

He has dissolved Representative Houses repeatedly, for opposing with manly firmness his invasions on the rights of the people ...

He has made judges dependent on his Will alone, for the tenure of their offices, and the amount and payment of their salaries.

He has erected a multitude of New Offices, and sent hither swarms of Officers to harass our people, and eat out their substance.

He has kept among us, in times of peace, Standing Armies without the consent of our legislatures.

He has affected to render the Military independent of an superior to the Civil Power. ...

For abolishing the free System of English Laws in a neighboring Province, establishing therein an Arbitrary Government, and enlarging its Boundaries so as to render it at once an example and fit instrument for introducing the same absolute rule into these Colonies:

For taking away our Charters, abolishing our most valuable Laws, and altering fundamentally the Forms of our Governments. ...

We therefore, the Representatives of the United States of America, in General Congress, Assembled, appealing to the Supreme Judge of the world for the rectitude of our intentions do ... solemnly publish and declare, That these United Colonies are, and of Right ought to be Free and Independent States; that they are Absolved from all Allegiance to the British Crown. ... And for the support of this Declaration, with a firm reliance on the protection of divine Providence, we mutually pledge to each other our Lives, our Fortunes and sacred Honor.

4. "George Washington Asks the Continental Congress for an Effective Army" (1776)

Writing from Harlem Heights, New York, Washington was in the process of keeping his army from being destroyed by British general Howe, during Howe's mid-Atlantic campaign. As the commanding general of a supposedly national Continental Army, Washington's frustration regarding the difficulties presented him both by state militias as well by the states themselves—through lack of funding—would be recurring concerns throughout the war, as well as afterward.

When men are irritated, and the Passions inflamed, they fly hastely and cheerfully to Arms; but after the first emotions are over, to expect ... that they are influenced by any other principles than those of Interest, is to look for what never did, and I fear never will happen. ... You must have good officers—there are no other possible means to obtain them ... but by giving your officers good pay. ...

To place any dependence upon Militia is ... resting upon a broken staff. ... Men accustomed to unbounded freedom, and no control, cannot brook Restraint which is indispensably necessary to the good order and Government of an Army. ... unhappily ... the little discipline I have been labouring to establish in the Army under my command is in a manner done away by having such a mixture of troops as have been [recently] called together. ...

The Jealousies of a standing Army, and the Evils to be apprehended from one are remote ... not at all to be dreaded ... but the consequence of [not having] one, according to my Ideas ... is certain and inevitable Ruin.

5. Oneida Indians Declare Neutrality (1775)

Writing to American patriot leaders, the Oneidan native tribe of Connecticut was the only tribe of the Iroquois Confederacy to generally support the patriots, once neutrality became impossible with the war's spread to upstate New York by 1778. But once the war ended, the Oneidans still found themselves under assault from land-hungry whites, and by the 1830s many of their number were forced to move to Canada. The poor treatment afforded the loyal Oneidan symbolizes how the American Revolution was at times simply a war of white supremacy and not much else.

"*Brothers!* We have heard of the unhappy differences ... between you and the old England. We wonder greatly and are troubled in our minds.

Brothers! Possess your minds in peace respecting us *Indians*. We cannot intermeddle in this dispute between two brothers. The quarrel seems to be unnatural; you are two brothers of one blood. We are unwilling to join on either side in such a contest, for we bear an equal affection to both of you, Old and New-England ...

Brothers! For these reasons, possess your minds in peace, and take no umbrage that we Indians refuse joining in the contest; we are for peace ... As we have declared for peace, we desire you will not apply to our Indian brethren in New-England for their assistance. Let us Indians be all of one mind, and live in peace with one another, and you white people settle your own disputes betwixt yourselves."

We the sachems, warriors, and female governesses of Oneida, send our love to you, brother Governour, and all the other chiefs in New-England.

6. Joseph Brant of the Mohawk Tribe to the British Secretary of State Lord Germain (1776)

Brant and his family had cultivated ties for many years with British officials such as William Johnson, responsible for native American affairs. Brant became a tribal chief for this reason; among other reasons, Brant felt that the future safety of his people would be best served by Great Britain. But it is questionable just how well the British protected tribes such as Brant's.

Brother—The Disturbances in America give great trouble to all our Nations, as many strange stories have been told to us by the people in the country. The Six Nations have always loved the King, and sent a number of their Chiefs and Warriors with their Superintendent to Canada last summer, where they engaged their allies to join with the British in defense of that Country, when it was invaded by the New England [patriots], the natives alone defeated [the patriots]. …

The Mohawks, our particular Nation, have on all occasions shown their loyalty to the Great King; yet they have been very badly treated by his people in that country, the City of Albany laying an unjust claim to the lands on which our Lower Castle is built … we have been assured that the King would do us justice; but this notwithstanding all of the applications has never been done, and this makes us uneasy …We have only this request that his Majesty attend to this matter … indeed it is very hard for us when we have let the King's subjects have so much land for so little value, that they should want to cheat more from us. …

7. Lord Dunmore (John Murray) Promises Freedom to Slaves (1775)

As the royal governor of Virginia during the uncertain period surrounding the Boston Tea Party and the Battles of Lexington and Concord, Dunmore took a gamble on offering some slaves freedom if they supported the British cause. Many historians feel that this gesture only further pushed white Virginians out of the British Empire.

I do, in virtue of the power and authority to me given, by his majesty, determine to execute martial law, and cause the same to be executed throughout this colony; and to the end that peace and good order may the sooner be restored, I do require every person capable of bearing arms to resort to his majesty's standard, or be looked upon as traitors to his majesty's crown and government, and thereby become liable to the penalty the law inflicts upon such offences; such as forfeiture of life, confiscation of lands … And I do hereby further declare all indented servants, negroes, or others (appertaining to rebels) free, that are able and willing to bear arms … for the more speedily reducing this colony to a proper sense of their duty to his majesty …

8. Lemuel Haynes, New England Mulatto, Attacks Slavery (1776)

Haynes had been freed in 1774, and fought with the Massachusetts militia after the Battles of Lexington and Concord. He became a Congregationalist minister and pastor to a white congregation in Vermont after the war ended. He consistently preached for the complete abolition of slavery.

To affirm, that an Englishman has a right to his Liberty, is a truth which has Been so clearly Evinced, Especially of Late, that to spend time illustrating [it] … would be superfluous. …

But I query, whether Liberty is so contracted a principle as to be Confin'd to any nation under Heaven; nay, I think it not hyperbolical to affirm, that Even an African, has Equally as good a right to his Liberty in common with Englishmen …

It hath pleased god to 'make of one Blood all nations of men, for to dwell upon the face of the Earth. …' Those privileges that are granted to us By the Divine Being, no one has the Least right to take them from us without our consent; and there is Not the Least precept or practice, in the Sacred Scriptures, that constitutes a Black man a Slave, any more than a white one. … [therefore] Break these intolerable yokes … least they be [placed] on your own necks, and you Sink under them, for god will not hold you guiltless.

9. Benjamin Rush Contrasts Loyalists and Patriots (1777)

Rush was an important early American medical doctor, as well as an active supporter of the patriot cause and signer of the Declaration of Independence from Pennsylvania. However, his reputation was marred by his early caustic remarks regarding General Washington as an inept leader of the Continental Army.

Tories and Whigs were actuated by very different motives in their conduct or by the same motives acting in different degrees of force. … There were Tories (1) from an attachment to power and office. (2) From an attachment to the British commerce which the war had interrupted or annihilated. (3) From an attachment to kingly government. (4) From an attachment to the hierarchy of the Church of England … (5) From a dread of power of the country being transferred into the hands of the Presbyterians (or other democratic forces). …

There were besides [Whigs and Tories] a great number of persons who were neither Whigs nor Tories. They had no fixed principles and accommodated their conduct to their interest, to events, and to their company. …

Perhaps the inhabitants of the United States might have been divided nearly into three classes, viz. Tories, Whigs, and persons who were neither Whigs nor Tories. The Whigs constituted the largest class. The 3rd class were a powerful reinforcement to [the Whigs] after the affairs of America assumed a uniformly prosperous appearance. …

10. Anonymous letter from Loyalists to the King (1782), printed in Hezekiah Niles's *Principles and Acts of the Revolution in America* (1822)

This letter reveals the desperate condition of mainland white loyalists at the end of the Revolutionary War. These loyalists, like many others, also tended to overstate the size of loyalist support in the colonies, which helped to mislead the British regarding how many Americans were actually available to aid the redcoats.

The penalty under which any American subject enlists in his majesty's service, is no less than the immediate forfeiture of all his goods and chattels, lands, and tenements; and if apprehended, and convicted by the rebels, of having enlisted, or prevailed on any other person to enlist into his majesty's service, it is considered as treason, and punished with death: Whereas, no forfeiture is incurred, or penalty annexed, to his entering into the service of congress; but, on the contrary, his property is secured and himself rewarded. ...

The desultory manner also in which the war has been carried on, by first taking possession of Boston, Rhode Island, Philadelphia, Portsmouth, Norfolk, etc. and then evacuating them, whereby many thousands inhabitants have been involved in the greatest wretchedness, is another substantial reason why more loyalists have not enlisted into his majesty's service, or openly espoused and attached themselves to the royal cause; yet, notwithstanding all these discouraging circumstances, there are many more men in his majesty's provincial regiments, than there are in the continental service. Hence it cannot be doubted but that there are more loyalists in America than there are rebels; and also, that their zeal must be greater, or so many would not have enlisted into the provincial service. ...

Our cause is the cause of legal and constitutional government, throughout the world; that, opposed by principles of republicanism, and convinced, from recent observation, that brutal violence, merciless severity, relentless cruelty, and discretionary outrages are the distinguished traits and ruling principles of the present system of congressional republicanism, our aversion is unconquerable, irreconcilable—That we are attached to monarchical government, from past and happy experience—by duty, and by choice. That, to oppose insurrections, and to listen to the requests of people so circumstanced as we are, is the common interest of all mankind in civil society.

11. Recollections of an Army Cook and Washerwoman (Sarah Osborn) of the Battle of Yorktown, Virginia (October 1781)

Sarah Osborn was a servant in a blacksmith's household in Albany, New York, when she met and married Aaron Osborn, a blacksmith and Revolutionary War veteran, in 1780. When he reenlisted as a commissary sergeant without informing her, Sarah agreed to accompany him. They went first to West Point, and Sarah later traveled with the Continental Army for the campaign in the Southern colonies, working as a washerwoman and cook.

Deponent's attention was arrested by the appearance of a large plain between them and Yorktown and an entrenchment thrown up. She also saw a number of dead Negroes lying round their encampment, whom she understood the British had driven out of the town and left to starve ...

Deponent took her stand just back of the American tents ... and busied herself washing, mending, and cooking for the soldiers ... She saw the roar of the artillery for a number of days, and. ... later deponent cooked and carried in beef, bread, and coffee to the soldiers [there]. On one occasion when deponent was thus employed carrying in provisions ... George Washington asked her if she "was not afraid of the cannonballs?" She replied ... 'It would not do for [only] the men to fight and starve too.'

Deponent stood on one side of the road and the American officers upon the other side when the British officers came out of the town and rode up to the American officers and delivered up their swords. ... The British general at the head of the army was a large, portly man, full face, and the tears rolled down his cheeks as he passed along. ...

Questions to Consider:

1. How did the patriots (though never a majority of the colonial population) manage to win the Revolutionary War?
2. How did the Revolutionary War expose weaknesses in the ability of colonists to govern themselves?
3. How did the patriots address the fact that certain subordinate groups might use the Revolution as a chance to strike out for their own freedom? How willing were the patriots to make their revolution a movement for greater equality in terms of race, class, or gender?

Credits

- United States Military Academy, "Population Density in the American Colonies 1775." Copyright in the Public Domain.
- Excerpts from Thomas Paine, *Common Sense*. 1776. Copyright in the Public Domain.
- Excerpts from Abigail Adams, *Adams Family Correspondence*, vol. 1. 1963. Copyright in the Public Domain.
- The Declaration of Independence. 1776. Copyright in the Public Domain.
- George Washington, "George Washington Asks the Continental Congress for an Effective Army," *American Archives, Series 5, Vol. 2*, pp. 495. 1776. Copyright in the Public Domain.
- "Speech of the Chiefs and Warriors of the Oneida Tribe of Indians to the four New-England Provinces," *American Archives, Series 5, Vol. 2*, ed. Peter Force, p. 1117. 1775. Copyright in the Public Domain.
- Excerpt from Joseph Brant, "Speech of Captain Brant to Lord George Germain," *Documents Relative to the Colonial History of the State of New York*, vol. 8, ed. E.B. O'Callaghan, pp. 671. 1853. Copyright in the Public Domain.
- Excerpt from John Murray, *By His Excellency the Right Honorable John Earl of Dunmore...A Proclamation*. 1775. Copyright in the Public Domain.
- Lemuel Haynes, *Liberty Further Extended: Antislavery Manuscript*, ed. Ruth Bogin. 1776.
- Benjamin Rush, "An Account of Political and Military Events and Observations," *A Memorial Containing Travels Through Life of Sundry Incidents in the Life of Dr. Benjamin Rush*, ed. Louis Alexander Biddle, p. 89. 1905. Copyright in the Public Domain.
- Excerpt from 'An Address, Of American Loyalists to the King and Parliament, 1782'," *The London Chronicle*, March 9, 1782. Copyright in the Public Domain.
- Sarah Osborn; ed. John C. Dann, "Selections from 'The Revolution Remembered'," *American Heritage*, vol. 31, no. 3. 1980. Copyright in the Public Domain.

★ CHAPTER 7
★ FORMING A GOVERNMENT AND
★ SECURING THE REPUBLIC, 1783–1789

As mentioned earlier, the recurring difficulty of making thirteen independent former colonies cede power to some new national authority dogged the revolutionaries during the war against Britain from 1775 to 1783. Although they established new state constitutions, as we have seen, it took some time before any of these states trusted the governor or the Senate enough to give them as much (or more) power than the lower houses of the assemblies. But in the process of writing and revising the state constitutions (an ongoing struggle between 1776 and 1783), there were signs of hope for those who sought to provide stability to the United States with a new, powerful central government. For example, the state of Massachusetts eventually devised a constitution providing the governor with veto power, which vested the Senate with equal advisory powers as the lower house. It also provided for a popular Constitutional Convention so that the people of the state could modify the constitution as they saw fit—it would be a living document responsive to the will of the people. Many historians see in the Massachusetts state constitution the germ of the eventual federal constitution. Still, many events had to transpire before the white American male majority became desperate enough in a sense to cede power to some new, distant, federal government entirely separate from that of the states.

During the course of the war, George Washington constantly found himself demanding more financial support from the states to support the Continental Army; his requests were rebuffed. The jealousy of the states toward giving the Confederation any power can be seen in the Articles of Confederation itself, finally ratified after nearly five years of debate in 1781. This Confederation was simply a meeting of representatives from the states, and was not a separate body with separate powers regarding things such as raising a military or raising taxes. Instead, the members of the Confederation had to vote unanimously—and with state approval—to raise any sort of revenue, such as an impost on foreign goods, which was constantly voted down. In this regard, the Confederation more resembled the modern United Nations than an actual sovereign power in its own right. Although the Confederation government was largely a failure, agreement existed among the states regarding ceding Western land west of the Appalachians to the confederation for it to be sold. Eventually what came to be known as the Northwest Ordinance established the process by which territories comprising the future states of Illinois, Indiana, Ohio, Michigan, and Wisconsin would become coequal states with the Eastern states. In this way, hope existed that the original thirteen states might give up even

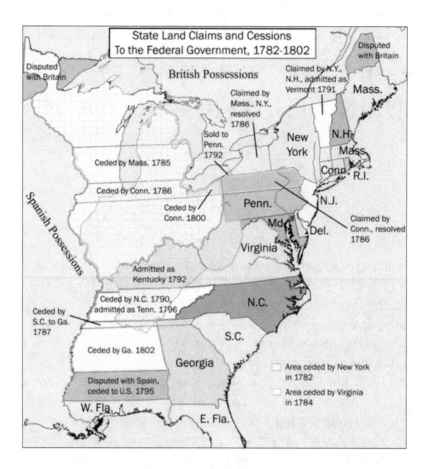

The United States in 1783. The fact that the original states decided to cede their vast westward land claims to the federal government constituted one of the few successes of the Confederation Period from 1777–1787.

more of their power to a new national government. The Northwest Ordinance also signaled that Western farmers would not be treated as distant colonial subjects of the Eastern capitals, and would be able to form states potentially equal in power to older states in the east.

But in nearly every other regard, the Confederation failed miserably. Nowhere was this more apparent than with finances: because the states could not agree on new taxes, the United States defaulted on its debts incurred during the Revolutionary War (including from France) in 1785. Of course, the paper currency was also nearly worthless, since it was backed by nothing other than the taxing power and the promise of American financial solvency (which turned out to be illusory). The unpaid debts—and the resulting lack of investor or taxpayer confidence engendered by them—threatened to destroy the country, as well as individual states such as Massachusetts. There, in the winter of 1786–1787, Daniel Shays, a former officer of the Continental Army, led a number of poorer farmers in closing down courts and debtors' prisons as the economic situation deteriorated, and as poor people were losing everything. More than this, Shays and his men nearly took over the U.S. arsenal (an ammunition and weapons stockpile) in Springfield, Massachusetts. The state government was so unpopular and the federal government so weak that a privately funded police force had to be hurriedly assembled to put down the rebellion and scatter the insurgency. But this crisis sent shockwaves through an already fragile national edifice; now, by the winter of 1787, many leading colonial Americans were ready for dramatic change. The country appeared to be not only bankrupt, but unable to defend itself: in addition to the troubles with Shays, there were still British troops in parts of New York and modern-day Michigan, and the Spanish were making things difficult for frontiersmen trying to sell their products in New Orleans.

And so it was not difficult to convince more cosmopolitan, wealthier Americans that the nation was in danger of being dismembered either by foreign powers, or by internal dissension (or both). These men then began to envision creating a much more robust and powerful separate federal government, and they agreed to convene the Philadelphia Constitutional Convention. This convention came together in the summer of 1787 with the consent of the Confederation Congress (even though that body was divided over whether or not the Articles of Confederation should be scrapped completely). The meeting in Philadelphia more or less represented a "who's who," as it were, of the colonial elite. The 55 men who sat in the chamber of the Pennsylvania State House in Philadelphia included many of the wealthiest and best-educated men in the former mainland colonies. This fact would later be used against the entire proceedings by those who viewed it as an attempt by the rich and well connected to take over the country. But during the convention in 1787, the Virginian delegation really set the tone from the beginning, once their "plan"—largely conceived by the young but brilliant James Madison—was agreed to as a basic blueprint for debates. This plan, in opposition to the plan put forth by William Patterson of New Jersey, got rid of the Articles of Confederation in favor of a new two-body Congress, based completely on proportional representation, and entirely separate from the state governments. Although there was opposition from the small states who feared the influence of larger states in this new federal government, the majority of delegates at the convention settled on a framework that not only established a separate House of Representatives, Senate, president, and Supreme Court, but which also enumerated the principle of proportionality in the election of the House of Representatives: larger states did have a larger say in that body, and this was a direct attack on the notion held by many that the states would all have equal power in this new government. (However, the "one state, one vote" model was retained in the Senate.) Also, the office of the president, a separate branch of government which empowered one person to be the "commander in chief" of the armed forces, spoke to the desire of the delegates to have a far greater concentration of power in one person than was desired by many others who had fought the Revolutionary War. Some feared that this "president" would become a monarch, but then, most men at the time understood that George Washington, a man they trusted and highly revered, would likely ascend to the office.

By September 1787, a finished draft of the Constitution was in place: The House would originate money bills, the Senate would ratify treaties, as well as appoint government officials such as judges, and although the president possessed veto power over acts of Congress, the veto could be overridden with a two-thirds majority of both houses of Congress. The president would be chosen by an electoral college (enumerated by the individual states' House and Senate membership), but the delegates to the college would be chosen by the state legislatures. A supreme court would determine the constitutionality of the acts of Congress (though its role was vague in the initial document), and amendments to the constitution could be ratified by a two thirds majority of the states. In this way, there were supposed to be numerous checks and balances on this government, though it remained unclear who was checking whom—were the elites restricting the rights of the commoners, or vice versa? In general, historians have focused on the conservatism of the founding fathers, who distrusted mankind in general, and who hoped to devise a government that would be non-radical and able to do the business, as it were, of raising taxes and funding a military. Nowhere can the conservatism of the founders be seen more clearly than concerning slavery and race. These men would not allow the unpopularity of the institution among certain Americans to override the desire of the Constitution's authors for a new federal government: according to the federal constitution, the slave trade would be allowed to exist for at least twenty years, and of more importance, all Americans—whether they lived in slave states or not—were legally responsible for returning runaway slaves to their masters under the so-called "Fugitive Slave Act" provision of the Constitution. In addition, sectional balance between free and slave states would be maintained through the enumeration of slaves as three fifths of a person when it came time to allocate congressional seats.

The slavery issue proved to be only one among many controversial aspects of the federal constitution. First and foremost, the Constitution, drafted in private by 50 men who represented the wealthiest and best-connected people in the United States, looked like an elite coup d'état to many of the white male Americans called upon to vote the document up or down. Who was to say that the men at the convention would not dominate the federal government for years to come? And of course there was the recurring concern about the loss of power from individual states to the new central government when this document was ratified. As the Constitutional Convention stipulated, this new federal constitution had to be ratified by a majority of the states in special ratifying conventions that were separate from the state assemblies. In these conventions, it can be said that the desire for merchants, lawyers, and the wealthy to provide a stable nation, able to defend itself and pay its bills, overrode the more local concerns of those who opposed the Constitution. Those who favored the Constitution donned the term "federalist" after the *Federalist Papers*, a group of letters written by Alexander Hamilton, John Jay, and James Madison, as a kind of script for those supportive of the Constitution to argue with those in the opposition. The "antis," as they were called, had no similar organizing document from which they could fire back at the points made by the Federalists (though there were dissenting public editorials voiced by men such as Patrick Henry). In addition, the fact that the Anti-Federalists tended to be poorer men from counties away form the Eastern seaboard reveals how the ratification of the Constitution can be seen as signaling the dominance of wealthier men with a more cosmopolitan vision over those with more local interests and influence.

Still, the ratification process that occurred between the fall of 1787 and 1789, when all but two states (North Carolina and Rhode Island) had approved the Constitution, proved extremely contentious. The Anti-Federalists included such Revolutionary era leaders as the aforementioned Patrick Henry and Richard Henry Lee, men who really believed that the Revolution's mission to restore government to the people, at the most local level possible (some might have called it "pure democracy") was being betrayed. Yet, the prior events of the 1780s had revealed to many Americans that such idealistic dreams simply could not be brought to realization. Besides this, the "Federalist Papers" sought to assuage those opposed to the Constitution that the various checks and balances deployed against the power of any one branch of government would prevent power from falling into a small clique of greedy leaders.

Finally, the Federalists agreed to a Bill of Rights, a demand made by the Anti-Federalists, to further provide checks on this new federal government. These first ten amendments to the Constitution would include such well-known American rights as the freedom of the press, the right to bear arms, and the idea that all powers not specifically enumerated to the federal government were reserved to the states.

The fact that the supporters of the federal constitution barely won out in many counties of the United States speaks to the divided nature of many in the polity regarding whether this new federal government in fact possessed sovereignty over the states—an issue that would not be resolved until the Civil War. As we will see at various points before 1860, different groups in the United States might try to leave the union if they felt their needs were not being adequately addressed by the federal government. In addition, the Constitution helped set a tone for the young nation, which often leaned in the direction of racial exclusion or white supremacy. As noted earlier, slavery not only was still in effect at the Constitutional Convention, but it was recognized as a legitimate form of private property in the federal constitution. It would prove difficult even for free blacks to attain voting rights in the new American republic, and slavery itself would spread west with the development of the cotton gin in the early 1800s. On the other hand, the violence of war freed several thousand slaves, and these freedmen could work on the consciences of many whites (particularly in New England and in the Quaker strongholds around Philadelphia) to free other bondspeople. Also in the North, gradual emancipation laws slowly came into existence. While hardly freeing all slaves at once, such laws laid the framework, whereby eight states would be free of slavery by the early 1800s. Enlightenment ideals about human freedom did make some headway among some revolutionaries, and these would lay the foundations for later abolitionist movements. Yet, most white Americans did not and could not see African Americans as equals until the necessity of war made emancipation feasible in the 1860s during another war (the Civil War), which in many ways proved to be more revolutionary than the actual Revolution.

Although white women fared better than slaves in the young United States, a similarly ambivalent legacy can be seen for the Revolution when it came to gender. The Revolution did nothing to immediately change divorce or property laws, both of which worked to the detriment of women. Anglo-American law operated under the assumption that a woman's legal identity was literally merged into that of her husband's, so that she was not even considered a person, in many respects. These debilities existed in addition to the lack of voting rights or the lack of employment options in the male-dominated world of the professions of law, medicine, education, or the religious ministry. Yet as was the case with African Americans, the Revolution allowed women to take small steps toward realizing a greater sphere of influence and responsibility within the republic. During the imperial protests against Britain in the 1760s and 1770s, for example, women signed documents pledging their families' support for the boycott, and during the war, several elite women published articles in newspapers or ran charity drives for the support of troops. Some women even accompanied Washington's army into battle. In these ways and in others, women were politicized. Indeed, the logic of a republic, where the leaders of polity can be no more moral nor educated than the citizens they lead, also mandated that women receive some sort of education if only for the benefit of the sons who were then responsible for being mature citizens or political leaders. It should not be surprising, then, that beginning in the late 1700s, several female academies came into existence, which offered some women (usually elite ones) a better education than had been available earlier. The fact that American women eventually embraced all sorts of reform efforts in the nineteenth century—including even a women's rights movement, whose founding document echoed the Declaration of Independence—all address the longer-term challenges to patriarchy originating with the Revolutionary generation's assault on entrenched privilege.

However, there was one group who benefited little from all of the "rights talk" of the Revolutionary era: native Americans. Subject to white disease, land fraud, and often addicted to commodities sold to them at ridiculously high prices by whites, natives repeatedly found themselves pushed to the margins (or worse) within the new American polity. And unlike for the minority of free African Americans living in northeastern towns and cities, it seemed that assimilation was never an option for the indigenous tribes. Beginning in the 1780s and 1790s, a determined American power decided to back up its Western settlers with military force to clear away large sections of the Ohio Valley and lower Mississippi Valley for white settlement. As will be discussed in the following chapter, the 1780s and 1790s saw an increase in so-called "Indian hating" in the Trans-Appalachian west, best associated with the career and ideas of "mad" Anthony Wayne. The Constitution made no reference to natives, but did restrict naturalization for citizenship to white males. This simple reference to race, made almost as an afterthought, revealed the cultural and racial limitations of a republic that would be built in large part by expropriating slave labor and native land.

Documents:

1. Congressman Charles Pinckney to the New Jersey Legislature (1786)

This document is significant because it reveals the growing sense of desperation among small-state leaders; if the states didn't give more money to the Confederation, they would lose much more power with a revision of the Articles themselves. It is worth evaluating how prescient Pinckney turned out to be.

The united states in congress assembled have been informed that this house had ... resolved that they could not. ... assent to the requisition [money] of September last, for federal supplies.

When these states united, convinced of the inability of each to support a separate system, and that their protection and existence depended upon their union- policy ... dictated forming one General and Efficient Government. ... The states having thus by their voluntary act, formed one government as essential to the protection of the whole ... each state is bound to furnish a proportion of the expences...for the public engagements, foreign and domestic. ... If this legislature thinks with me that [the Article of Confederation's] powers are inadequate to the ends for which it was instituted, and they should be increased ... she ought to instruct her delegates in congress to urge the calling of a general convention of the states, for the purpose of revising and amending the federal system ... It is certainly more the interest of the small, than it can be of the large states to preserve the confederation upon its present principles ... but is it not to be reasonably expected that the large states would contend and insist upon a greater influence than they presently possess. Would they again consent to unite upon principles ... to give [smaller states] and equal vote with themselves? It is not even to be hoped ... It ought therefore appear exceedingly important to the small states to maintain a system so advantageous to their interests

[by giving money to it] ... Though our present disorders must be attributed ... to the weakness and inefficacy of the general government, it must still be confessed they have been precipitated by the refractory and inattentive conduct of the states, most of whom have neglected the performance of federal duties.

2. Petition from the Town of Greenwich, Massachusetts, to the State Senate and House of Representatives (January 1786)

This petition—not unlike the demands from regulators in North Carolina—laid out the numerous frustrations Western farmers possessed regarding Eastern interests, especially once the economy collapsed in the mid-1780s. The tight money and high-tax policies pursued by the General Court in Massachusetts as a response to the financial crisis only made the situation worse for poorer farmers such as these.

We are sensible that a great debt is justly brought upon us by the war and are willing to pay our shares towards it ... but we believe that if prudent measures were taken a moderate quantity of [paper money]. ... were allowed to circulate our property might sell for the real value, and we might in time pay said debt ... with the greatest submission we beg leave to inform your Honours that unless something takes place more favourable to the people, in a little time at least, one half of our inhabitants in our opinion will become bankrupt—how can it be otherwise—the constable are daily selling our goods, our land after it is prised by the best judges under oath is sold for about one third of the value of it, our cattle about one half. ... And when we compute the taxes laid upon us the five preceding years ... the amount is equal to what our farms will rent for. ... know that many of our good neighbors are now confined in jail for debt and for taxes. ...

3. Thomas Grover Petitions the Printer of the Hampshire Herald, on Behalf of the Massachusetts Regulators (1786)

Grover, later a supporter of Daniel Shays, further reveals the frustrations of Western farmers toward government authority in Boston.

It has some how or other fallen to my lot be employed in a more conspicuous manner than others of my fellow citizens in stepping forth in defense of the rights and privileges of the people, more especially of the county of Hampshire [Massachusetts].

Therefore, upon the desire of the people now at arms, I take this method to publish to the world of mankind in general, particularly the people of this Commonwealth, some of the principal grievances we complain of, and of which we are now seeking redress...

1st—The General Court must be removed out of the town of Boston [closer to the Western counties for purposes of transportation]

2nd—A revision of the state constitution is absolutely necessary.

3rd—All kinds of government securities [should no longer be paying such high rates of interest] ... to save this Commonwealth thousands of pounds.

4th—Let the land belonging to this Commonwealth, at the eastward, be sold at the best advantage, to pay the remainder of our domestick debt. ...

7th—The total abolition of the Inferiour Court of Common Pleas and Sessions of the Peace [which were prosecuting foreclosures for debt]

8th—Deputy Sheriffs totally set aside, as a useless set of officers in the community ... and if this is done, by which means a large swarm of lawyers will be banished from their wonted haunts, who have been more damage to the people at large, especially the common farmers, than the savage beast of pretty.

4. James Madison to George Washington, New York City (February 1787)

Madison, the brilliant young political theorist educated by John Witherspoon at the College of New Jersey (now Princeton), quickly became the voice for those in Virginia (and elsewhere) who demanded an abolition of the Articles of Confederation in favor of a new central government.

Our latest information from Massachusetts gives hopes that the mutiny or as the Legislature now style it, the Rebellion is nearly extinct. If the measures however on foot for disarming and disfranchising those concerned in it should be carried into effect, a new crisis may be brought on. I have not been here long enough to gather the general sentiments of leading characters touching our affairs and prospects. I am inclined to hope that they will gradually be concentered in the plan of a thorough reform of the existing system. ...

5. James Madison to Edmund Pendleton, New York City (February 1787)

The present system neither has nor deserves advocates; and if some very strong props are not applied will quickly tumble to the ground. No money is paid into the public Treasury; no respect is paid to the federal authority. Not a single state complies with the requisitions, several pass them over in silence, and some positively reject them. The payments ever since the peace have been decreasing, and of late fall short even of the pittance necessary for the Civil list of the Confederacy. ... The late turbulent scenes in Massachusetts and the infamous ones in Rhode Island [farmers' revolt over lack of money], have done inexpressible injury to the republican character in that part of the United States; and a propensity towards Monarchy is said to have been produced by it in some leading minds. The bulk of the people will probably prefer the lesser evil of a partition of the Union into three more practicable and energetic Governments ... The latter idea is beginning to find expression in newspapers. But tho it is a lesser evil, I trust it will rouse all the real friends of the Revolution to exert themselves in favor of such an organization ... as will perpetuate the Union.

6. *The Federalist Papers*, Number 10, Factions and Their Remedy, James Madison

The Federalist Papers are a series of 85 articles or essays advocating the ratification of the United States Constitution. Seventy-seven of the essays were published serially in the Independent Journal and the New York Packet between October 1787 and August 1788. Alexander Hamilton actually wrote more articles than Madison, although Madison's contributions are often the ones best remembered by historians and scholars. The two men also collaborated on many of the entries. It should be remembered that John Jay also wrote five of the articles. Taken together, the articles were an attempt to provide pro-Constitution forces a playbook of arguments to combat those who opposed the proposed Constitution.

The two great points of difference between a Democracy and a Republic are, first, the delegation of the government, in the latter, to a small number of citizens elected by the rest: secondly the greater number of citizens, and great sphere of country, over which the latter [the Republic] may be extended ... the effect of [the size of the republic] is ... to refine and enlarge the public views, by passing them through the medium of a chosen body of citizens, whose wisdom may best discern the true interest of their country. ... It will not be denied, that the Representation of the Union will be most likely to possess ... the greater security afforded by a greater variety of parties, against the event of any one party being able to outnumber and oppress the rest. ... [a large republic like the United States] consist[s] in the greater obstacles opposed to the concert and accomplishment of the secret wishes of an unjust and [self] interested majority. Here again, the extent of the Union gives it the most palpable advantage. ...

7. *The Federalist Papers*, Number 51, The System of Checks and Balances, James Madison and Alexander Hamilton

The great security against a gradual concentration of the several powers in the same department [of the federal government] consists in giving to those who administer each department the necessary constitutional means and personal motives to resist encroachments of the others. The provision for defence must in this, as in all cases, be made commensurate to the danger of attack. Ambition must be made to counteract ambition. The interest of the man must be connected with the constitutional rights of the place. It may be a reflection on human nature, that such devices should be necessary to control the abuses of government. But what is government itself, but the greatest of all reflections on human nature? If men were angels, no government would be necessary. If angels were to govern men, neither external nor internal controls on government would be necessary. ... It is not possible to give to each department an equal power of self-defence. In republican government, the legislative authority necessarily predominates. The remedy for this inconveniency is to divide the legislature into different branches. ... As the weight of the legislative authority requires that it should be thus divided, the weakness of the executive may require, on the other hand that it should be fortified. ...

8. *The Federalist Papers*, Number 69, A Defense of the Presidency, Alexander Hamilton

[Comparing the office of the president with the British monarch] The President of the United States would be an officer elected by the people for four years. The King of Great Britain is a perpetual and hereditary prince. The [president] would be subject to personal punishment and disgrace. The persons of the other is sacred and inviolable. The one would have a qualified negative upon the acts of the legislative body: The other has an absolute negative. ... The [president] would have a concurrent power with a branch of the Legislative in the formation of treaties: the other is the sole possessor of the power of making treaties. ... What answer shall we give to those who would persuade us that things so unlike resemble each other? The same that ought to be given to those who tell us that, a government the whole power of which would be in the hands of the elective and periodical servants of the people, is [instead] an aristocracy, a monarchy, and a despotism.

9. Patrick Henry, Speech to the Virginia Ratifying Convention (1788)

Henry's credentials as a radical republican dated from the late 1750s with his opposition to the king interfering in how the colony of Virginia paid Anglican ministers. Unlike his fellow Virginians, James Madison and George Washington, Patrick Henry felt that the new federal Constitution betrayed the Revolution. His efforts certainly helped to slow down the ratification process in his home state, but they could not stop it.

Have they said, We, the state? Have they made a proposal of a compact between states? If they had, this would be a confederation. It is otherwise most clearly a consolidated government. ... The rights of conscience, trial by jury, liberty of the press, all your immunities and franchises, all pretensions to human rights, and privileges, are rendered insecure, if not lost, by this change. ... Here is a revolution as radical as that which separated us from Great Britain. It is as radical, if in this transition our rights and privileges are endangered, and the sovereignty of the states be relinquished: And cannot we plainly see that this is actually the case? The rights of conscience, trial by jury, liberty of the press, all your immunities and franchises, all pretensions to human rights and privileges are rendered insecure, if not lost, by this change so loudly talked of by some, and inconsiderately by others. ...

Consider your own situation, sir: go to the poor man, and ask him what he does. He will inform you that he enjoys the fruits of his labor, under his own fig tree, with his wife and children around him, in peace and security ... Why, then, tell us of danger, to terrify us into an adoption of this new form of government? And yet who knows the dangers that this new system may produce?

10. Amos Singletary, Speech before the Massachusetts Ratifying Convention (1788)

Singletary was one of the many debt-ridden, illiterate farmers from Western Massachusetts who despised wealthier politicians and landowners, not only in a place like Boston, but also in his own home county. His presence in the ratifying convention was part of the reason why the vote in that state turned out to be so close, even though the state did eventually vote in favor of the Constitution.

We contended with Great Britain [during the Revolution], some said for a threepenny duty on tea; but it was not that; it was because they claimed a right to tax us and bind us in all cases whatever. And does not this Constitution do the same? Does it not take away all we have—all our property? Does it not lay all taxes, duties, imposts, and excises ...? They tell us that Congress won't lay [direct] taxes upon us, but collect all the money they want by impost. I say there has always been a difficulty about the impost. ... they won't be able to raise money enough by impost, and then they will lay it on the land, and take all we have got. These lawyers, and men of learning, and moneyed men, that talk so finely, and gloss over matters so smoothly, to make us poor illiterate people swallow down the pill, expect to get into Congress themselves; they expect to be the managers of this Constitution, and get all the power and all the money into their own hands, and then they will swallow up us little folks, like the great Leviathan, Mr. President; yes just like the whale swallowed up Jonah.

11. Petition of North Carolina Blacks to Congress, from the Annals of Congress (January, 1797).

Led by Absalom Jones, the influential freed black minister in Philadelphia, these free persons of color tried to get Congress to act regarding the forced re-enslavement of freed blacks in North Carolina. But acting under pressure from Southern representatives, this petition was refused for discussion on the floor of the House. This is the earliest known petition to Congress from African Americans.

To the President, Senate, and House of Representatives

That, being of African descent, late inhabitants and natives of North Carolina, to you only, under God can we apply with any hope of effect, for redress of our grievances, having been compelled to leave the State wherein we had a right of residence, as freemen liberated under the hand and seal of human and conscientious masters, the validity of which act ... was affirmed by a decision of the Superior Court of North Carolina ... yet not long after the decision, a law of that State was enacted under which men of cruel disposition and void of just principle, received countenance and authority in violently seizing, imprisoning, and selling into slavery, such as had been so emancipated; whereby we were reduced to the necessity of separating from some of our nearest and most tender connexions, and of seeking refuge in such parts of the Union where more regard is paid to the public declaration in favor of liberty and the common right of man, several hundreds, under our circumstances, have been hunted day and night. ... We beseech your impartial attention to our hard condition, not only with respect to our personal sufferings, as freemen, but as a class of that people who, distinguished by color, are therefore considered unentitled to that public justice and protection which is the great object of Government. ... we hope for a share of your sympathetic attention ... and that some deep inquiry into this evil is worthy of the supreme Legislative body of the land. ...

12. Chickasaw Message to Congress (July 1783)

The Chickasaw tribe in present-day Mississippi later became hired allies of the Americans in their efforts to suppress tribes in the Ohio Valley, though in this document they were threatening to not do so. Eventually, however, this tribe shared in the same fate as other Southern tribes that were removed to Oklahoma in the 1830s.

Brother, ... Our Brothers, the Virginians call upon us to a Treaty, and want part of our land, and we expect our Neighbors who live on Cumberland River will in a little time demand, if not forcibly take part of it from us, also as we are informed they been marking Lines through our hunting grounds: we are daily receiving talks from one Place or other, and from People we know nothing about. We know not who to mind or who to neglect. We are told that the Americans have 13 councils composed of chiefs and Warriors. We know not which of them to listen to ... but we hope that you [Congress] will also put a stop to any encroachments on our lands, without our consent, and silence all those People who sends us such talks as inflame and exasperate our Young men, as it our earnest desire to remain in peace and friendship with our Brother, the Americans forever. ...

Brothers, we are very poor for necessaries, for Ammunition particularly. We can supply ourselves from the Spaniards but we are averse to hold any intercourse with them, as our hearts are always with our Brothers the Americans. We have advised our young men to wait with patience for the answer to this talk, when we rest assured of having supplied, and every thing so regulated that no further confusion may ensue. We wish that this land may never again be stained with the blood of either white or Red men. ...

13. Naturalization Act of 1790

This early decision by Congress is one early indication of the racial chauvinism present at the founding of the American republic.

Be it enacted by the Senate and House of Representatives of the United States of America in Congress assembled, That any alien, being a free white person, who shall have resided within the limits and under the jurisdiction of the United States for the term of two years, may be admitted to become a citizen thereof, on application to any common law court of record. ...

Questions to Consider:
1. Many contemporaries, as well as many historians, referred to the early 1780s as a period of crisis. Is this true? How might have the idea of a crisis been useful for certain groups in the United States at the time?
2. Were the men who drafted the constitution influenced in any way by the likely concern of common Americans that a new central government would be dangerous? Did the Federalists try to accommodate the concerns of poorer, less powerful men in the final document?
3. Some of the men who opposed the federal Constitution felt that the document, as well as the new government it created, represented a "betrayal of the Revolution." Was this accusation fair?
4. What does it mean that there were unclear implications of the Revolutionary War for African Americans, native Americans, and white women? How would you characterize the treatment afforded each of these three groups after the federal government was established in 1790?

Credits
- Copyright © Kmusser (CC BY-SA 2.5) at https://commons.wikimedia.org/wiki/File:United_States_land_claims_and_cessions_1782-1802.png.
- Excerpt from Charles Pinckney, "Account of a Deputation From Congress to the Assembly of New Jersey," *The American Museum or Repository of Ancient and Modern Fugitive Pieces*, vol. 2, pp. 154-155. 1787. Copyright in the Public Domain.
- Petition from the Town of Greenwich. 1786. Copyright in the Public Domain.

- Excerpt from Thomas Grover, List of Grievances by Shaysite Thomas Grover. *Hampshire Gazette*, 1786. Copyright in the Public Domain.
- Excerpt from James Madison, James Madison to George Washington. 1787. Copyright in the Public Domain.
- Excerpt from James Madison, James Madison to Edmund Pendleton. 1787. Copyright in the Public Domain.
- Excerpt from James Madison, *The Federalist Papers,* No. 10. 1787. Copyright in the Public Domain.
- Excerpt from James Madison or Alexander Hamilton, *The Federalist Papers, No. 51*. Copyright in the Public Domain.
- Excerpt from Alexander Hamilton, *The Federalist Papers,* No. 69. Copyright in the Public Domain.
- Excerpts from Patrick Henry, Patrick Henry's Speech to the Virginia Ratifying Convention. 1788. Copyright in the Public Domain.
- Excerpts from Amos Singletary, "Swallowing Up the People," *American Patriots and Statesmen from Washington to Lincoln*, vol. 2, ed. Albert Bushnell Hart, pp. 335-336. 1916. Copyright in the Public Domain.
- Excerpt from The Annals of Congress of the United States, 4th Congress, 2nd Session. 1849. Copyright in the Public Domain.
- Excerpts from "Chickasaw Message to Congress," Calendar of Virginia State Papers and other Manuscripts from January 1, 1752 to December 31, 1784 Preserved in the Capitol at Richmond, ed. William P. Palmer, pp. 315-317. 1883. Copyright in the Public Domain.
- Excerpt from Naturalization Act of 1790. Copyright in the Public Domain.

★ CHAPTER 8
★ THE ASCENDANCY OF THE FEDERALISTS
★ AND THE CRISES OF THE 1790S

With the final ratification of the federal Constitution made official by the fall of 1789, the Federalists—those who believed a new, separate, stronger central government was needed to coordinate fiscal and military policy for the disparate states—possessed the upper hand within the government of the United States. The policies of the next decade would be set by these men, who felt that the local prerogatives of the states had led to a near breakdown of order in the 1780s, and men who frankly believed that only the wealthiest, most educated men should hold the reins of government. The stability provided by the Federalists was no doubt appreciated by many in the United States, but their elitism, secrecy, and lack of interest in negotiating with their opponents would soon destroy the Federalists as a viable political party in American public life. The 1790s represented a moment where the United States nearly returned to instability, not so much from external warfare (though that was a possibility) but instead from an internal civil war over the scope of federal power.

The first presidential election led to the unsurprising choice of George Washington as commander in chief. Washington then went about appointing the two most important cabinet posts in the new administration, those of the secretary of the treasury and the secretary of state. The two men he chose for the posts, however, could not have been more different. At the Treasury Department, Washington placed Alexander Hamilton, Washington's aide-de-camp during the war (some have called him Washington's adopted son). Hamilton was born in the Caribbean, and did not share any particular attachment to any one state, therefore making him something of an arch-Federalist, or as he would later be called, a "high" Federalist in his support of national or federal power. Hamilton also consistently took some of the most conservative positions during the drafting of the Constitution: he was a believer in something close to monarchy for the United States, and he envisioned the American nation as an imperial rival to Great Britain. On the other hand, the man chosen to be secretary of state, Thomas Jefferson, was diametrically opposed to Hamilton's views. Jefferson can best be described as a small-government libertarian who detested Britain and hoped to preserve the United States as a simple, agrarian republic. Jefferson also believed that the common man should have a greater say in the day-to-day affairs of government than did the Federalists—indeed, Jefferson would soon form his own faction to oppose the Federalists by the mid-1790s.

Since Hamilton believed in a vigorous government, and since his views were closer both to President Washington and Vice President John Adams than to Jefferson, Hamilton was able to propose and implement important financial plans for the first Congress in 1790. The most significant aspect of his financial plan, as part of his Report on the Public Credit, advocated that all state debt become national debt and be financed with new taxes. In this way, investors—both foreign and domestic—would have much more confidence lending the United States money (remember that the United States had defaulted on its debts in 1785). To pro-business Federalists, this plan made perfect sense as a means of building the economy of the United States; but to people such as Jefferson, it appeared to be a move toward financial speculation and the creation of a class of people dependent upon government taxation for survival. After agreeing to move the federal capital to an as yet unbuilt swamp in Maryland (to become Washington, D.C.), there were enough votes in Congress to approve the plan. But the resentments toward the federal government were building in those areas which had previously hated and feared the federal Constitution in the first place. One such place, frontier Pennsylvania, saw outright resistance toward the sales tax on whiskey advocated by Hamilton lead to courts being closed down, in addition to threats that Pittsburgh would be burned to the ground. Attempting to scatter this resistance to federal authority, George Washington himself took to the field with 13,000 soldiers in order to intimidate the lawbreakers. It worked, but the beginnings of opposition to Federalist policies could not be contained, and by 1794 several self-styled "Democratic societies" were being launched in numerous cities around the country. These societies also owed part of their inspiration to events in France, where the king had recently been executed (in 1793). As a result, a European war ensued to protect monarchy from the chaos of Republican France, and Americans found themselves having to choose between support for France or for Great Britain, since so much American trade took place on the ocean, which was now a theater of battle. The opponents of the Washington administration felt that the French were carrying forward the revolutionary principles of limited government and the right of citizen expression, and should thus be loudly supported by all Americans. However, the Federalists—perhaps predictably—had different ideas regarding France and liberalism. The Federalists feared the social, economic, and political instability generated by the French Revolution, and so tended to lean in the direction of Great Britain. The foreign policy debate concerning the level of support owed France by the United States would also further alienate the Democrats (also known as Democratic-Republicans) from Federalists like Washington, Adams, and (especially) Hamilton.

With time, the new French government came to expect support from the Washington administration, but Washington and the Federalists not did not want to support France (Washington issued his Declaration of Neutrality in 1793). Yet the Federalists actually negotiated a treaty with Great Britain over commercial relations, as well as other issues left over from the Revolution, such as the presence of British troops on American soil in New York and present-day Michigan. To the Federalists, negotiating with Britain made sense because Britain was the stronger naval power and had the ability to make life difficult for the United States on the high seas during wartime. As was customary at the time, any power trying to claim neutrality in warfare was essentially fair game for attack on the ocean, since neither power at war could know if the "neutral" power was in fact "neutral." Furthermore, it was the British, not the French, who still occupied forts on American soil, so the Federalists sought to talk things over with the British out of national self-interest. The resulting treaty, named for Chief Justice John

Jay, led to the eventual evacuation of British troops from all parts of the United States, and provided for some trading rights in the Caribbean. Of course, many Americans were shocked that the treaty did not do more to recover lost American property from the Revolutionary era (including slaves lost to the British), and also forced Americans to pay pre-Revolutionary debts to Britain. Yet, given the relative weakness of the United States on the foreign stage, not much else could be hoped for with a treaty of this sort.

The larger problem with Jay's Treaty was the message it sent to France and to pro-French Americans: the U.S. government essentially wanted to cozy up to Great Britain, as it were, in defiance of the alliance which had existed between France and the Americans since 1778 (of course, that alliance was made with a king who had since been executed, and that was the excuse Hamilton would give for rejecting this alliance). Thus the French, insulted by Jay's Treaty, began seizing American vessels—at least 300 of them by 1797. In this climate, Washington left the White House, and the election of 1796 placed John Adams in the White House, with Thomas Jefferson as vice president. However, with three Hamiltonians in the cabinet posts of treasury, state, and war (Hamilton himself returned to his law practice in New York), hard-line Federalists really called the shots in the Adams administration. Thomas Jefferson, therefore, was even more estranged from the White House; by 1797, he had retreated from the administration altogether. He was in many ways the not-so-informal head of the growing opposition to the Federalists in the late 1790s.

With Vice President Jefferson absent from the White House, the high Federalists began murmuring about war preparations against France in retaliation for the French seizure of American vessels. Publicly led by President Adams, there was a desire for negotiation, and in the fall of 1797, three ministers were dispatched to Paris to negotiate with the French foreign minister, Talleyrand. But instead of being greeted, the American ministers were informed that Talleyrand would only meet with the Americans if the Americans paid an immediate bribe of $250,000, in addition to a $12 million loan to France, literally as the price of peace. Needless to say, most Americans—even several Democratic-Republicans—were shocked. In this climate, it was all the easier for those Federalists sympathetic with the militarist Hamilton to demand that the army and navy be readied for war with France. A naval war in the Caribbean ensued, which was not that eventful; rather, the real fireworks came on the home front when the Federalists overstepped their bounds in trying to silence domestic antiwar opposition. As mentioned earlier, the Democratic-Republican opposition believed in mobilizing the common man to protest political acts even when there was no election. In addition, the Republicans believed in using newspaper editorials to skewer their Federalist opponents. This kind of rough-and-tumble partisan politics deeply disturbed the Federalists, who really possessed quite elitist sentiments regarding the ability of average white men to loudly condemn the decisions of their social betters. In this way, the Federalists were out of touch with various democratic impulses within white American culture, and would soon pay for their imperiousness.

What nearly caused a domestic civil war came from the Federalist-supported Alien and Sedition Acts. The Alien Act lengthened naturalization time for foreigners and empowered the president to deport or imprison any foreigner suspected of being a "danger" to the United States (such as various French and Irish radicals then circulating in the country.) The Sedition Act made it a crime not only to conspire to revolt but to publicly "defame" the President or Congress. This last act smacked of traditional British restraints on public speech against the king, and there were plenty of Republicans who made connections between the Federalists and the British aristocracy. The Sedition Act was in many ways a likely assault upon the First Amendment, so strongly supported by Anti-Federalists and later by Jeffersonians. During 1798–1799, ten men were jailed under these laws, although given the scope of the law, there could have been many more prosecutions. But the damage was done. With the leadership of Vice President Jefferson, Republicans in Virginia and Kentucky responded to the Alien and Sedition Acts with resolutions of their own, which basically affirmed the ability of states to reject federal laws and even to secede from the Union, if they felt threatened by a tyrannical federal government. The state of Virginia, it has been claimed, actually began to stockpile arms in the capital of Richmond in the anticipation of civil war. In these events, historians can discern the fragility of the American federal union, and can see how less than 17 years after the end of the Revolutionary War, it appeared that Americans would be at each others' throats again over not being able to agree upon the power and prerogatives of a central government. But President John Adams understood the seriousness of the situation, and that he had been irresponsibly misled by Hamilton and his supporters within the cabinet, in terms of supporting such a bellicose program. Therefore, in January of 1799, once Adams learned that the French, headed by Napoleon, did not want to continue the unofficial naval war in the Caribbean, Adams agreed to a peace commission to France headed by Vans Murray. This peace commission may very well have prevented an internal civil war within the United States, even if it nearly assured that Adams would lose support among Federalists, as well as the presidential election (which did come to pass). And with Adams' defeat at the polls in 1800, the elitist view of the Federalists was also soundly defeated, and could never mount a successful comeback. Slowly, by the early 1800s, it would no longer be possible to prevent average white males from participating fully in the public sphere of the American republic.

And yet, as has been mentioned, this white man's democracy often depended upon the expropriation both of slave labor and native land. On these issues, Jeffersonians, who often hailed from the South and the West, were more likely to be implicated in racially exclusive policies, yet most white Americans—regardless of party—shared sentiments considered "racist" to later generations. This is a significant limitation on the meaning of a "democracy" influenced by slave owners and Indian-haters, who hardly believed that all men really were created equal. In the case of the natives, the early defeats for the American military suffered by generals such as Josiah Harmar and Arthur St. Clair testify to the inexperience of American troops in the Ohio Valley region. These troops attempted to move north and west from Fort Washington (present-day Cincinnati, Ohio) in the late 1780s and early 1790s, only to meet stiff native resistance. It should be noted that this region contained numerous tribes, foremost amongst them the Shawnee, Delaware, and Miami, who preferred death over negotiating land away to an American government they deeply distrusted. But beginning with the actions of President Washington in the early 1790s, the American government doubled the size of its military presence in Ohio, and appointed a new commander to oversee its operations against the natives, General Anthony Wayne of Pennsylvania. Wayne established two new forts in Ohio, Fort Wayne and Fort Recovery, and soon launched new offensives culminating in the Battle of Fallen Timbers in August 1794, where the Shawnee-led coalition of natives was routed. By 1795, Wayne's strategy of intimidation worked to bring many of these natives to the bargaining table at the Treaty of Greenville. This treaty, whereby the Americans pledged money and trade goods to the natives, led to the tribal leaders ceding most of Ohio to the Americans. George Washington claimed that he sought to help the natives become sedentary farmers, and that white Americans were supposed to leave tribes alone, but Washington realized the likely futility of such actions. Moreover, he appointed his secretary of war, Henry Knox to be the man to "handle" native affairs—hardly an endorsement of peace between whites and the tribes. And as we shall see, if native tribes dared to conceive of themselves as independent nations within the United States, this would only encourage whites to view tribes as military enemies worthy of being destroyed by force.

To the south in the Caribbean came another, more troubling reminder of the limitations of the American Revolution. On the Western half of the island of Hispaniola, the French colony of Saint Domingue slipped into revolution, after the local whites challenged the monarchist government shortly after the French Revolution began in 1789. This initial revolution set off several chain reactions, where mixed-race planters began to demand rights, and soon enough armed bands of slaves also got in on the action. To compound matters, British and Spanish troops sought to take advantage of France's travails in order to move in on the island, possibly to restore not only order, but to gain advantages for their countries with access to the lucrative sugar crop on the island. A leader of the revolution soon emerged, Toussaint L'Ouverture, who tried to use these foreign troops to his advantage, all the while trying to establish a government led by people of color. By the late 1790s, when it was apparent that the French had been at least temporarily defeated, all sorts of rumors began to be heard in the American South regarding the possibility of coordinated slave revolts. This seemed all the more likely now that several thousand Haitian refugees managed to find their way to numerous seaport towns from Charleston to Philadelphia (in addition to the larger community of refugees in Spanish New Orleans). Thomas Jefferson, for one, was petrified of black revolution spreading north, and when he eventually became president, he did all he could to deny diplomatic recognition to the new black nation of Haiti. Jefferson's hostile stance toward Haiti also came after authorities in Virginia unearthed the plot of an attempted slave insurrection in Richmond, Virginia, in 1800 (the so-called Gabriel's Rebellion). The ostracizing of Haiti—also shared by France and other European powers—badly damaged this black republic. But it also reveals how many white, supposedly democratic Americans had no intention of allowing nonwhite races their rights as equal citizens of the nation or of the world.

Documents:

1. Alexander Hamilton on the Public Credit (1790)

As the newly appointed secretary of the treasury, Hamilton felt he was the second-in-command after Washington in the federal government, since he saw his position as similar to the chancellor of the exchequer in Britain. Hamilton, therefore, went on the offensive in his efforts to create a British-style financial and commercial power in the United States. It is worth considering to what extent the average American would agree with Hamilton's thinking on economics.

States, like individuals, who observe their engagements are respected and trusted; while the reverse is the fate of those, who pursue an opposite conduct.

Every breach of the public engagements, whether from choice or necessity, is in different degrees hurtful to public credit ...When such a necessity does truly exist, on the part of the government, [they] ... should manifest ... a sincere disposition to make reparation, whenever circumstances shall permit ...

Those who are most commonly creditors of a nation, are, generally speaking, enlightened men; and ... they will understand their true interest too well to refuse their concurrence in such modifications of their claims, as any real necessity may demand ... To justify and preserve their confidence; to promote the increasing respectability of the American name ... to furnish new resources both to agriculture and commerce ... these are the great and invaluable ends to be secured ... for the support of public credit.

2. Alexander Hamilton, *Report on Manufacturers* (1791)

Unlike his report on the credit, Hamilton's desire to see federal support for internal improvement was not supported by the first Congress, even though such support would come in the following century.

Manufacturing establishments not only occasion a positive augmentation of the Produce and Revenue of the Society, but they contribute essentially to rendering them greater than they could possibly be without such establishments. ... It has been observed that there is scarcely any thing of greater moment in the economy of a nation, than the proper division of labor. The separation of occupations causes each to be carried to a much greater perfection, than it could possibly acquire, if they were blended ... And from these causes ... the mere separation of the occupation of the cultivator from that of the Artificer, has the effect of augmenting the productive powers of labour and with them, the total mass of the produce or revenue of a Country. In this single view of the subject, therefore, the utility of Artificers or Manufacturers, towards promoting an increase of productive industry, is apparent.

3. Thomas Jefferson *Notes on the State of Virginia* (1785)

Jefferson's notes were an attempt to create a kind of encyclopedia describing the New World. But in this book, Jefferson also expounded upon his views of economics, which were diametrically opposed to those of Hamilton.

... [W]e have an immensity of land ... it is best that all our citizens should be employed in its improvement ... Those who labor in the earth are the chosen people of God, if ever He had chosen people, whose breasts He has made His peculiar deposit for substantial and genuine virtue. It is the focus in which he keeps alive that sacred fire, which otherwise might escape from the face of the Earth. Corruption of morals in ... [farmers] is [unknown] in the modern age. It is the mark of those who do not look ... to their own soil or industry. ... While we have land to labor then, let us never wish to see our citizens occupied at the work bench ... for the general occupations of manufacture, let our workshops remain in Europe. ... The mobs of great cities add just so much to the support of pure government, as sores do to the strength of the human body.

4. From the Minutes of the Democratic Society of Pennsylvania, Civic Festival (May 1, 1794)

This democratic society was one of several dozen formed to protest the Federalist policy, as well as to support the French Revolution.

Resolved unanimously, that they would commemorate the successes of their Republican French Brethren in a Civic Festival on the first day of May 1794 and that to this Festival they would invite their Sister Society the German Republican, and all other citizens who harmonized with them in sentiment ...

On the first day of May ... about 800 citizens assembled [in Philadelphia] ... and the following toasts were drunk:

A Revolutionary Tribunal in Great Britain—May it give lessons of liberty to her king, examples of Justice to her Ministry, and honesty to her corrupt legislature.

The Fair Daughters of America and France—May they ever possess virtue to attract merit, and sense to reward it.

To Democratic and Republic societies of the United States—May they preserve and disseminate their principles, undaunted by the frowns of powers ... till the Rights of Man shall become the Supreme Law of the land. ... May every Free Nation consider a public debt as a public curse; and may the man who would assert a contrary opinion be considered as an Enemy to his Country. ...

5. A Pennsylvania Democrat, Regarding the Whiskey Rebellion (1796)

This anonymous account of the Whiskey Rebellion downplayed the insurrectionary tendency of those who opposed the whiskey tax. It also highlighted the perspective of poorer farmers regarding what they saw as the unfair nature of Federalist tax policy.

As no riots that I knew of were attempted in the county where I reside, or by the people of it previous to the insurrection, and as I had never heard any person threaten any other kind of opposition other than laying aside their stills, I consequently knew nothing of the insurrection until it took place ... In endeavoring to restore order, and submission to the laws, the most arduous talk with people otherwise of good morals was to convince them of the error of this principle. ... Their objections are obvious and easily comprehended, and address themselves powerfully to their interests; whereas the arguments arising from the unequal pressure of imposts on the inhabitants of towns and people generally who manufacture little themselves, and consequently consume much of foreign manufacturers or luxuries, not coming under their observation, are not understood nor admitted in abatement of their own complaints; consequently citizens in situations remote from market are advocated for direct taxes, proportioned to the value of their property, and always pay them without complaint.

6. George Washington, By the President of the United States of America, a Proclamation (1794)

Fearing destabilizing events both in Europe and at home, Washington took a dim view of what he saw as an excess of democracy. He speaks here of those involved in the Whiskey Rebellion, but his dislike for democratic societies did not stop with the events in Pennsylvania.

Whereas combinations to defeat the execution of the laws laying duties upon spirits distilled within the United States and upon stills have from the time of commencement of those laws existed in some of the Western parts of Pennsylvania; and

Whereas the said combinations, proceeding in a manner subversive equally of the just authority of government and of the rights of the individuals, have hitherto effected their dangerous and criminal purpose by the influence of certain irregular meetings whose proceedings have tended to encourage and uphold the spirit of opposition by misrepresentations of the laws calculated to render them odious; by endeavors to deter those who might be so disposed from accepting offices under them through fear of public resentment and of injury to person and property, and to compel those who had accepted such offices by actual violence to surrender or forbear the execution of them. …

Whereas the endeavors of the Legislature to obviate objections to the said laws by lowering the duties and by other alterations conducive to the convenience of those whom they immediately effect … have been disappointed by their effect by the machinations of persons who industry to excite resistance has increased with every appearance … [and many other persons have therefore] been hardy enough to perpetrate acts which I am advised amount to treason, being overt acts of levying war against the United States … it shall be lawful for the President of the United States to call forth the militia of such State to suppress such combinations and to cause the laws to be duly executed …. and I George Washington, President of the United States do hereby command all persons being insurgents … on or before the 1st day of September next to disperse and retire peaceably to their respective abodes. …

7. Thomas Jefferson's Letter to Philip Mazzei (April 1796)

As the election of 1796 drew near, Jefferson revealed himself to be the head of a growing opposition to the Federalist program. According to the following, is Jefferson calling for a new revolution?

[Over the past few years] … in place of that noble love of liberty and republican government which carried us triumphantly through the war, an Anglican monarchical aristocratical party has sprung up, whose avowed object is to draw over us the substance, as they have already done the forms, of the British government. The main body of our citizens, however, remain true to their republican principles: the whole landed interest is republican, and so is a great mass of talents. Against us are the Executive, the Judiciary, two out of three branches of the Legislature, all the officers of the government, all who want to be officers … speculators and holders in the banks and public funds, a contrivance invented for the purposes of corruption. … In short we are likely to preserve the liberty we have obtained only by unremitting labors and perils. But we shall preserve it. …

8. George Washington, Farewell Address (1796)

Washington's farewell address is an important statement of the Federalist worldview relating to domestic politics. But his address also was used later as a justification for nonintervention in European affairs.

All obstructions to the executions of the laws, all combinations and associations, under whatever plausible character with the real design ... to control, counteract, or owe the regular deliberation and action of the constituted authorities ... serve to organize faction ... [and] to put in the place of the delegated will of the nation the will of a party, often small but artful and enterprising minority. ...

As a very important source of strength and security, cherish public credit. One method of preserving it is to use it as sparingly as possible, avoiding occasion of expense by cultivating peace, but remembering also that timely disbursements to prepare for danger frequently prevent much greater disbursements to repel it. ...

Observe good faith and justice toward all nations. Cultivate peace and harmony with all. Religion and morality enjoin this conduct. ...

In the execution of such a plan nothing is more essential than that permanent, inveterate antipathies against particular nations and passionate attachments for other should be excluded, and that in place of them just and amicable feelings toward all should be cultivated. ...

The great rule of conduct for us in regard to foreign nations is, in extending our commercial relations to have with them as little political connection as possible. So far as we have already formed engagements let them be fulfilled with perfect good faith. Here let us stop. ...

It is our true policy to steer clear permanent alliances with any portion of the foreign world, so far, I mean, as we are now at liberty to do it; for let me not understood as capable of patronizing infidelity to existing engagements. I hold the maxim no less applicable to public than to private affairs that honesty is always the best policy. I repeat, therefore, let those engagements be observed in their genuine sense. But in my opinion, it is unnecessary and would be unwise to extend them.

9. Thomas Jefferson, The Kentucky Resolutions (1798)

As vice president under John Adams, Jefferson secretly wrote these resolutions as a way of trying to protect the sanctity of the First Amendment to the Constitution. The Kentucky State Legislature passed the first resolution on November 16, 1798, and the second on December 3, 1799.

... *3. Resolved,* That it is true as a general principle, and is also expressly declared by one of the amendments to the Constitution, that 'the powers not delegated to the United States by Constitution, nor prohibited by it to the States, are reserved to the States respectively, or to the people;' and that no power over the freedom of religion, freedom of speech, or freedom of the press being delegated to the United States by the Constitution, nor prohibited to it by the States, all lawful powers respecting the same did of right remain and were reserved to the States. ... [they have the] right of judging how far the licentiousness of speech and of the press may be abridged without lessening their useful freedom. ... [therefore] the act of Congress of the United States, passed on the 14th day of July 1798, entitled, 'An Act in addition to the act intituled an Act for the punishment of certain crimes against the United States,' which does abridge the freedom of the press, is not law, but is altogether void, and of no force.

4. *Resolved*, That alien friends are under the jurisdiction and protection of the laws of the State wherein they are: that no power over them has been delegated to the United States, nor prohibited from the individual States, distinct from their power over citizens ... [and therefore] the act of Congress of the United States, passed on ___ day of July, 1798, intituled, 'An Act concerning aliens,' which assumes power over alien friends, not delegated by the Constitution, is not law, but is altogether void, and of no force. ... Where powers are assumed which have not been delegated, a nullification of the act is the rightful remedy; that every State has a natural right in cases not within the compact (casus non foederis) to nullify of their own authority all assumptions of power by others within their limits; that without this right, they would be under the dominion, absolute and unlimited, of whosoever might exercise the right of judgment for them ... [and] that nevertheless this commonwealth, from motive of regard and respect for its co-States, has wished to communicate [with the other states] on this subject ... [because of the usurpation of civil liberties by Congress and the President] no rampart now remains against the passions and the powers of a majority of Congress to protect against a like exportation or other more grievous punishment against a minority. ...

10. Joseph Brant, "Article in the American Museum" (1789)

Brant was one of the most outspoken loyalist natives during the Revolution. He relocated to Canada once the war ended.

I was, sir, born of Indian parents, and lived while a child, among those you are pleased to call savages; I was afterwards sent to live among the white people, and educated at one of your schools ... and have been honored with an acquaintance with a number of principal characters in Europe and America. After all this experience, and after every exertion to divest myself of prejudice, I am obliged to give my opinion in favour of my own people ... We have no prisons—we have no pompous parade of courts ... we have no robbery under the colour of law—daring wickedness here is never suffered to triumph over helpless innocence—the estates of widows and orphans are never devoured by enterprising sharpers. ... No person, among us, desires any other reward for performing a brave and worthy action, than the consciousness of serving his nation. ... The palaces and prisons among you, form a most dreadful contrast ... [and] for what are many of your prisoners confined? For debt! Astonishing! And will you ever again call the Indian nations cruel?—Liberty, to a rational creature, as much exceeds property, as the light of the sun does that of the most twinkling star; but you put them on a level, to the everlasting disgrace of civilization. ... I would rather die by the most severe tortures ever inflicted by any savage nation on the continent, than languish in one of your prisons for a single year. Great Maker of the world! And do you call yourselves Christians! ... Cease to call other nations savage, when you are tenfold more the children of cruelty, than they.

Questions to Consider:

1. Many Americans currently see Alexander Hamilton as the father of the American economy. How is this true? Is Thomas Jefferson's economic vision irrelevant to our present age?
2. How did the French Revolution impact the economy and society of the United States? Why was debate over support of the French such a contentious issue in the 1790s?
3. How did the Federalists possess assumptions regarding government and society that differ from those held by later generations of Americans?
4. What were the limitations of the term "democracy" in the United States around the turn of the nineteenth century?

Credits

- Excerpts from Alexander Hamilton, "Hamilton's Report on Public Credit, January 9, 1790," Senate Documents, 60th Congress, 1st Session, vol. 8. 1790. Copyright in the Public Domain.
- Excerpts from Alexander Hamilton, Report on *Manufactures*, Communicated to the House of Representatives, December 5, 1791, pp. 10-11. 1791. Copyright in the Public Domain.
- Excerpt from Thomas Jefferson, "Query XIX," *Notes on the State of Virginia*, pp. 176. 1853. Copyright in the Public Domain.
- Excerpt from Democratic Society of Pennsylvania minutes. 1794. Copyright in the Public Domain.
- Excerpt from *History of the Insurrection in the Four Western Counties of Pennsylvania*, pp. 301-302. 1796. Copyright in the Public Domain.
- Excerpts from George Washington, Proclamation, 7 August 1794. Copyright in the Public Domain.
- Excerpts from Thomas Jefferson, Thomas Jefferson's Letter to Philip Mazzei. 1796. Copyright in the Public Domain.
- Excerpts from George Washington, Farewell Address. 1796. Copyright in the Public Domain.
- Excerpts from Thomas Jefferson, The Kentucky Resolutions of 1798. Copyright in the Public Domain.
- Joseph Brant, "Article in the American Museum," *The Indian and White Man or The Indian in Self-Defense*, ed. Rev. D. W. Risher, pp. 467-469. 1880. Copyright in the Public Domain.

CHAPTER 9

JEFFERSONIAN AMERICA AND THE WAR OF 1812

Once upon a time, historians referred to the election of Thomas Jefferson to the presidency as the "Revolution of 1800." The reasons for this should be clear, given the role that Jefferson played in thwarting Federalist efforts to dominate domestic politics and build a huge fighting force to do battle with France. Jefferson identified himself with the values of small government, and hoped that the United States would avoid the severe concentration of wealth associated with modern banking and industrialization (two aspects of British society Jefferson disliked). His inaugural address claimed that "we are all republicans, we are all federalists," but in fact this phrase really meant that Federalists were encouraged to support his policies if they so chose, not that Jefferson saw much to admire in the Federalist world view. The fact that Jefferson's inauguration occurred in the new capital of Washington, D.C., is a telling sign of the simplicity that he saw as indispensable to the proper functioning of an American government: the nation's capital was half built, and was more or less located in the middle of nowhere. Therefore, few bureaucrats or other government officials would want to live in this capital, and in some sense that was the way men such as Jefferson liked it.

Thus, in the spirit of smaller government, Jefferson embarked on what could be termed a fairly radical effort to dismantle most of the Federalist program of the prior ten years. He repealed the Alien and Sedition Acts, he dramatically reduced the size of the federal bureaucracy by firing employees, and more or less retired the Federalist debt through other cost-saving measures. In addition, Jefferson and his party (which also controlled Congress) tried to wage war on the Federalist judiciary, men who were appointed by Adams in an attempt to influence laws according to Federalist principles. For example, the House impeached Samuel Chase for being too partisan in his prosecution of the Sedition Acts (though he was not ultimately convicted), and John Pickering was convicted for misconduct (he was mentally deranged and an alcoholic). Another part of the Federalist program in Congress distasteful to Jeffersonians had been legislation giving the Supreme Court the power of "writ of mandamus," which was a court order forcing the president to appoint certain judges to the district courts. Of course, the Jeffersonians challenged this and Jefferson himself, by denying the last-minute appointment of William Marbury, and triggered a Supreme Court case over the legality of these writs of mandamus, passed into law by a Federalist Congress. However, the Supreme Court, led by Jefferson's cousin, John Marshall, proved very effective at carving out a space for its autonomy when it was still unclear how much power the Court should have. In the decision for *Marbury v. Madison*, Marshall came up with the ingenious solution whereby he would deny the Court

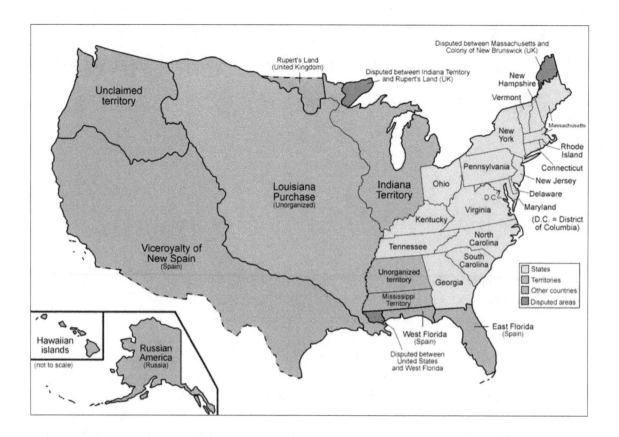

The Louisiana Purchase of 1803.

the power to issue writs of mandamus, but in so doing, the Court was establishing its larger ability to determine which acts of Congress were constitutional or which were not. So in denying itself the relatively smaller ability to determine whom the president could appoint and whom he could not, the Court was nonetheless giving itself the much more important right to judge acts of Congress unconstitutional.

In the foreign policy arena, meanwhile, Jefferson also wanted to pursue peaceful measures when dealing with European foes, and he sought to reject the belligerent militarism both of men such as Hamilton (who had recently been killed in a duel with Aaron Burr), as well as of other European powers. Jefferson hoped that negotiation or other nonviolent measures could lead to positive results for the Americans. In the case of the Louisiana Purchase, Jefferson simply got lucky in that Napoleon wanted to sell the territory to the Americans rather than risk a confrontation, since Napoleon needed money for his war efforts in Europe. Napoleon also had recently lost Haiti and therefore did not need a commodity supply from mainland America to sustain his sugar island. So Jefferson agreed to buy the vast territory to the west of the Mississippi River for the amazing sum of approximately $14 million (including debt forgiveness). Jefferson then encouraged the expedition of Lewis and Clark to map and otherwise document the geography, resources, and peoples of this vast domain. Many Americans at the time believed that it would take up to one thousand years for Americans to populate the Western reaches of their continent, and this fact is a reminder of how small the American republic was, and how little white Americans understood about the Western reaches of the

North American continent. But with Lewis and Clark, the federal government began one of many projects to fund overland exploration in anticipation of territorial growth. Jefferson was an expansionist—he believed that American farmers should comprise an "empire of liberty," where the production of crops for export would create a stable, healthy society free of cities, factories, or concentrations of paper wealth.

But in order to defend his "empire of liberty," Jefferson would have to stand up to foreign powers, both internally and externally. Standing up to "foreign" powers first of all meant further belligerent behavior toward the already badly treated native tribes of the Ohio and lower Mississippi valleys. As mentioned in the last chapter, these natives had been constantly pushed around, attacked, or otherwise exploited by an expanding white American power, and the resentments of the tribes had hardly diminished by the early 1800s. A Shawnee tribal leader named Tecumseh began to organize disparate native tribes in the Ohio Valley in an attempt to opt out of any contact or compromise with white society. Tecumseh called on natives to present a united front against white Americans by, for example, not selling land and not going into debt to buy Western trade goods—most notably alcohol. Tecumseh inspired natives to return to their own culture, and even articulated a type of racial pride in Indian-ness, which represented an attempt to combat Anglo-American racial chauvinism. Because many natives in the Ohio Valley soon began to meet at the community dubbed Prophetstown, there was widespread fear among the whites that there would be a native American uprising. Soon enough, the British would also be implicated in aiding men like Tecumseh, since the British had tried to use natives against the Americans in the Revolutionary War. In reality, many whites in the West were itching to take on tribes they suspected of being weak enough to be broken once and for all, so that whites would not have to share any of the farmland east of the Mississippi River.

The other foreign threat faced by Jefferson came from Great Britain. The wars in Europe instigated by the execution of the French monarch in 1793 only briefly died down and were rekindled after 1803. Once again, American ships found themselves imperiled by the prospect of war on the high seas. And this time Great Britain proved quite eager to crack down on American attempts to trade on the high seas as a neutral power (again, remember that the free trade neutrality advocated by the Americans was not how Europeans fought wars; a country was supposed to declare support for one side or else face reprisals from both). American ships were searched and cargo was seized. To make matters even worse, British naval forces began boarding American vessels and taking American sailors off of American ships. In some cases there were British sailors hiding out in American vessels—since American maritime service was easier than in Britain—but often the more powerful British naval forces simply took advantage of the weaker U.S. ships to steal men away. Soon enough, Jefferson, motivated by an attempt to protest these policies without war, tried to revive the same kind of boycott measures used against Britain before the Revolution. And so Jefferson and Congress instituted an embargo (boycott) against Britain, but really all this did was damage the domestic economy and help to revive the nearly defunct Federalist Party. The Federalists also benefited from the fact that as the French began boarding and seizing material from American ships as a way of punishing American neutrality, Jefferson did not try to strike out at France. Even though the French were not nearly as large a naval power as Britain, the Federalists began to make an issue out of Jefferson's apparent laxity in dealing with the government of the dictator Napoleon. Jefferson ended up leaving the White House with the gathering storm of war hardly abating. His successor, James Madison, more or less continued Jefferson's economic measures designed to stop

Great Britain, but again to no avail. Soon enough, a number of so-called "war hawks" from more Western regions of the United States demanded action, and saw in these foreign policy headaches an opportunity to strike boldly against both the British in Canada and the natives in the Ohio and lower Mississippi valleys. With time and with a deteriorating economy, congressional leaders found the votes for war, even though Great Britain claimed at the last moment that it was interested in negotiations. The War of 1812 had begun.

In general, the U.S. military was not up to the task of fighting, and the war can best be described as a stalemate in the various regions of battle. (Although the fact that the United States held its own against the most powerful navy in the world was nothing to sneeze at.) The American invasion of Canada was more or less a disaster, even though U.S. troops did manage to burn the Canadian capital of York. The mid-Atlantic campaign proceeded along a similar line, with the American militia proving so ineffective that Washington, D.C., was not only invaded but badly damaged by British troops. (President and Mrs. Madison fled the city during their dinner.) But the fact that Americans held Fort McHenry in Baltimore Harbor at least showed that the Americans could put up some sort of fight. Also in the North, American troops killed Tecumseh after he joined the British, thus signaling that the American war against Britain was really a war against various rebellious tribes. In addition, in what was then called the "Southwest"—modern-day Tennessee, Alabama, Mississippi, and Louisiana—a young, daring militia general from Tennessee named Andrew Jackson would really give American nationalists something to boast over with his bloody and vicious defeat of the native Creek tribe at the battle of Horseshoe Bend, Alabama. Jackson then followed this up with a decisive defeat of British forces at the Battle of New Orleans in 1815. This last victory in New Orleans appeared to vindicate the war hawks who wanted to fight with Great Britain and served to discredit the Federalists, who not only opposed the war, but who went so far as to flirt with disunion in the Hartford Convention, which was meeting around the same time as Jackson's victory in New Orleans. The Hartford Convention made several ludicrous demands (such as no two sequential presidents should come from the same state, an obvious attack on the Virginians so often in the White House), as well as implying that the New England states would secede from the Union if their demands were not met. But with victory, these actions simply looked treasonous.

On the other hand, the end of the war saw power continue to shift to the south and west. The fact that Andrew Jackson, a rough-and-tumble Indian killer and slave owner from Tennessee, became such a huge military and political figure after 1815 further testifies to the belligerent nature of American nationalism in the early nineteenth century. And the biggest consequence of the War of 1812 was the consolidation of white American power over lands once occupied by various proud native tribes in places like modern-day Indiana or Alabama. The rising American confidence and assertiveness in the foreign policy realm only continued in the 1810s with moves made by Jackson to detach Florida from Spanish control, even though he was reprimanded for such behavior. In many ways, the Spanish lost interest in maintaining control of Florida when they were losing their Latin American empire, and when Southerners such as Jackson wanted it so badly. The Spanish therefore sold Florida to the United States for $5 million in 1819 and also ceded their claims to the Oregon Territory and part of Louisiana. The assertiveness of the United States also manifested itself in the foreign policy statement known as the Monroe Doctrine, promulgated in 1823. President James Monroe, who followed Madison in the White House, was encouraged by Secretary of State John Quincy Adams to boldly declare both American support for the recently independent Latin American republics

This is a map of American territorial growth to 1820, including the results of the Adams-Onis Treaty and the Missouri Compromise, both approved by 1820.

(such as Mexico, Colombia, or Argentina), and to state that former colonizers such as Spain had no business being involved in the affairs of the Western hemisphere (or otherwise try to claim them back). These expressions of support for Latin American republics may seem harmless in hindsight, but it could be said that the United States was trying to establish a sphere of influence in the Western hemisphere, especially given that Americans already eyed large tracts of land to the west that belonged to Mexico.

Indeed, by the 1820s, American settlers began moving into what is now Texas (although they were technically invited by the Mexican government, something that, as we will see, was not very smart on Mexico's part). Over the next several decades, numerous trailblazers and explorers would map routes for travelers either to the northwest toward Oregon, or the southwest toward California. Men such as William Becknell, who helped to chart the Santa Fe Trail so as to increase the fur trade, and Jedediah Smith, who opened up the so-called "South Pass" of the Rocky Mountains in present-day Wyoming, aided both trappers and settlers in their efforts to trade in and then occupy Western North America. Beginning with Lewis and Clark's Corps of Discovery, the federal government also sponsored expeditions to chart the trans-Mississippi West, and within a few years the fabulously successful American Fur Company, led by John Jacob Astor, was a testament to the ability of Americans to penetrate the trade of the far West with the help of the American government, which passed laws excluding foreign competition. Between 1805 and 1807, Zebulon Pike produced detailed accounts of present-day Minnesota; in 1820 Stephen Long did the same thing with modern-day Oklahoma, Kansas, and Nebraska, and both men worked for the U.S. Army. The years after the War of 1812 coincided with several efforts made by individual Americans to extend commercial contacts far beyond the geographical confines of their nation-state. For example, by 1840 clipper ships and other oceanic vessels helped American merchants gain exposure to Japan and to China. These commercial endeavors reveal a desire for commercial trade with Asia; by the 1850s, it was an American naval officer, Matthew C. Perry, who compelled the Japanese to open up trade with all Western powers.

There were other, important consequences of the end of war in 1815 besides travel and exploration. With the defeat of Napoleon in Europe, the Western world would be more or less free of major military conflict for the next century; thus, many powers could focus on building up their economies and making money. The United States proved no exception in this regard, and turned toward economic modernization in the years after 1815. During the war itself, American capitalists invested in the development of domestic textile manufacturing (clothing), with pirated technology from Great Britain. The Slater mills in New England were primarily concerned only with making thread, not finished clothing, but their use of water power revolutionized the production of textiles and laid foundations for even greater achievements in the mass production of clothing. It is significant that many of the political heirs of Thomas Jefferson soon lessened their once-stiff opposition to industrialization or banking, while they insisted that state and local governments—and not the federal government in Washington—take the lead in these endeavors. These efforts at economic modernization also included support for newer military institutes such as West Point, which encouraged the development of engineering skills. It is also important to note that the Democratic-Republicans were now the only party in Washington, D.C., since the Federalists had discredited themselves for their involvement in the Hartford Convention of 1815. Many of these Jeffersonian Republicans hoped that the farming republic would not be entirely destroyed by this compromise with the forces of mechanization, urbanization, and modern finance. A flurry of road building and the beginnings of canal construction in the North typified the postwar period as a way of encouraging the growth of an internal market for farm goods. These achievements came in addition to the rechartering of the Bank of the United States by President Madison in 1816, as a means of extending credit for the various development projects which seemed necessary to meet the demands of a growing economy and society. However, the confidence many Americans had in the burgeoning market economy represented by credit expansion and the development of technological innovation was shaken by the banking panic of 1819. The panic was caused primarily by the overinvestment in unsustainable investments—especially in land—in order to supply war-ravaged Europe with foodstuffs. But once Europe recovered, demands for crops (and therefore for land) failed, and many Americans found themselves over-indebted and banks found that they had made too many bad loans. As many Americans discovered, there were consequences to borrowing and lending on credit, and plenty of Americans in the coming years (including Andrew Jackson) would demand that the republic not be seduced by the apparent "magic" of paper money issued by banks.

Documents:

1. Thomas Jefferson's Inaugural Address (1801)

As the first inaugural address delivered in the new capital of Washington, D.C., Jefferson laid out the small-government agenda that would typify his party in power. Going forward, it is debatable just how committed Jefferson's supporters were to his agenda, however.

Let us, then, with courage and confidence pursue our own federal and republican principles, our attachment to our union and representative government. Kindly separated by nature and a wide ocean from the exterminating havoc of one quarter of the globe; too high minded to endure the degradations of others; possessing a chosen country, with room enough for our descendants to the thousandth and thousandth generation ... with all these blessings what more is necessary to make us a happy and prosperous people? ... Still one more thing, fellow citizens—a wise and frugal government, which shall restrain men from injuring one another [and] which shall leave them otherwise free to regulate their own pursuits of industry and improvement. ... The vital principle of republics, from which there is no appeal but to force ... a well disciplined militia—our best reliance in peace and for the first moments of war, till regulars may relieve them; the supremacy of the civil over the military authority; economy in the public expense, that labor may be lightly burdened; the honest payment of our debts and sacred preservation of the public faith; encouragement of agriculture, and of commerce as its handmaid; the diffusion of information and the arraignment of all abuses at the bar of public reason; freedom of religion; freedom of the press; freedom of person under the protection of habeas corpus—these principles form the bright constellation which has done before us, and guided our steps through an age of revolution and reformation.

2. Thomas Jefferson, Annual Message to Congress (1808)

Jefferson's attempt at "peaceable coercion" demonstrated his belief that the United States should pursue peaceful forms of protest against European powers in wartime. Once again, it is debatable how peaceful were the implications of Jefferson's foreign policy ideas.

[The embargo] necessarily remains in the extent originally given to it. We have the satisfaction, however, to reflect that in return for the privations imposed upon the measure, and which our fellow citizens in general have borne with patriotism; is has had the important effects of saving our mariners and our vast mercantile property, as well as of affording time for prosecuting the defensive and provisional measure called for by the occasion. It has demonstrated to foreign nations the moderation and firmness which govern our councils, and to our citizens the necessity of uniting in support of the laws and the rights of their country, and has thus long frustrated those usurpations and spoliations, which, if resisted, involved war; if submitted to, sacrificed a vital principle of our national independence.

3. Resolutions of the Town of Beverly, Massachusetts (1809)

This is a short example of the hundreds of resolutions that poured into Congress demanding that Presidents Jefferson and Madison rescind trade restrictions, which nearly destroyed the economy of New England.

The citizens [of Beverly] have witnessed with regret too strong a propensity to palliate and overlook the unjust aggressions of one foreign nation [France], and to exaggerate and misrepresent the conduct of another [Great Britain]; that the measures [embargo] are calculated and designed to force us into a war with Great Britain—a war which would be extremely detrimental to our agriculture, fatal to our commerce, and which would probably deprive us forever of the Bank fishery—and to unite us in alliance with France, whose embrace is death.

4. Tecumseh Confronts Governor William Henry Harrison (1810)

This confrontation came after the Treaty of Fort Wayne, prosecuted by Harrison, the Indiana territorial governor, in 1809. Tecumseh felt that certain leaders of groups such as the Kickapoo and Wea tribes had sold out their members, and that Harrison and the Americans would use whatever tactics necessary to steal native land.

On the 12th day of August, Tecumseh arrived at Vincennes [Indiana Territory], accompanied by a large number of his warriors. When the council convened, he rose and said … "The white people have no right to take the land from the Indians who had it first … We may sell, but all must agree; any sale made by a part [of a tribe] is no good. The last sale is bad. … [Many] promises of peace were made to the Shawnee people. One was at Fort Finney, where some of my people were forced to make a treaty. Flags were given to my people, and they were told they were now the children of the Americans. We were told, if any white people mean to harm you, hold up these flags and you will then be safe from all danger. We did this in good faith. But what happened? Our beloved chief Moluntha stood with the American flag in front of him and that very peace treaty in his hand, but his head was chopped off by an American officer, and that American officer was never punished …

It is you, Americans, by such bad deeds, who push the red men to do mischief. You do not want unity among the tribes, and you destroy it. You try to make differences between them. We, their leaders, wish them to unite and consider their land the common property of all, but you try to keep them from this. You separate the tribes and deal with them that way, one by one, and advise them not to come into this union. Your states have set an example of forming a union among all the Fires, why should you censure the Indians for following that example? … The only way to stop this evil is for all the red men to unite in claiming an equal right in the land. That is how it was first, and should be still, for the land never was divided, but was for the use of everyone … Sell a country! Why not sell the air, the clouds, the Great Sea, as well as the earth? Did not the Great Good Spirit make them all for the use of his children?

I am a Shawnee! I am a warrior! My forefathers were warriors. From them I took only my birth into this world. From my tribe I take nothing. I am the maker of my own destiny!

William Henry Harrison, in reply, declared to Tecumseh, that he and his band had no right to interfere or say one word in this matter, as he said the Shawnees had been driven from Georgia by the Creek Indians, and therefore, had no claim to land in this country. This exasperated the chief, and he pronounced the declaration of Harrison a falsehood. Harrison told his he was a bad man, and for some time it was apprehended that a serious conflict would ensue, … Harrison informed Tecumseh, before they separated, that he would lay the case before the President of the United States, and await his decision on the subject. Tecumseh replied … "I hope the Great Chief will put sense enough in his head to cause you to give up those lands. It is true that he may sit in his fine house and drink his wine, while you and I shall have to fight it out."

5. Felix Grundy, Speech in Congress (1811)

Tennessee congressman Grundy typified the views held by new, Western politicians eager to go to war against Britain in order to solidify American power in the Ohio Valley and in the old Southwest.

What, Mr. Speaker are we now called upon to decide? It is, whether we will resist by force the attempt made by the British government to subject our maritime rights to the arbitrary and capricious rule of her will; for my part I am not prepared to say that this country shall submit to have her commerce interdicted and regulated, by any foreign nation. Sir I prefer war to submission. ...

It cannot be believed by any man who will reflect, that the savage tribes, uninfluenced by other Powers, would think of making war on the United States. They understand too well their own weakness, and our strength. ... How then, sir, are we to account for their late conduct? In one way only; some powerful nation must have intrigued with them, and turned their peaceful disposition toward us into hostilities. Great Britain alone [has done this].

This war, if carried on successfully will have its advantages. We shall drive the British from our Continent—they will no longer have an opportunity of intriguing with our Indian neighbors, and setting on the ruthless savage tomahawk our women and children. That nation will lose her Canadian trade, and, by having no resting place in this country, her means of annoying us will be diminished [also]. ... When Louisiana shall be fully peopled, the Northern states will lose their power; they will be at the discretion of others; than can be depressed at pleasure, and then this Union might be endangered—I therefore feel anxious not only to add the Floridas to the South, but the Canadas to the North of this empire. ...

6. "The Congressional War Report" (1812)

This report was submitted by John C. Calhoun to the House of Representatives. It exemplifies the views of the so-called "war hawks" who pushed America to war with Britain, even though that country was interested in negotiation.

Your committee, believing that free-born sons of America are worthy to enjoy the liberty which their fathers purchased at the price of so much blood and treasure, and seeing in the measures adopted by Great Britain, a course commenced and persisted in, which must to a loss of national character and independence, feel no hesitation in advising resistance by force; in which the Americans of the present day will prove to the enemy and to the world, that we have not only inherited that liberty which our fathers gave us, but also the will and power to maintain it. Relying on the patriotism of the nation, and confidently trusting that the Lord of Hosts will go with us to battle in a righteous cause, and crown our efforts with success, your committee recommend an immediate appeal to arms. ...

7. Daniel Webster, Speech Before Congress Against the War (1812)

Representative Webster embodies the New England Federalist response to the Jefffersonian Republican desire for war. It is worth considering whether or not the complaints made by the Jeffersonians in fact justified war. Did the Jeffersonians want war because they sensed the western tribes and the British could be easily beaten?

If we could perceive that the present war was just; if we could perceive that our rights and liberties required it; if we could perceive that no Administration, however wise, honest, or impartial, could have carried us clear of it; if we could perceive its expediency, and a reasonable hope of obtaining its professed objects ... the war would, in some measure, cease to be horrible. It would grow tolerable, in idea, as its expediency should be made manifest. ... But we are constrained to say, that we cannot, in conscience ascribe the foregoing characteristics to the present war. ... The impressments of our seamen, which forms the most plausible and popular of the alleged causes of war, we believe to have been the subject of great misrepresentation. We have as much sympathy as others, for those who suffer under this abuse of power. We know there are instances of this abuse ... but the number of these cases has been extravagantly exaggerated. ... If so many of our sea-faring brethren had actually been taken, they must have been taken from amongst the inhabitants of the Atlantic coast. They would be from among our brethren, sons, relations, and friends. We should be acquainted with them, and their misfortunes ... It is well worthy of notice, that the greatest apparent felling on this subject of impressments, and the greatest disposition to wage war ... are entertained by those states, which have no seamen at all of their own. ...

It is well known that England pretends no right of impressing our seamen. She insists that she has a right to the service of her own subjects, in time of war ... is our nation to plunge into a ruinous war, in order to settle a question of relative right, between the government of a foreign nation and the subjects of that government? Are we to fight the battles of British seamen?

8. Resolutions of the Hartford Convention (1814)

In October of 1814, the State Legislature of Massachusetts called a convention ostensibly for the defense of the New England states, but it was widely known that many in Massachusetts, Connecticut, Rhode Island, New Hampshire, and Vermont wanted to secede from the Union, or perhaps try to detach Western states from the Union over their support for the War of 1812. The Hartford Convention was discredited, along with the Federalist party, when the fortunes of the American military effort in war changed within weeks of the convention meeting.

Therefore resolved, That it be and hereby is recommended to the legislatures of the several states represented in this Convention, to adopt all such measures as may be necessary effectually to protect the citizens of the said states [of New England] from operation and effects of all acts which have been or may be passed by the Congress of the United States, which contain provisions subjecting the militia or other citizens to forcible drafts, conscriptions, or impressments, not authorized by the constitution of the United States.

Resolved, That is be and hereby is recommended to the said Legislatures, to authorize an immediate and earnest application to be made to the government of the United States, requesting their consent to some arrangement, whereby the said states may, separately or in concert, be empowered to assume upon themselves the defense of their territory against the enemy. ...

Resolved, That the following amendments of the constitution of the United States be recommended to the states represented as aforesaid. ...

First, Representatives and direct taxes shall be apportioned among the several states which may be included within this Union, according to their respective number of free persons ... and excluding Indians not taxed, and all other persons. ...

Third, Congress shall not have power to lay any embargo on the ships or vessels of the citizens of the United States, in the ports or harbors thereof, for more than sixty days. ...

Seventh, The same person shall not be elected president of the United States a second time; nor shall the president be elected from the same state two terms in succession.

Resolved, That if the application of these states to the government of the United States, recommended in a foregoing resolution, should be unsuccessful, and peace should not be concluded [with Great Britain], and the defense of these states should be neglected, as it has been since the commencement of the war it will, in the opinion of this convention, be expedient for the legislatures of the several states to appoint delegates to another convention, to meet at Boston in the state of Massachusetts, on the third Thursday of June next, with such powers and instructions as the exigency of a crisis so momentous may require. ...

9. Francis Scott Key, "The Star-Spangled Banner" (The Defense of Fort McHenry) (September 20, 1814)

Key was onboard the British vessel HMS Tonnant attempting to negotiate with the British over the release of a prisoner during the British bombardment of Fort McHenry near Baltimore in 1814. Inspired by the fact that the American flag at the fort had survived the bombardment, he wrote the following poem, which was set to the tune of the British drinking song, Anacreon in Heaven, a few years later. However, The Star-Spangled Banner did not become the national anthem of the United States until 1931.

Oh, say can you see, by the dawn's early light,
What so proudly we hailed at the twilight's last gleaming?
Whose broad stripes and bright stars, through the perilous fight,
O'er the ramparts we watched, were so gallantly streaming?
And the rockets red glare, the bombs bursting in air,
Gave proof through the night that our flag was still there.
O, say does that star-spangled banner yet wave
O'er the land of the free and home of the brave?

On the shore, dimly seen through the mists of the deep
Where the foe's haughty host in dread silence reposes.
What is that which the breeze o'er the towering steep
As is fitfully blows, now conceals, now discloses?
Now it catches the gleam of the morning's first beam,
In full glory reflected now shines on the stream:
'Tis the star spangled banner! O long may it wave
O'er the land of the free and the home of the brave.

And where is that band who so vauntingly swore
That the havoc of war and the battle's confusion
A home and a country should leave us no more?
Their blood has wiped out their foul footstep's pollution.
No refuge could save the hireling and slave
From the terror of flight, or the gloom of the grave:
And the star spangled banner in triumph doth wave
O'er the land of the free and home of the brave.

Oh! Thus be it ever, then freemen shall stand
Between their loved home and the war's desolation!
Blest with victory and peace, may the heaven-rescued land
Praise the Power that hath made and preserved us a nation.
Then conquer we must, for our cause it is just,
And this be our motto: "In God is our trust."
And the star-spangled banner forever shall wave
O'er the land of the free and the home of the brave!

10. Anonymous, The Hunters of Kentucky; or the Battle of New Orleans (undated, ca. 1816).

The following was a well-known song lauding the success of Andrew Jackson at the Battle of New Orleans in early 1815. It symbolizes the rising fame of this militia general who would later become president.

I suppose you've read it in the prints,
How Packenham attempted
To make Old Hickory Jackson wince
But soon his scheme respected;
For we with rifles ready cock'd
Thought such occasion lucky
And soon around the general flocked
 Oh the hunters of Kentucky
 The Hunters of Kentucky
 Oh Kentucky
 The Hunters of Kentucky

You've heard I suppose, how New-Orleans
Is famed for wealth and beauty
There's girls of every hue, it seems,
From snowy white to sooty,
So Packenham made his brags
If he in fight was lucky
He'd have their girls and cotton bags,
In spite of old Kentucky,

Oh Kentucky, etc.
But Jackson was wide awake,
And wasn't scared at trifles
For well he knew what aim we take
With our Kentucky rifles.
So he led us up to a Cyrus swamp,
The ground was low and mucky,
There stood John Bull [England] in martial pomp
And here was old Kentucky. ...

They did not let their patience tire,
Before they showed their faces,
We did not choose to waste our fire
So snugly kept our places
But when so near we saw them wink
We thought it time to stop 'em
And it would have done you good, I think,
To see Kentuckians drop 'em.

They found, at last, 'twas vain to fight,
Where lead was all their booty,
And so they wisely took to flight,
And left us all the beauty.
And now if danger e'er annoys,
Remember what our trade is,
Just send for us Kentucky boys,
And we'll protect ye, ladies

11. Nathaniel Appleton, *Introduction of the Power Loom; and Origin of Lowell* (1858)

Appleton was a cousin of Francis Lowell and an early supporter of Lowell's efforts to establish the first power loom in the United States. Appleton had hoped that industrialization would not be nearly as traumatic or exploitative in the United States as in Britain. Appleton therefore tried to convince factory owners to pay factory workers well and to provide them with adequate living conditions.

My connection with the Cotton Manufacture takes date from the year 1811, when I met my friend Mr. Francis C. Lowell, at Edinburgh, where he had been passing some time with family. We had frequent conversations on the subject of the Cotton Manufacture, and he informed me that he had determined before his return to America, to visit Manchester, for the purpose of obtaining all possible information on the subject, with a view to the introduction of the improved manufacture in the United States. I urged him to do so, and promised my co-operation. He returned in 1813. He and Mr. Patrick T. Jackson, came to me one day on the Boston exchange, and stated that they had determined to establish a Cotton manufactory, that they had purchased a water power in Waltham, (Bemis' paper mill), and that they had obtained an act of incorporation, and Mr. Jackson had agreed to give up all other business and take the management of the concerns. …

The power loom was at this time being introduced in England, but its construction was kept very secret, and after many failures, public opinion was not favorable to its success. Mr. Lowell had obtained all the information which was practicable about it, and was determined to perfect it himself. He was for some months experimenting at a store in Broad Street, employing a man to turn a crank. It was not until the new building at Waltham was completed, and other machinery was running, that the first loom was ready for trial. Many little matters were to be overcome or adjusted before it would work perfectly. Mr. Lowell said to me that he did not wish me to see it until it was complete, of which he would give me notice. At length the time arrived. He invited me to go out with him and see the loom operate. I well recollect the state of admiration and satisfaction with which we sat by the hour, watching the beautiful movement of this new and wonderful machine, destined as it evidently was, to change the character of all textile industry. This was in the autumn of 1814. …

From the first starting of the first power loom, there was no hesitation or doubt about the success of this manufacture. The full capital of four hundred thousand dollars was soon filled up and expended. An addition of two hundred thousand dollars was afterwards made, by the purchase of the place below in Washington.

12. James Monroe, First Inaugural Address (March 1817)

President Monroe's inaugural address demonstrates how the Jeffersonian Republicans began to support efforts at strengthening internal improvements and otherwise binding the nation together in the aftermath of the War of 1812. Historians at one time characterized this period as an "era of good feelings," because most Americans seemed to agree on the need to invest in the technological and material development of the United States.

Just as this constitution was put into action several of the principal States of Europe had become much agitated and some of them seriously convulsed. Destructive wars ensued, which have of late only been terminated [over 20 years later]. In the course of these conflicts, the United States received great injury from several of the parties. It was [the United States'] to stand aloof from the contest, to demand justice from the party committing the injury … War at length became inevitable, and the result has shown that our Government is equal to that, the greatest of trials, under the most unfavourable of circumstances. …

Such, then is the happy Government under which we live—a Government adequate to every purpose for which the social compact is formed. …

Our fellow citizens of the North engaged in navigation find great encouragement in being made the favored carriers of the vast productions of the other portions of the United States, while the inhabitants of these are amply recompensed, in their turn, by the nursery of seaman and naval force thus formed and reared up for the support of our common rights. …

Other interests of high importance will claim attention, among which the improvement of our country by roads and canals, proceeding always with a constitutional sanction, holds a distinguished place. By this facilitating the intercourse between the states we shall add much to the convenience and comfort of our fellow citizens, much to the ornament of the country, and what is of greater importance we shall shorten distances ... [to] bind the Union more closely together. ...

Our manufacturer will likewise require the systematic and fostering care of the Government ... It is important too that the capital which nourishes our manufacturers should be domestic, as its influence in that case instead of exhausting, as it may do in foreign hands, would be set advantageously on agriculture and every branch of industry. Equally important is it to provide at home a market for our raw materials, as by extending the competition it will enhance the price and protect the cultivator against the casualties incident to foreign markets. ...

13. James Monroe, The Monroe Doctrine (1823)

Monroe laid out an ostensibly idealistic vision of the relationship of the United States to Europe, since the United States was not militarily able to enforce its own declaration. It is worth comparing his ideas with those of Washington; it is also worth considering to what extent the following declaration was motivated more by self-interest than by concern over protecting the autonomy of Latin American states.

As a principle in which the rights and interests of the United States are involved, that the American continents, by the free and independent condition which they have assumed and maintain, are henceforth not to be considered as subjects for future colonization by any European powers. ... With the movements in this hemisphere, we are, of necessity, more immediately connected, and by causes which must be obvious to all enlightened and impartial observers. The political system of the allied [European] powers is essentially different, in this respect from that of America. This difference proceeds from that which exists in their respective governments ... We owe it, therefore, to candor and to the amicable relations existing between the United States and those powers, to declare, that we should consider any attempt on their part to extend their system to any portion of this hemisphere as dangerous to our peace and safety. ...

Our policy in regard to Europe ... is not to interfere in the internal concerns of any of its powers. ... But in regard to these continents, circumstances are eminently and conspicuously different.

It is impossible that the allied powers [of Europe] should extend their political system to any portion of either continent ... nor can anyone believe that our Southern Brethren, if left to themselves, would adopt it of their own accord. ...

Questions to Consider:

1. Some historians claim that Jefferson's ideas (as well as those of his supporters) about an American "Empire of Liberty" were contradictory and hypocritical. Why? Is this assessment fair?
2. Americans liked to claim that their ideas about foreign policy differed significantly with European ones, that the United States represented a more "enlightened" force in the world. From what you have read in this chapter, is this true?
3. How did the United States emerge from the War of 1812 as a stronger nation, both politically and economically? Is it fair to say that the War of 1812 represented a turning point whereby the United States might become a major world power?

Credits

- Copyright © Golbez (CC BY-SA 3.0) at https://commons.wikimedia.org/wiki/File:United_States_1789-03-1789-08.png.
- U.S. Geological Survey, H. George Stroll, "Map of American territorial growth to 1820." 1970. Copyright in the Public Domain.
- Excerpts from Thomas Jefferson's Inaugural Address. 1801. Copyright in the Public Domain.
- Excerpts from Thomas Jefferson, State of the Union Address. 1808. Copyright in the Public Domain.
- Excerpt from Henry Adams, "Chapter 18," *History of the United States of America During the Second Administration of Thomas Jefferson*, vol. 2, pp. 413-414. 1909. Copyright in the Public Domain.
- Excerpt from Henry Harvey, *The First American West: The Ohio Valley, 1750-1820*. 1855. Copyright in the Public Domain.
- Excerpts from *Felix Grundy, Annals of Congress, 12th Congress, 1st Session*, vol. 1, pp. 424-426. 1811. Copyright in the Public Domain.
- John C. Calhoun, "The Congressional War Report," *Official Letters of the Military and Naval Officers of the United States, During the War with Great Britain*, ed. John Brannan, p. 24. 1823. Copyright in the Public Domain.
- Excerpt from Daniel Webster, "To James Madison, Esq. President of the United States," *Extra Globe*, vol. 6, no. 24, ed. Francis Preston Blaire. 1812. Copyright in the Public Domain.
- Excerpts from Amendments to the Constitution Proposed by the Hartford Convention. 1814. Copyright in the Public Domain.
- Francis Scott Key, "The Star-Spangled Banner." 1814. Copyright in the Public Domain.
- Excerpt from *Hunters of Kentucky, Or Half Horse and Half Alligator*. 1822. Copyright in the Public Domain.
- Excerpts from Nathaniel Appleton, *Introduction of the Power Loom*. 1858. Copyright in the Public Domain.
- Excerpts from James Monroe, First Inaugural Address of James Monroe. 1817. Copyright in the Public Domain.
- Excerpts from James Monroe, Monroe Doctrine. 1823. Copyright in the Public Domain.

★ CHAPTER 10
★ THE RISE OF THE COTTON SOUTH, 1815–
★ 1860

The years following the end of the War of 1812 saw a growing sectional difference in the United States between an increasingly free-labor, industrializing North, and a slave-labor, agrarian South. Up until this time, it was not guaranteed that newer states in the South such as Alabama, Mississippi, Arkansas, and Tennessee would become so attached to slave labor; many older areas such as Virginia and North Carolina appeared at least ambivalent regarding the profitability of slavery in the late eighteenth century, if slaves were only needed to grow rice or tobacco. But the invention of the cotton gin by Eli Whitney in 1793 provided a whole new impetus for the use of slave labor. The cotton gin suddenly made it profitable to grow short-staple cotton (the kind much more prevalent in the Deep South), because the machine separated the fibers from the seeds in the cotton plant in ways previously impossible to do by hand. And so it became much easier for farmers in the South to grow and harvest cotton at a profit. Additionally, with the rise of the textile industry by 1815 (mentioned in the last chapter), demand for cotton increased dramatically since the new factories could produce much more clothing for consumption at much cheaper prices. Because of the textile industry and the cotton gin, cotton became something akin to oil in the twentieth century: cotton was needed by the entire industrializing world, and this commodity was in relatively short supply. Those who produced cotton could therefore amass larger fortunes than most people in the Western world. Many Southern whites more or less invested everything in slaves and in cotton land, and the Southern United States became more, not less, attached to an agrarian economic system with black slavery at its cornerstone.

This economic system possessed several social and political consequences that made the South increasingly different from the North after 1815. Obviously, since all or most of the available capital in the slave states was poured into slavery and the production of cotton, that left little investment in labor-saving machinery, or anything else which might lead to industrialization. Cities were also not particularly necessary in the Southern economic system (although they existed), and there were not nearly as many public schools, colleges, or universities as in the free states. Literacy rates were lower, and families were more isolated from each other, as the physical development of the South was spread out with the farms and plantations. Since the slave-labor system was based upon brutality and force (notwithstanding what the planters claimed), there was a martial culture in the South, and Southern whites took the need to defend one's honor very seriously, or to otherwise live under the constant threat of having to physically defend their homes or property. The violence of Southern society can be seen in the internal slave trade, as well as in the treatment afforded native tribes in the years after

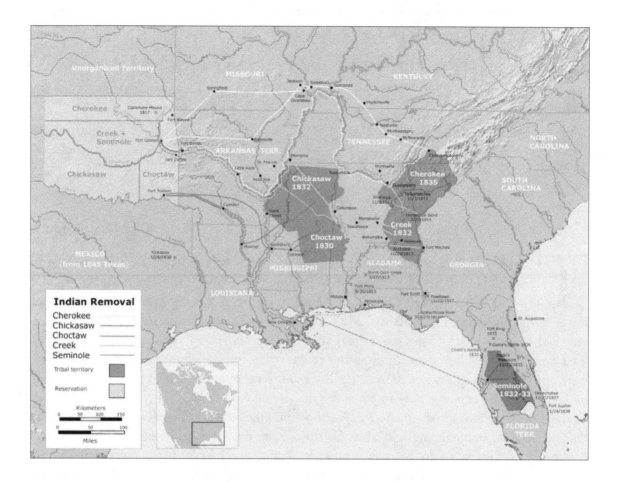

This map of the removal of tribes from the South reveals the dependence of the cotton kingdom on acquiring (or stealing) land from the natives.

1815. Because native tribes stood in the way of whites trying to gain access to the best cotton land in the Deep South, there was all the more reason for Southern whites to justify tactics approaching mass murder in order to develop cotton plantations. Therefore, the expansion of slavery became contingent upon the removal of thousands of native peoples in states such as Georgia, Alabama, and Mississippi.

Although the War of 1812 significantly damaged the Creek tribes of Alabama, there were several others—most notably the Cherokees—who still tried to maintain their tribal identity even as they found themselves surrounded by land-hungry whites desirous of becoming cotton planters. And wherever whites and natives came into contact in large numbers, several familiar themes emerged: the natives became victims of land fraud (usually due to certain tribal members selling out the rest), and the natives were also victims of dependency upon white consumer items. The Cherokees of Georgia tried to resist these problems through a partial assimilation to European ways, and many tribal members succeeded in agriculture, some even becoming slave owners. The Cherokees also declared themselves a civilized nation with a constitution that supposedly forbade land sales to Americans without widespread consent. But the dynamics of white/native relations would not lead to a bicultural society in Georgia—usually because of white racism, in addition to the hatred of the Cherokees for daring to declare themselves an autonomous state within a state. Increasingly, "removal" of natives to areas further west became the option most favored by white politicians in Washington. While this was a humane option when compared to the outright murder and extermination of tribes, such "removal" never went as planned, and resulted in thousands of deaths for the tribes involved. By 1830, President Andrew Jackson more or less mandated that the Cherokees be forcibly ejected from their lands—again ostensibly to prevent white Georgians from carrying out a kind of genocide against the tribe—but Jackson's attitude to the tribes (and his complete lack of willingness to try to stop Georgia from dealing so harshly with the natives) has earned him the opprobrium of most historians. During the so-called "Trail of Tears," roughly 4,000 Cherokees died in a forced march toward present-day Oklahoma, revealing that when push came to shove, native rights were easily sacrificed to the demands of land-hungry Southerners driven by cotton fever for more and more land.

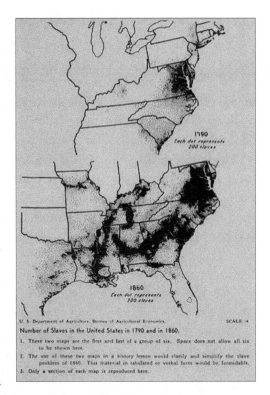

The Growth of Slavery, 1790–1860. This map captures the explosion of slavery in the mid-1800s and the development of a cotton belt in the deep South.

The internal slave trade is another aspect of Southern slaveholding society that revealed how whites used brutal, naked force to build their economy and society. Because slaves in the United States naturally reproduced (for various reasons), it was not necessary to import new slaves from Africa in order to meet the demands for more labor from a growing plantation society. Rather the "extra" slaves grown in the older Eastern lands with lower crop yields could be sold on the market and transported (often marched in chains) from several hundred to a thousand miles away from their homes on the Atlantic seaboard. The constant movement of slaves meant that there needed to be slave-trading firms as well as slave pens, as they were called, to move and otherwise manage this human merchandise. White Americans now had a domestic slave trade on their own shores, where many of the horrid scenes of the African trade were now reenacted in the United States. For example, there were reports of suicides of slaves who did not want to leave behind the family ties they had made on their old plantations, and there would always be slaves who caught diseases or who were beaten to death by their slave drivers during the march to their new "home." The nation's capital, Washington, D.C., also saw a growth in slave-trading firms, since slavery was legal in the city. And so visitors or politicians from around the country could see firsthand the brutality of human beings chained up and sold to the highest bidder during slave auctions.

The brutality of the domestic slave trade was of course simply the tip of the iceberg, as it were, in terms of the numerous ways that slaves could be terrorized by their masters. On plantations or farms, slaves could be whipped to death or locked up for years in closets or other makeshift prisons, women could be sexually brutalized, and others might be fastened with all sorts of inhuman metal contraptions to stifle their ability to fight back against their owners. Slaves might only be fed just enough to stay alive, clothed just enough to avoid being killed by the elements, and old slaves might literally be thrown out into the woods to fend for themselves and to die quietly. While slave owners might claim that the large financial investment made in slaves would discourage such treatment, the facts told a different story: Slave owners needed to show slaves who the boss was, as it were; besides, if slaves produced enough cotton, or reproduced children enough times, it wouldn't matter so much to the bottom line of profits for whites if one or two were accidentally killed in a fit of rage. Female slaves were helpless, in many cases, against the sexual advances of their masters (though in some cases they may have tried to make the best of a bad situation in order to become a more privileged house servant), and the plantations of the South were filled with light-skinned slaves who were the product of such unions. In this way, slavery completely dehumanized workers, even in an age where other free workers were similarly taken advantage of in a new, industrialized system. But the reality of never having the chance to be legally free, of never having the right to legally marry, of never having the right to learn to read or write or the chance to better oneself, made the enslavement of African Americans increasingly anachronistic in the modern world. Freedom may not have been much for some industrial free workers, but it was infinitely better than being owned completely, in every sense, by another human being.

To say that slavery was brutal does not properly convey some of the complexity and different gradations of enslavement, however. The institution could vary according to the size of the farm or plantation, depending on how much direct supervision or force that whites could bring to bear on certain communities of the enslaved. Not all slaves were working all day in the fields on a labor gang—some privileged slaves were able to work in the master's house—and others might even be trusted with certain basic artisanal skills, where they might avoid some of the drudgery of menial labor. Likewise, there were masters who treated their slaves better than most, or who were more attuned to the basic humanity of their chattel "property." Usually by pointing to the exceptional situations where slaves were not treated as badly as the norm, slave owners would often enough advance elaborate justifications for the paternalism of their system. Slave owners chose to see themselves as kindly father figures looking over all of the helpless subordinates on their plantations. These masters would insist that in the South an older, chivalric ideal was in place, dating back to feudal times, where masters understood that they "owed" something to those who served them. But the slave owners could never adequately explain away why they constantly lived in fear of slave rebellions, or of slaves trying to rise up to slit their masters' throats.

Those men who owned even one slave never constituted more than 20 percent of the white population in the South, but they were never the same 20 percent in the same generation (meaning that many men went in and out of the slave-owning class during their lifetimes), and still additional numbers of whites rented slaves. Furthermore, because of the amazing rags-to-riches stories achieved by the boom in cotton prices in the period from 1815–1860, it can be argued that most whites aspired to be slave owners, or otherwise saw in slave ownership a variant of the "American dream" of making a fortune. But also because of the dominance of the planter class in the political and social life of the slave states, being involved in the slave-based, cotton economy constituted the only way to achieve upward social mobility. Additionally, what could be termed the agrarian ethic, where each family owned their land and produced a sufficiency of crops to maintain themselves, certainly took deep root in the slave states, especially in opposition to the urbanizing, socially atomizing, industrial "free states." Yet, many farmers in the slave states lived on the margins of poverty, prompting some historians to wonder why these poor whites did not rise up against the planter elite or otherwise make trouble for them. One plausible answer rests in the constant threat of slave revolts and the resulting racial conservatism of the slave states: In other words, why would poor whites stir up social unrest if it might lead to the deadly consequences of a Haitian-style revolution?

It was the growing threat of slave resistance that represented a constant fact of life for antebellum white Southerners. As we have seen, the American Revolution inspired a white-led movement to abolish slavery; by the 1820s, the British government was leaning toward abolition in the Caribbean, due to the unprofitability of its sugar plantations in the West Indies. But blacks took part in the growing move toward freedom when the Haitian revolution established the first black republic in the Western hemisphere, and when the number of attempted black revolts in the Caribbean increased after 1800. In this environment, one could say that liberty for slaves was "in the air," and many slaves in the American South were not oblivious to this fact. However, within the American South, slave resistance took many forms, most of which fell far short of outright violence. Slaves tried to maintain families even though they were forbidden from doing so. They would also attempt to slow down work routines, break tools, or even kill animals. Slaves might try to bury money (even though they were usually forbidden from keeping any), and they might try to hold prayer meetings where they could learn of news from different and far away places. Others sought to run away, and looked to build networks of slaves, free blacks, and sympathetic whites called the Underground Railroad, helping fugitives run away to Canada. Sometimes individual house slaves stood accused of poisoning their masters; sometimes slaves fought back against male masters to the point of causing severe bodily harm.

Finally, there were more radical attempts at outright slave rebellion in the United States. These were rare between 1815 and 1860, but the best known, led by a slave named Nat Turner in Virginia in 1831, revealed to white Southerners that all was not well with their society. Turner was the son of an escaped slave, he was literate, and he was a lay preacher of sorts. He fashioned himself something of a prophetic religious leader, seeking to lead his people out of an American Egypt of human bondage. And so Turner and his band of committed believers succeeded in killing over fifty whites in their beds in the night as they made their way through Southampton County, Virginia. As a result, renewed attempts were made to strengthen the existing slave codes to further restrict movement, literacy, and any other effort slaves might make to attempt to assert their own freedom. What has been termed a police state mentality in many ways descended upon the white South, as whites closed ranks against a world they believed to be unfairly aligning against them. As mentioned above, chattel slavery came under increased attack in the Western world by the 1830s; most of the new Latin American republics were abolishing slavery by this time, and Great Britain also decided to end slavery in its Caribbean possessions in 1833. This last fact galvanized many in the free states to fight for slavery's end, including many free blacks, heirs of the first emancipation made during the Revolutionary era.

One such free black, David Walker, encouraged by a diffuse and growing black reform and self-help movement in the North, began to assert something approaching black nationalist ideals within the United States. In 1829, Walker decided to write a strong denunciation of both slavery and racial prejudice generally in a pamphlet entitled *Appeal to the Coloured Citizens of the World* in 1829. Among other things, the pamphlet called upon slaves to rise up and to resist their masters, while also loudly condemning the customary notion that black people should not be able to use the same discourse of natural rights so often used by whites in their movement for national self-determination. When news spread in the South that this pamphlet was being read to slaves, attempts to search the mail were made, and many whites publicly wanted a price placed on his head (Walker did in fact die under mysterious circumstances less than a year after the publication of his pamphlet). As a result of attacks upon their way of life, many white Southerners went on the ideological offensive to try to fight a media battle against the forces of abolition after 1830. This represented an important cultural shift, because many white Southerners now began to assert elaborate justifications for slavery, not merely as a necessary evil, but rather as a "positive good." Authors such as Thomas Roderick, and later George Fitzhugh and James Henry Hammond, all explained how slavery was the basis for a superior, refined civilization in the South. These men insisted that African slaves were saved from barbarism by being brought to the United States as slaves. Hammond coined the term "King Cotton" to describe the superior economic system that enabled whites in the South to live with far more security and affluence than their average Northern white counterpart. It is important to note that when stripping out the status of black slaves in the South, it is possible that the average white net worth was higher in the South than the North by 1860.

The loud determination of these white men to defend their slaveholding civilization from the outside world also led to an aggressive desire among many Southerners for Western land. This can be seen most clearly in the fight for Texas (or Tejas to Mexicans), which also ensued in the 1830s. By the 1820s, the Spanish and then Mexican governments had allowed thousands of Americans to enter the province of Tejas, with the idea that these Americans would assimilate and help develop the territory. In hindsight, of course, this was foolish, as these Americans simply wanted the land, and wanted to be left alone. One important sticking point between the Texas Americans and the Mexicans was over the American insistence upon bringing their black slaves into the territory, since slavery had been abolished in Mexico. As time passed, the Mexican government grew alarmed at the number of Anglo-Americans moving into its territory, and the Mexican government also tried to restrict the trade of its American subjects with the United States. Eventually those Americans who wanted more autonomy from Texas took over a tax collection station at Galveston Bay in 1835 in protest. Such action also came in solidarity with other Northern Mexican provinces bucking at the authority of the central government in Mexico City, even if they were not in open rebellion. But in response to the anti-federal sentiments shared by many in Northern Mexico, a hard-liner named Antonio Santa Anna rose to power in Mexico City and essentially declared war on the Americans in Tejas. After a bitter defeat at the Alamo and at Goliad in 1836, the American Texans managed to defeat Santa Anna by the end of the year. But victory for the Americans in Texas did not mean annexation to the United States, since Mexico might still make war over the issue. In addition, if annexed to the United States, Texas would be a large slaveholding state, something that many in the North found abhorrent. Annexation of Texas would not occur until the 1840s, and not until Northerners would become involved in settling other Northern territories (like Oregon), which were unfavorable to slavery's spread west. Moving forward, however, the battle over slavery's future in the West began to reveal deep sectional divisions within the United States—divisions that could not be easily dismissed by politicians.

Documents:

1. Andrew Jackson, Second Annual Message to Congress (1830)

In this message to Congress, Jackson made it clear he felt powerless to stop the forced removal of native tribes to the west. An important debate among historians has focused on the degree to which Jackson could have helped the Southern tribes avoid forced relocation, if he had so desired.

Our conduct toward these people is deeply interesting to our national character. Their present condition, contrasted with what they once were, makes a most powerful appeal to our sympathies. ... By persuasion and force they have been made to retire from river to river and from mountain to mountain, until some of the tribes have become extinct. ...

It is too late to inquire whether it was just in the United States to include them and their territory within the bounds of the new States, whose limits they cannot control. That step cannot be retraced. A state cannot be dismembered by Congress or restricted in the exercise of her constitutional power. ... I suggest for your consideration the propriety of setting apart an ample district west of the Mississippi ... to be guaranteed to the Indian tribes as long as they shall occupy it. ...

Can it be cruel in this Government when, by events which it can not control, the Indian is made discontented in his ancient home to purchase his lands, to give him a new and extensive territory, to pay the expense of his removal, and support him a year in his new abode? How many thousands of our own people would gladly embrace the opportunity of removing to the West on such conditions! If the offers made to the Indians were extended to them, they would be hailed with gratitude and joy. ... Taken together the policies of the General Government toward the red man is not only liberal, but generous. He is unwilling to submit to the laws of the States and mingle with their population. To save him from this alternative, or perhaps utter annihilation, the General Government kindly offers him a new home. ...

2. Memorial of the Cherokee Nation (1830)

The Cherokee Nation tried to hold for as long as possible against the Americans' desire to move them west. It is worth comparing and contrasting the Cherokees' words below with those of President Jackson.

We are aware that some persons suppose it will be for our advantage to remove beyond the Mississippi. We think otherwise ... We wish to remain on the land of our fathers. We have a perfect and original right to remain without interruption and molestation. The treaties with us, and laws of the United States made in pursuance of treaties, guarantee our residence and our privileges securing us against intruders. ... Judge then, what must be the circumstances of a removal when a whole community embracing persons of all classes and every description, from the infant to the man of extreme old age ... are compelled to remove by odious and intolerable vexations and persecutions, brought upon them in the forms of law, when all agree only in this ... that we have been most cruelly robbed of their country, in violation of the most solemn compacts ... if they are forcibly removed ... how is it possible that we should pursue our present course of improvement, or avoid sinking into utter despondency? ... there is not a man within our limits so ignorant as not to know that he has a right to live on the land of his fathers. ...

3. Solomon Northup Recalls Life Under Slavery (1853)

Northup was born a free black in New York in 1808 and was tricked into traveling with white men for work, after which time he was forcibly sold into slavery. He found himself in Louisiana, but after a few years remarkably managed to escape. His slave narrative was one of the many publicized in the mid-nineteenth century among whites in the free states, in order to awaken the antislavery conscience.

In the latter part of August begins the cotton picking season. At this time each slave is presented with a sack ... When a new hand, one unaccustomed to the business, is sent for the first time into the field, he is whipped up smartly, and made for that day to pick as fast as he can possibly. He must bring in the same weight each night following. If it falls short, it is considered evidence that he has been laggard, and a greater or less number of lashes is the penalty.

There may be humane masters, as there certainly are inhuman ones—there may be slaves well-clothed, well-fed, and happy. ... Nevertheless, the institution that tolerates such wrong and inhumanity as I have witnessed is a cruel, unjust and barbarous one. [White] men may write fictions portraying lowly life as it is, or as it is not ... but let them toil with [the slave] in the field—sleep with him in the cabin—feed with him on husks. ... Let them know the heart of the poor slave—learn his secret thoughts ... and they will find that ninety-nine out of every hundred are intelligent enough to understand their freedom, and to cherish in their bosoms the love of freedom, as passionately as themselves.

4. Harriet Jacobs, The Trials of Girlhood (1861)

Born a slave in North Carolina, Jacobs endured sexual abuse from her master for years. At one point she hid in the crawlspace of a relative's home in order to avoid her master, but was eventually able to escape slavery. Through an efficacious marriage to a free white lawyer, she was able to secure freedom for her children as well.

I now entered on my fifteenth year—a sad epoch in the life of a slave girl. My master began to whisper foul words in my ear. Young as I was, I could not remain ignorant of their import. I tried to treat them with indifference or contempt. ... He was a crafty man, and resorted to many means to accomplish his purposes. Sometimes he had stormy, terrific ways, that made his victims tremble ... He peopled my young mind with unclean images, such as only a vile monster could think of ... He told me I was his property; that I must be subject to his will in all things ... No matter whether the slave girl be as black as ebony or as fair as her mistress. In either case, there is no shadow of law to protect her from insult, from violence, or even from death. ... The mistress [wife of the master] who ought to protect the helpless victim, has no other feeling towards her [who is taken advantage of by her master] but those of jealousy and rage. The degradation, the wrongs, the vices, that grow out of slavery, are more than I can describe. They are greater than you would willingly believe. ... I once saw two beautiful children playing together. One was a fair white child; the other was her slave, and also her sister. When I saw them embracing each other, and heard their joyous laughter, I turned sadly away from the lovely sight. I foresaw the inevitable blight that would fall on the little slave's heart. I knew how soon her laughter would be changed to sighs. The fair child grew up to be a still fairer woman. From childhood to womanhood her pathway was blooming with flowers, and overarched by a sunny sky. ... How had those years dealt with her slave sister, the little playmate of her childhood? ... She drank the cup of sin, and shame and misery, whereof her persecuted race are compelled to drink.

5. David Walker, Appeal to the Colored Citizens of the World (1829)

Walker's writings signaled to many in the free and slave states that a new generation of free blacks was going on the offensive to try to stop slavery. His pamphlet created substantial controversy, and Walker was found dead under mysterious circumstances after several Southern leaders called for his assassination.

Remember, Americans, that we must and shall be free and enlightened as you are, will you wait until we shall, under God, obtain our liberty by the crushing arm of power? Will it not be dreadful for you? I speak Americans for your good. We must and shall be free I say, in spite of you. ... wo, wo will be to you if we have to obtain our freedom by fighting. Throw away your fears and prejudices then, and enlighten us and treat us like men, and we will like you more than we do now hate you, and tell us no more about colonization, for America is as much our country, as it is yours—

See your Declaration, Americans!!! Do you understand your own language? Hear your language, proclaimed to the world, July 4, 1776 ... Compare your own language ... with your cruelties and murders inflicted by your cruel and unmerciful fathers ... on our fathers and us. ... The whites have had us under them for more than three centuries, murdering, and treating us like brutes; and, as Mr. Jefferson wisely said, they have never *found us out*—they do not know, indeed, that there is an unconquerable disposition in the breasts of the blacks, which, when it is fully awakened and put in motion, will be subdued, only with the destruction of the animal existence. Get the blacks started, and if you do not have a gang of tigers and lions to deal with, I am a deceiver of the blacks and of the whites. ... [I]f you commence, make sure work—do not trifle, for they will not trifle with you—they want us for their slaves, and think nothing of murdering us in order to subject us to that wretched condition—therefore, if there is an *attempt* made by us, kill or be killed. Now, I ask you, had you not rather be killed than to be a slave to a tyrant, who takes the life of your mother, wife, and dear little children? Look upon your mother, wife and children, and answer God Almighty; and believe this, that it is no more harm for you to kill a man, who is trying to kill you, than it is for you to take a drink of water when thirsty. ...

6. From *The Confessions of Nat Turner, The Leader of the Late Insurrection in Southampton, VA* (1831)

Not long after Walker's Appeal was issued, Southern whites saw firsthand the desire of black slaves to live free when Turner led the only coordinated black slave revolt in the antebellum United States.

On the 12th of May 1828, I heard a loud voice in the heavens, and the Spirit instantly appeared to me and said the Serpent was loosened, and Christ has laid down the yoke he had borne for the sins of men, and that I should take it on and fight against the Serpent, for the time was fast approaching when the last shall be the first. ... That night it was agreed that we should meet at the home of Mr. Travis ... Hank went to the door with an axe, for the purpose of breaking it open, as we knew we were strong enough to murder the family, if they were awakened by the noise, but reflecting it might cause an alarm in the neighborhood, we determined to enter the house secretly, and murder them whilst sleeping. Hank got a ladder ... and it was observed that I should be the first to spill blood, on which armed with a hatchet I entered and came down the stairs ... it being dark I could not give the death blow, the hatchet glanced from his head, he sprang up in bed and called his wife, it was his last word, Will laid him dead, with a blow of his axe, and Mrs. Travis shared the same fate, as she lay in bed. The murder of this family, five in number, was the work of a moment ... we got here four guns that would shoot, and several old muskets, with a pound or two of gunpowder. We remained some time at the barn, where we paraded, I formed them in a line as soldiers, and ... carrying them through all the maneuvers I was masters of. ...

7. A North Carolina Law Forbidding the Teaching of Slaves to Read and Write (1831)

In response to the Turner insurrection, many Southern states strengthened laws aimed at suppressing black autonomy and freedom. Such laws signaled to Northerners that the slave states intended to quash any effort to end their "peculiar institution."

Whereas the teaching of slaves to read and write, has a tendency to excite dissatisfaction in their minds, and to produce insurrection and rebellion, to the manifest injury of the citizens of this State: Therefore, Be it enacted by the General Assembly of the State of North Carolina, and it is hereby enacted by the authority of the same, That any free person who shall hereafter teach, or attempt to teach any slave within the State to read or write, the use of figures, excepted, or shall give or sell to such slave or slaves any books or pamphlets, shall be liable to indictment in any court of record in the States ... and if found guilty may either be fined or imprisoned ... if they are a free person of color that shall be fined, imprisoned, or whipped, at the discretion of the court, not exceeding thirty nine lashes nor less than twenty lashes.

Be it further enacted, that is any slave shall hereafter teach, or attempt to teach, any other slave to read or write, the use of figures excepted, he or she may be carried before any justice of the peace and on conviction thereof, shall be sentenced to receive thirty nine lashes on his or her bare back.

8. James Henry Hammond Defends Slavery (1836)

Hammond was a congressman, governor, and senator from South Carolina who became known as an outspoken defender of the "positive good theory" of slavery after 1830.

The question of emancipation ... has become with us the first and most important question; partly because the levelers here have not yet felt the heavy pressure of political oppression, and partly because they have regarded our institutions of slavery as most assimilated to an aristocracy. In this they are right. ... It is a government of the best. Combining all the advantages, and possessing but few of the disadvantages, of the aristocracy of the old world, without fostering to an unwarrantable extent the pride, the exclusiveness, the selfishness ... which distinguish the nobility of Europe, it gives us their education, their polish, their munificence, their high honor, their undaunted spirit. Slavery does indeed create an aristocracy—an aristocracy of talents, of virtue, of generosity and courage. In a slave country every freeman is an aristocrat ... slavery ... produces ... the best organization of society that has ever existed on the face of the earth.

9.   George Fitzhugh, *Sociology for the South* (1854)

A Virginia lawyer and early sociologist, Fitzhugh sought to provide an intellectual defense of slavery in order to argue with abolitionists such as Gerrit Smith and Wendell Phillips, with whom he personally contended in the 1850s.

At the South all is peace, quiet, plenty, and contentment. We have no mobs, no trade unions, no strikes for higher wages, no armed resistance to the law, but little jealousy of the rich by the poor. We have but few in our jails, and fewer in our poor houses. We produce enough of the comforts and necessaries of life for a population three or four times as numerous as ours. We are wholly exempt from the torrent of pauperism, crime ... and infidelity which Europe is pouring from her jails ... [In the South] the poor are as hospitable as the rich, the negro as the white man. Nobody dreams of turning a friend, a relative, a stranger from his door. The very negro who deems it no crime to steal, would scorn to sell his hospitality. We have no loafers, because the poor relative or friend who borrows our horse, or spend a week under our roof, is a welcome guest. The loose economy, the wasteful mode of living at the South, is a blessing when rightly considered; it keeps want, scarcity, and famine at a distance, because it leaves room for retrenchment. The nice, accurate economy of France, England, and New England keeps society always on the verge of famine, because it leaves no room ... to live on only a part of what they now consume. Our society exhibits no symptoms of decay. A long course of continuing improvement is in prospect before us, with no limits which human foresight can descry. Actual liberty and equality with our white population has been approached much nearer than in the free States. Few of our whites ever work as day laborers, none as cooks, scullions ... body servants or in other menial capacities. One free [white] citizen does not lord it over another; hence that pride of self respect, that give us ascendancy when we come in contact with Northerners. It is a distinction to be a Southerner, as it was once to be a Roman citizen.

10. Mary Chestnut, Excerpts from Her Diary (1861)

Mary Chestnut was the wife of South Carolina senator and future Confederate general, James Chestnut. Her diary is an invaluable resource regarding many aspects of the sectional crisis and Civil War, but this excerpt represents one of the most candid admissions from within the white plantation world regarding the injustice and hypocrisy of slavery.

Under slavery, we live surrounded by prostitutes, yet an abandoned woman is sent out of any decent house. Who thinks any worse of a Negro or mulatto woman for being a thing we can't name? God forgive us, but ours is a monstrous system, a wrong and an iniquity! Like the patriarchs of old, our men live all in one house with their wives and their concubines; and the mulattoes one sees in every family partly resemble the white children. Any lady is ready to tell you who is the father of all the mulatto children in everybody's household but their own. Those, she seems to think, drop from the clouds. My disgust sometimes is boiling over. Thank God for my country women, but alas for the men! They are probably no worse than men everywhere, but the lower their mistresses, the more degraded they must be. ...

Someone said: "Oh I know half a Legree [the villain of *Uncle Tom's Cabin*]," a man said to be as cruel ... But the other half of him did not correspond. He was a man of polished manners, and the best husband and father and church member in the world. "Can that be so?" Yes I know it. And I knew the dissolute half of Legree. He was high and mighty, but the kindest creature to his slaves; and the unfortunate results of his bad ways [his children] were not sold. ... they were provided for, handsomely, in his will. His wife and daughters ... are supposed never to dream of what is as plain before their eyes as the sunlight ...

11. General Manuel Mier y Terán, "Reports to His Superiors Regarding American Emigration in Texas" (1830)

This excerpt reveals how American Southerners were on the move in the early nineteenth century. The expansionist designs of Anglo-Americans were also likely misunderstood by the Mexican government when they invited Americans into their province of Tejas in the 1820s.

In the town of Nagadoches ... the naturalized North Americans in the town maintain an English school, and send their children north for further education; the poor Mexicans not only do not have sufficient means to establish schools, but they are not of the type that take any thought for the improvement of its public institutions or the betterment of its degraded condition. Neither are their civil authorities or magistrates; one insignificant little man—not to say more—who is called an alcalde, and an ayuntamiento that does not convene once in a lifetime is the most that we have here at this important point on our [Mexican] frontier. ... The North American colonists murmur against the political disorganization of the frontier and the Mexicans complain of the superiority and better education of the colonists ... Meanwhile the incoming stream of new settlers is unceasing; the first news of these comes by discovering them on land already under cultivation ... the old settlers make a claim for which there are no records, on a law of the Spanish government; and thus arises a lawsuit in which the alcalde has a chance to come out with some money. ... this section is being settled without the consent of anybody ... In spite of the enmity that usually exists between the Mexicans and the foreigners, there is a most evident uniformity of opinion on one point, namely, the separation of Texas from Coahuila and its organization into a territory of the federal government ... The whole population here is a strange and incoherent parts without parallel in our federation: numerous tribes of Indians ... armed at any moment ready for war ... among the foreigners are fugitives from justice, honest laborers, vagabonds, and criminals, but honorable and dishonorable alike travel to this colony. ...

Questions to Consider:

1. Describe the Southern proslavery worldview as it evolved in the years after 1830. Why was this view so attractive even to non-slaveholders in the South?

2. How did slavery differ from the so-called "wage slavery" extant in the industrial North and in Europe? Were the two forms of labor similar in any way?

3. Explain the various ways in which slaves resisted their masters. Do you agree that slave masters genuinely believed that their slaves were content?

4. Is it fair to say that white people were nearly as enslaved by chattel slavery as were the slaves? What effects did slavery have on other white people, besides the slave master?

Credits

★ CHAPTER 11
★ THE MARKET REVOLUTION AND
★ INDUSTRIALIZATION IN THE FREE
STATES, 1815–1865

In contrast with the slave states, the free states took part in the general trend begun by Great Britain toward a greater degree of industrialization in the years following the War of 1812. It was during that war, for example, that Northern capitalists began to invest more in domestic manufacturing concerns, especially textile mills, which began the increased reliance upon a division of labor. Such a division of labor dramatically increased the output of any one worker (in addition to cheapening the cost of some laborers), because specific, individual human skills were being replaced either by machines or by new manufacturing techniques (or both). Early factories, most famously those associated with the Waltham mills in Massachusetts, consolidated the entire process of making products such as clothes under one roof. Previously it had been necessary to have several different people or companies turn cotton to yarn, to cloth, to finished clothing, but newer technologies made this more cumbersome process obsolete. And now that production times were cut down, a new mass industry of "ready-made" clothing took off, which was far cheaper than earlier items of similar quality. In turn, the affordability of these items spurred new retail industries and employment, which further enriched those in the position of building such businesses. And as such capitalists made more money, they also took more risks on any number of new technologies in the early nineteenth century, starting with the steam engine. The steam engine revolutionized travel with steamboats, which could dramatically cut down on transportation time (usually by allowing flatboat operators faster ways to get home and conduct more business once they delivered their merchandise with the older, cheaper flatboats). As a result, it became much easier for farmers to get goods to market, which worked as a stimulant to trade. A similar argument can be made about the early railroad industry, which was just getting its start in the 1830s. In terms of military technology, the development by the 1830s of interchangeable parts in guns (essentially mass-produced parts, which are all standard and less dependent upon individual craftsmanship) also furthered the development of technologies for mass production and later, the assembly line.

Labor-saving technologies in turn revolutionized agriculture, as has already been seen by the cotton gin, but also by the McCormick reaper (1834) and John Deere's steel plow (1837), which greatly increased yields of wheat production in the North. Although historians focus on how mechanization and industrialization were slowly being born in the early 1800s, the United States remained a largely rural, agricultural country until 1900. But the nature of that agricultural work changed, as more farmers were incorporated into larger and larger markets. Furthermore, many farmers tried to take in work such as making shoes, thread, or cloth—again

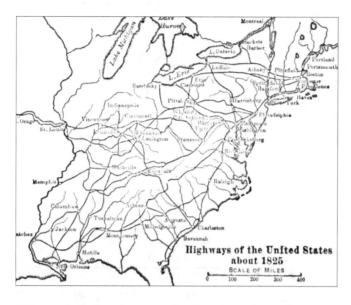

Highways of the United States about 1825

SCALE OF MILES

0   100   200   300   400

This map depicts the growth of roads in the early 1800s. These roads were one way Americans developed an internal market after 1815.

revealing how an increased chance to make money meeting the demands of consumers impacted even those far away from urban areas. And so what historians refer to as the process of industrialization owed its start to an increase in certain technologies, which in turn increased labor productivity, and which also enabled a greater volume of trade over an ever-larger range of distance. And these processes impacted people throughout the country, regardless of their occupation or of their involvement with industry.

However, it was not only private capitalists who were responsible for greater investment in different technologies or industries that stimulated greater productivity and market orientation in the early nineteenth century. The government, especially at the state level, also took steps to encourage new internal improvements, such as newer roads and canals. The Erie Canal, which was completed in 1825, speaks to the desire of politicians and other state officials to allocate tax dollars toward new technologies responsible for the increases in labor productivity and increased market interaction. This canal, which connected New York City with the Great Lakes (something that had eluded colonial Americans), encouraged a massive amount of trade (mostly with flatboats, not steamboats) and was largely responsible for making New York City a metropolis several times larger than any other American city. Legal entities as well, especially the Supreme Court, the highest court in the land, also defined the law in ways amenable to the desire for market competition as well as for the growth of corporations. Two Supreme Court cases made by the Marshall Court stand out as emblematic of these changes: *Gibbons v. Ogden* (1824) and *Charles River Bridge v. Warren Bridge* (1837). In the Gibbons case, the court ruled that individual states could not grant exclusive monopolies to companies (in this case steamboat operators) because the federal government's power to license new enterprises such as corporations forbade it. As a result of this law, the number of steamboat operators in New York increased from 6 to 43. The Charles River Bridge case later curtailed the ability of states to grant monopolies—in this case to the owners of the sole bridge connecting Cambridge to Boston, Massachusetts—and was therefore friendlier to the proliferation of corporations that might increase competition and lower costs for things such as building bridges.

The related processes of mechanization, urbanization, and the spread of markets produced winners and losers. In general, economic historians point to the increases in wages in real terms for most American workers, in addition to increases in average household wealth as evidence that this new market economy worked overall to improve the standard of living for the white American majority. It was also the case that immigration from Europe dramatically increased in the early and mid-nineteenth century, and such an increase presumably could not have been possible if the economy of the United States did not function as a kind of magnet for labor from other parts of the world. But such statistics and facts accenting how the "majority" benefited from this growing economic system—as usual—mask the real pain, hardship, and suffering endured by those at the bottom of the income ladder. And as may be the case with capitalist systems, the bottom fifth or tenth of the society not taking part in the improvement aiding the majority likely suffered disproportionately in terms of living standards, health, or both (to say nothing of the horrendous experiences facing slaves described in the last chapter). One of the most notable changes in the nature of the work force was the number of young people, often women, who were brought in to do the menial, laborious, and highly strenuous work required of making thread and clothing in the textile mills of New England. Elsewhere could be found evidence of the "bastardization" of once honored crafts such as shoemaking or cabinetmaking when newer production techniques were brought in, or simply when more and more people found the time to supplement farming with attempts at making extra money from the fabrication of these items.

The growth of canals, depicted above, also furthered a domestic market in the United States in the early 1800s.

As would be the case over the course of the nineteenth century, it would prove harder and harder for artisans to simply make a living from their trade: they would have to try to become miniature capitalists by, for example, getting access to cheap labor and opening a small factory of their own. But when this option did not work out as planned, many fell into the ranks of those who would never attain the economic status of the independent small proprietor or "master," as the term usually was used. Together with the factory workers, these badly paid artisans epitomized what was called at the time "wage slavery," implying that these low-paying, difficult jobs led nowhere and were contributing to the kind of rigid class system then found in England. In response, many workers tried to organize strikes or other forms of protest to fight for better pay, shorter hours, or better working conditions in many of the new factories in the free states. At the Lowell mills, for example, 1834 saw the first limitedly successful walkout. The same could be said for the short-lived Workingman's Party, primarily focused in New York City, and which also clamored for things such as public education and a shorter work day. Some progress was made in these years in the courts, however. In 1842, the Massachusetts State Supreme Court ruled that shoemakers were in fact allowed to strike for better wages. Although historians concede that early-nineteenth-century workers achieved success to a degree, they nonetheless laid the foundations for later reforms, particularly in terms of workplace safety. The competition for good-paying wage work in the nineteenth century could be intense, and this trend increased once thousands of new immigrants flooded ashore in Eastern cities after 1840. As mentioned earlier, the American economy functioned as a magnet for people down on their luck in Europe. Further, by the 1840s the potato famine in Ireland essentially forced thousands of desperate, half-starved peasants onto the shores of the United States where they settled into miserable conditions in places such as Boston or New York. But at least they were not starving (or at least not as many were). The deluge of Irish immigrants had all sorts of implications for the economy and society of the northeastern states. But the concern regarding an uncertain economic future facing native-born Americans who had to compete with these desperate laborers helped to fuel middle-class angst about the newly emerging industrial market–oriented culture of the urban Northeast.

The flood of migrants only furthered the explosive growth of urban areas in the free states: Between 1820 and 1860, the number of towns over 10,000 in size grew nearly four times. These growing cities became symbols of the extremes of wealth, where the newer middle and upper classes would reside in their own neighborhoods, and tried to distance themselves from the newer urban slums. Nowhere was this more evident than New York City, which saw extravagant new mansions built further north on Manhattan Island, while the Southern parts of the city increasingly housed dilapidated slums. The so-called "Five Points" in this area was often referred to as one of the worst slums in the Western world—even in comparison with some of the urban poverty of London. The problems associated with increased crime, violence, or sanitation represented a huge challenge to government as well as to other civic-minded re-formers, who wondered if America's republican experiment could survive with so many people who did not seem to have much of an economic stake in society. Yet, these new, scary urban centers clearly served a purpose in the emerging industrial Northeast and Midwest. Cities allowed for merchants to have access to as many laborers as possible, and allowed businesses to tap more easily into an educated workforce. Entire cities could devote their energies to meeting the demands of the new technologies so highly desired by American companies to keep the economy going. For example, the relatively new Ohio city of Cincinnati became increasingly devoted to the production of the steamboats so essential to river traffic and trade in the early nineteenth century. It was usually in or near the urban areas that a new middle class emerged, which consisted of clerks or corporate officers who would help coordinate and consolidate the many specialized and detailed aspects of running new industries like textile mills, department stores, or railroads. As the facilitators of this new market economy, such new middle-class workers were well paid, and constituted those who "won" in this new economy. These people nearest to the power centers of this new economic engine—those at the top of the corporations or those affiliated with the banking and lending industries—disproportionately benefited from their connections to the areas making the most profits. As a result, by 1860, the top 5 percent of the population owned more than half of the nation's wealth. Of course, those who defended such a concentration pointed out that in real terms the entire wealth of the country grew by at least 50 percent over the course of the early mid-nineteenth century, and so many other Americans benefited from the "trickle-down effect," as it were.

In addition, the changing, modernizing economy of the free states could be the catalyst to enable some people at the margins of the economy to move up or to gain new skills. For example, the increased attention to education and literacy, coupled with other factors (such as evangelical Protestantism) allowed women to assume a greater role as schoolteachers. Catharine Beecher was only one of many white women who extolled the benefits of utilizing female labor in education, because women were supposedly more virtuous than males. Besides education, the expanding economy gave women other possible sources of income, such as the textile in-dustry. Of course, much of the labor allocated to women was not well paid, but simply having the ability to earn a wage (perhaps in anticipation of having a dowry for marriage) could be viewed as empowering. Furthermore, as was the case with teaching, female employment at least implied that women would not be under the direct supervision of their husbands during all waking hours. The subject of women's rights will be addressed below, but the logic of female emancipation in order to better serve a modern economy and a modern state could be heard from increasing numbers in the early nineteenth century. And legal change was coming in the form of more liberal divorce legislation, as well as women's rights to own property, even in marriage (something not normally allowed).

For free African Americans, a growing Northern economy did contribute to the growth of a tiny middle and even upper class, though any historian should be careful about claiming that free blacks as a whole were improving during the early and mid-nineteenth century. As mentioned in Chapter 7, there was a movement for gradual emancipation after the Revolutionary War, which resulted in tens of thousands of blacks gaining their freedom in states from Pennsylvania to Massachusetts. Even though these blacks suffered from discriminatory legislation (not to mention the possible threat of being kidnapped back into slavery), it was possible for some black artisans to gain business contacts and build enterprises that placed some free blacks among the wealthy in cities such as New York, Philadelphia, or Boston. Of course, all blacks suffered the stigma of second-class citizenship, but in many cases their wealth could contribute to numerous self-help organizations (often churches), which attempted to alleviate the worst aspects of racial oppression. The biography of James Forten is an excellent example of a free African American who managed not only to succeed, but to prosper in the first decades of the nineteenth century as a shipbuilder in Philadelphia. With his newfound wealth, Forten made significant contributions to black churches, to other African-American self-help organizations, as well as to the abolition movement, which would gain supporters with the American Anti-Slavery Society, formed in 1833. Although it was small, the presence of a black bourgeoisie in cities such as Philadelphia, New York, and Boston nonetheless existed as a challenge to the maintenance of white supremacy in the United States. If blacks could in fact achieve the "American dream" of upward social mobility, then why did so many Southerners insist that blacks were innately inferior and destined for nothing better than slavery? How was it that blacks could not vote in the free states, when such people as James Forten possessed as much talent and education as did many whites? Although the free states were hardly free of racism, the appeal to mobility that grew out of the free states' increased interest in industrialization would help fuel a dislike for the rural, slaveholding, "backward" South. Many in the North would increasingly view slave states as not only a separate region, but as a separate country.

Documents:

1. "John Jacob Astor to Albert Gallatin" (March 14, 1818)

As the founder of the American Fur Company, which traded furs and other commodities around the world, Astor was well on his way to becoming the wealthiest man in the United States in 1818. Because of his numerous business interests, he was quite knowledgeable on the banking crisis that enveloped the nation in the late 1810s.

Dear Sir:

The United States Bank is not doing so well as they might have done, there has been to much Speculation [in Real Estate] and too much assumption of Power on the Part of the Bank Directors which has caused the Institution to become unpopular and I may say generally ... Those who have sold out at 50% profit I think have done best to make Large Dividends. To Raise the price of the stock they have discounted too freely and made money so cheap that everything [tangible] has become Dear and the result is that our merchants in Stead of Shipping Produce [they] Ship Specie [gold and silver bullion], so much so that I tell you in confidence that it is not without difficulty that Specie payments are maintained. The Different states are still going on making more Banks and I shall not be surprised if by and by there be a general Blow up [failure] among them ...

2. James Flint, "Letters from America," Indiana (May 4, 1820)

The views of Flint, this English observer who traveled mostly around the Ohio Valley between 1818 and 1820, reveal some of the lingering problems caused by the 1819 banking panic in the areas he visited.

Agriculture languishes—farmers cannot find profit in hiring labourers. ... Labourers and mechanics are in want of employment. I think that I have seen upwards of 1500 men in quest of work within eleven months past, and many of these declared, that they had no money. ... Great numbers of strangers lately camped in an open field near Baltimore, depending upon the contributions of the charitable for subsistence. You have no doubt heard of emigrants returning to Europe without finding the prospect of a livelihood in America. ... I have seen several men turned out of lodging houses, where their money [paper currency from bad banks] would not be taken. They had no other resource left but to lodge in the woods, without any covering except their clothes. ...

3. Thomas Skidmore, *The Rights of Man to Property* (1829)

Skidmore was a Connecticut-born machinist who became the leading spokesman for the New York Workingman's Party in 1829. This indictment of the capitalist system would be one of many made throughout the Western world in the mid-1800s.

Whoever looks over the face of the world, and surveys the population of all countries; our own as well as any and every other, will see it divided into rich and poor; into the hundred who have everything, and the million who have nothing. Thomas Jefferson ... speaks of the rights of man [and that they are all created equal]. If ... property is to descend only to particular individuals from the previous generation, and if the many are born, having neither parents nor any one else, to give them property, equal in amount to that which the sons of the rich receive from their fathers and other testators, how is it established that they are created equal. ... If we are created equal—how has he [the rich man] have the right to monopolize all, or even an undue share of the property of the preceding generation. ...

Mankind have enquired too little to their rights, their interests, and their happiness. If it had not been so such enormities could not have been allowed to take place, daily and forever before our eyes, without having been remedied. …

If, then, it is seen that the Steam-Engine, for example, is likely to greatly impoverish, or destroy the poor, what have they to do but to lay hold of it and make it their own? Let them appropriate also, in the same way, the cotton factories, the woolen factories, the iron foundries. … & etc. It is an equal division of property that makes all right, and an equal transmission of it to posterity, keeps it so.

4. Harriet Hanson Robinson, excerpts from *Loom and Spindle: Or, Life Among the Early Mill Girls (1890)*

As a former worker in the textile industry, Robinson's perspective on life in a factory may not be as negative as one might imagine. It is worth evaluating how much worse factory life was from other forms of menial labor in nineteenth-century America.

[Regarding life in a textile mill] … they were a class of factory operatives, and were spoken of as a set of persons who earned their daily bread, whose condition was fixed, and who must continue to spin and to weave to the end of their natural existence. Nothing but this was expected of them, and they were not supposed to be capable of social or mental improvement … [but] it must be remembered that at this time woman had no property rights … the law took no cognizance of woman as a money spender. She was a ward, an appendage, a relict. … The cotton factory [was therefore] a great opening to these lonely and dependent women. From a condition approaching pauperism they were at once placed above want; they could earn money and spend it as they pleased …

One of the first strikes of cotton-factory operatives that ever took place in this country was that in Lowell in October, 1836. When it was announced that the wages were to be cut down, great indignation was felt, and it was decided to strike, en masse. … One of the girls stood on a pump, and gave vent to the feelings of her companions in a neat speech, declaring that it was their duty to resist all attempts at cutting down the wages. This was the first time a woman had spoken in public in Lowell, and the vent caused surprise and consternation among her audience. … It is hardly necessary to say that so far as results were concerned this strike did no good. The dissatisfaction of the operatives subsided, or burned itself out, and though the authorities did not acceded to their demands, the majority returned to their work, and the corporation went on cutting down the wages. …

5. Alonzo Potter, *The Political Economy: Its Objects, Uses, and Principles* (1841)

Potter, a noted Episcopal bishop and advocate of reforms such as temperance, was also a supporter of the Whig Party. His thinking demonstrates the connections between religious reform and support for the nascent system of industrial capital seen in many churches in the free states.

The great principles, in short, of free labor and free disposal of its produce, would seem, in such case, amply sufficient to secure and equitable distribution of property among the several classes who contribute to its creation. ... Under a system of free and equitable exchange, the recompense [wages] of every labourer will be by no means equal ... It must be determined by the value of his produce in the market. And this will increase in proportion to his talent, skill, application of the labourer, or any other circumstances which may his labour more productive than that of another ... The increased reward thus obtained by increased productiveness is the motive and necessary stimulus to most of those efforts for rendering labour more productive, which have carried mankind forward from the savage to the civilized state and must be depended upon for inciting his to yet farther advances. ...

[T]hose who observe the prevalence of great misery among the inferior classes of workmen in some wealthy countries—who witness and deplore the fact, that, in spite of all the manifold improvements which are continually adding to the productiveness of labour, the share of the gross production which falls to the common labourer does not increase ... that they should view something is wrong, is no source of astonishment to me, for I arrive at the same necessary conclusion from the same observation. But that any sane person should attribute the evil to the existence of capital—that is to the employment of wealth in aiding the production of farther wealth, instead of being unproductively consumed, almost, if not quite, as fast as it is created, or unproductively hoarded to satisfy the lust of the miser—is indeed wonderful. Why, without capital, the Island of Great Britain would not afford subsistence to a hundredth part of its present population. Destroy the security for the free enjoyment or disposal of capital, deny its owner the privilege of accepting what any one may find it for his advantage to give for its use, and every individual will soon be reduced to his unaided resources. He will find nowhere any store of food on which to live while he is digging, and sowing, and protecting his immature crop ... All trades would stop at once, for every trade is carried on by means of capital. Men would at once be reduced to the isolation and helplessness of barbarism.

6. Catharine Beecher, *A Treatise on Domestic Economy* ... (1846)

Beecher was the sister of the noted author of Uncle Tom's Cabin, *Harriet Beecher Stowe, as well as sister to the famed minister, Henry Ward Beecher. But Catharine garnered attention in her own right as an advocate for female education, even as she remained skeptical of the women's rights movement itself.*

In this country, it is established, both by opinion and by practice, that woman has an equal interest in all social and civil concerns; and that no domestic, civil, or political institution is right, which sacrifices her interest to promote that of the other sex. But in order to secure her the more firmly in all these privileges, it is decided that in the domestic relation, her interests be instructed to the other sex, without her taking part in voting or in making and administering laws ...

The success of democratic institutions, as is conceded by all, depends upon the intellectual and moral character of the mass of the people. If they are intelligent and virtuous, democracy is a blessing; but if they are ignorant and wicked, it is only a curse, and as much more dreadful than any other form of government as a thousand tyrants are more to be dreaded than one ... The mother forms the character of the future man; the sister bends the fibres that are hereafter to be the forest tree; the wife sways the heart, whose energies may turn for good or for evil the destinies of a nation. Let the women of a country be made virtuous and intelligent, and the men will certainly be the same. ...

But [women do suffer from] a delicacy of constitution, which renders them early victims to disease and decay. ... [therefore] much less time should be given to school, and much more to domestic employments, especially in the wealthier classes. A little girl may begin at five or six years of age to assist her mother, and if properly trained, by the time she is ten, she can render essential aid. From this time on ... it should be the principal object of her education to secure a strong and healthy constitution, and through a practical knowledge of all kinds of domestic employments. ... [we must] raise the science and practice of Domestic Economy to its appropriate place, as a regular study in female seminaries. ...

Every American woman, who values the institutions of her Country, and wishes to lend her influence in extending and perpetuating such blessings, may feel that she is doing this, whenever, by her example and influence, she destroys the aristocratic association, which would render domestic labor degrading.

7. Orestes Brownson, *The Laboring Classes* (1840)

Brownson was a noted New England Transcendentalist who later surprised his associates by joining the Catholic Church. Brownson also broke ranks with many New England reformers by emphasizing how the rise of industrial wage labor was seemingly as big a threat to human freedom as black slavery. It is worth considering whether "wage slavery" was in fact as bad as the plantation slavery experienced by African Americans in the South.

All over the world, the fact remains the case that the workingman is poor, while a large portion of the non-workingmen, in the sense we now use the term, are wealthy. It may be laid down as a general rule, with but few exceptions, that men are rewarded in an inverse ration to the amount of actual service they perform. ... It is our judgment that [African slavery] is the least oppressive form of labor. If the slave has never been a free man, we think, as a general rule, his sufferings are less than those of the free laborer at wages. ... The laborer at wages has all the disadvantages of freedom and none of the blessings, while the slave, if denied blessings, is freed from the disadvantages. We are no advocates of slavery, we are as heartily opposed to it as any modern abolitionist can be; but we say that if there must always be a laboring population distinct from proprietors and employers, we regard the slave system as decidedly preferable to the system at wages. ... In a [recent] account of the abolition of slavery in the West Indies, the fact is established that the employer may have the same amount of labor done 25% cheaper than the slave master. What does this fact prove, if not that wages is a more successful method of taxing labor than slavery.

8. British Cabinetmaker Describes Life in New York City *(1846)*

The anonymous recollections of this British workingman were actually published in London in 1846. His views are an important window on the white immigrant mindset in the mid-nineteenth century.

I was a cabinetmaker by trade, and one of the many who, between the years 1825–35, expatriated themselves [from Europe] in countless thousands, drawn by the promise of fair wages for faithful work, and driven by the scanty [pay] offered at home [to emigrate to New York]. ... I was fortunate enough to find employment from a master tradesman who had emigrated from England twenty years previously. ...

In the summer of 1836, when the inflated state of commerce and speculation had reached its height ... a strike took place among the cabinet-makers. They were dissatisfied with the wages then paid for their labour ... they held meetings; appointed committees; and on a given day, with very few exceptions, ceased working in all the shops of the city. The Americans of our workshop were among the noisiest of the strike, and naturally expected that I should join them but to this ... I was disinclined. First, I was disinclined that I was receiving quite as high wages as my manual skill deserved; next, I felt disposed to attach more importance to the claims of my family ... and last. ... [my striking] would have been an ill return for the kindness of my employer, who had given me work in the anxious time immediately following our arrival, and befriended me in various ways afterward.

9. Gustaf Unonius, Letters from a Swedish Man (1841–1842)

Unonius' letters are an invaluable resource documenting the views of the growing Scandinavian migration to the Midwest (and later to the Plains states) in the nineteenth century.

As far as we are concerned, we do not regret our [emigration to Wisconsin]. We are living a free and independent life in one of the most beautiful valleys the world can offer; and from the experiences of others we see that in a few years we can have a better livelihood and enjoy comforts that we now must deny ourselves ... I am partial to the republican form of government, and I have realized my youthful dream of social equality here in the United States ... I have found the Americans entirely different [than negative stereotypes of being greedy] ... There is something kindly in his speculation for profit and wealth and I find more to admire in his manner than in that of the European leaders. The merchant here is withal patriotic; in calculating his own gain he usually includes a share for his country ... the universities and other educational institutions, homes for the poor and other institutions of value to society are dependent on and supported by the American merchants. Canals, railroads, etc are all financed by companies composed of a few individuals whose collective fortunes serve the public for its common benefit and profit. One must therefore overlook an avariciousness which sometimes go to extremes.

10. George Templeton Strong (from New York City), Excerpts from his Diary (1838; 1857)

As a wealthy New York City lawyer and philanthropist, Strong's perceptions of the world around him were informed by certain ethnic and class prejudices. But his diary is valued for its frank assessments of the dramatic changes occurring in New York City from the 1830s though the 1860s.

November 6, 1838. It was enough to turn a man's stomach—to make a man adjure republicanism forever—to see the way they were naturalizing this morning at the Hall. Wretched, filthy, bestial-looking Italians and Irish, and creatures that looked as if they had risen from the lazarettos of Naples for this especial object; in short the very scum and dregs of human nature filled the clerk of Common Pleas Office so completely that I was almost afraid of being poisoned by going in. A dirty Irishman is bad enough, but he's nothing comparable to a nasty French or Italian loafer. …

July 7, 1858. Yesterday morning I was spectator of a strange, weird, painful scene. Certain houses of John Watts DePeyster are to be erected on the northwest corner of this street and Fourth Avenue, and the deep excavations therefore are in progress. Seeing a crowd on the corner, I stopped and made my way to a front place. The earth had caved in a few minutes before and crushed the breath out of a pair of ill-starred Celtic [Irish] laborers. They had just been dragged, or dug out, and lay white and stark on the ground where they had been working ten or twelve feet below the level of street. Around them were a few men who had got them out, I suppose, and fifteen or twenty Irish women, wives, kinfolk, or friends who had got down there in some way. I suppose they were "keening" all together were raising a wild, unearthly, cry—half shriek and half song, wailing as a score of daylight Banshees, clapping their hands and gesticulating passionately … It was an uncanny sound to hear … Our Celtic fellow citizens are almost as remote from us in temperament and constitution as the Chinese.

11. George Lawrence, *An Oration on the Abolition of the Slave Trade* (1813)

Lawrence was a relatively unknown free black writer in the early nineteenth century. But this excerpt below testifies to the cultural and economic vitality of the black community despite Northern racial prejudice.

My brethren, the land in which we live gives us the opportunity rapidly to advance to the prosperity of liberty … You who are enrolled and proudly march under the banners of the Mutual Relief, and Wilberforce Societies, consider your important standings as incorporated bodies, and walk worthy of the name you bear, cling closely to the paths of virtue and morality, cherish the plans of peace and temperance, by doing this you shall not only shine as the first stars in the firmament … but immortalize your names. Be zealous and vigilant, be always on the alert to promote the welfare of your injured brethren; then shall providence shower down her blessings upon your heads. It has been said be your enemies that your minds were not calculated to receive a sufficient store of knowledge, to fit you for beneficial or social societies; but your incorporation drowned that assertion. … There could be many reasons given to prove that the mind of an African is not inferior to that of an European, yet to do so would be superfluous. … My brethren the time is fast approaching when the iron hand of oppression must cease to tyrannize over injured innocence, and very different are the days that we see, from those that our ancestors did; yet I know that there are a thousand of our enemies who would rather see us exterminated from off of the earth, than partake of the blessings that they enjoy … O thou father of the universe and disposer of events, thou that called from a dark and formless mass this fair system of nature … Oh! Wilt thou crush that power that still holds thousands of our brethren in bondage, and let the sea of thy wisdom, wash its very dust from the face of the earth; let liberty unfurl her banners, freedom and justice reign triumphant in the world, universally.

Questions to Consider:

1. Who won and who lost out as the economy of the free states became more dependent upon increases in trade, technological innovation, and labor-saving techniques?
2. How did the "market revolution" reorganize American society, from the nature of the family to the nature of urban environments?
3. What were some of the remedies proposed by workers to make up for the shortcomings within this new market economy? How different are these complaints from ones which might be heard today?
4. What role did class interest play in influencing the views of those who defended this new capitalist class system, as well as in those who attacked the system?
5. How did the new economy redefine conventional thinking about race and gender?

Credits

- Allen Johnson, "Highways USA 1825." 1915. Copyright in the Public Domain.
- Allen Johnson, "Canals USA 1825." 1915. Copyright in the Public Domain.
- John Jacob Astor, "John Jacob Astor to Albert Gallatin." 1818. Copyright in the Public Domain.
- Excerpt from James Flint, "Letters from America," *Early Western Travels*, vol. 9, ed. Reuben Gold Thwaites, pp. 226-227. 1822. Copyright in the Public Domain.
- Excerpt from Thomas Skidmore, *The Rights of Man to Property.* 1829. Copyright in the Public Domain.
- Excerpts from Harriet Hanson Robinson, *Loom and Spindle or Life Among the Early Mill Girls.* 1898. Copyright in the Public Domain.
- Excerpt from Alonzo Potter, *The Political Economy: Its Objects, Uses, and Principles*, pp. 92-94, 137-138. 1841. Copyright in the Public Domain.
- Excerpts from Catharine Beecher, *A Treatise on Domestic Economy, For the Use of Young Ladies at Home and at School.* 1845. Copyright in the Public Domain.
- Excerpts from Orestes Brownson, *The Laboring Classes an Article from the Boston Quarterly Review,* 3rd ed., pp. 10-12. 1840. Copyright in the Public Domain.
- Excerpt from *A Working Man's Recollections of America*, p. 97. 1846. Copyright in the Public Domain.
- Excerpts from Gustaf Unonius, *Letters Relating to Gustaf Unonius and the Early Swedish Settlers in Wisconsin*, ed. George M. Stephenson, pp. 50, 68-69. Copyright © 1937 by Augustana Historical Society.
- Excerpts from George Templeton Strong, *The Diary of George Templeton Strong, volumes I & II,* ed. Allan Nevins and Milton Thomas, pp. I: 94, 318, II: 197, 348. 1952. Copyright in the Public Domain.
- Excerpt from George Lawrence, *An Oration on the Abolition of the Slave Trade, Delivered on the First Day of January, 1813*, pp. 11-13, 16. 1813. Copyright in the Public Domain.

★ CHAPTER 12
★ THE AGE OF JACKSON
★

The related processes of westward movement, the growth of a participatory political culture (among whites), and the dramatic economic changes associated with the market revolution all led to what has been called a more "democratic" political atmosphere in the nineteenth century for white Americans. We have seen already with the election of Thomas Jefferson in 1800 that a new political philosophy—one friendlier to the "common man" and one that was suspicious of elitist concentrations of wealth and power—began to impact American civil society in ways that George Washington would probably have found repugnant. After 1800, newspapers proliferated as a more robust civil society made its presence felt, and perhaps of more importance, states now lifted various property requirements for voting, so that white males possessed a greater voice in elections. Related to the expansion of white voting came increased support from states for the direct election of electors for president (as opposed to simply leaving the process of choosing presidential electors up to the state legislatures).

The rise of Andrew Jackson as a major political figure after 1815 symbolized many of these "democratic" developments; yet his life and career also revealed the serious limitations of the very democracy so often advanced by Western frontiersmen such as Jackson. His violent personal style (seen in his military exploits against the British and the natives) coupled with his deep hatred for Eastern elites (especially bankers) has led some historians to see Jackson as an opportunistic demagogue—someone simply playing on the fears, and not the hopes, of common white men. But many of the fears articulated by Jackson were rooted in actual events of the 1820s, which led some Americans to believe that the simple, agrarian republic envisioned by Jefferson was now under assault from various special interests in the centers of Eastern power, such as Washington, D.C., Philadelphia, or New York.

Several developments led to new resentments from Westerners and Southerners after the Panic of 1819. First, the banking panic itself, which saw urban unemployment skyrocket to over 50 percent (luckily, most Americans were still farmers), made an entire generation hate banks, or at least the Bank of the United States. This is because banks played a role in overextending credit for land speculation or business enterprises, only to see the whole house of cards collapse. Many people lost everything when bankers began to call in loans or otherwise tighten credit policy when they feared the loans would never be repaid. In many ways, the 1819 panic was the first "modern" banking depression in the United States, but the ire of many in the South and West was focused on the Bank of the United States in the East, because that bank

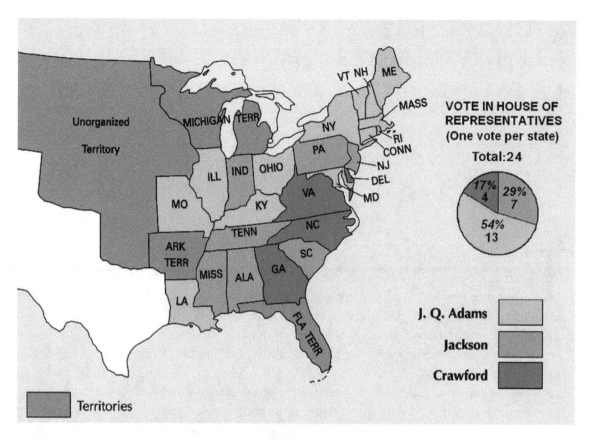

VOTE IN HOUSE OF REPRESENTATIVES
(One vote per state)

Total: 24

17% 4 — 29% 7 — 54% 13

J. Q. Adams

Jackson

Crawford

Territories

The Presidential Election of 1824, also known as the "corrupt bargain."

began the process of tightening back on the expansion of credit to other subordinate, weaker banks.

Another ominous sign of national disunity in the 1820s arose from sectional arguments over slavery. Southern planters, as well as more conservative Northerners, hated Rufus King and James Tallmadge's attempts to abolish slavery in Missouri (one of the first states carved out of the Louisiana Purchase), and many conservatives believed that Eastern moralists were trying to destroy private property and needlessly divide the country along sectional lines. Other Southerners, particularly those in South Carolina, also developed increasing critiques of federal tariff policy, whereby the products of Northern industry were made cheaper by taxes on foreign imports, but this hurt Southerners who imported foreign goods.

However, one of the biggest seismic shocks experienced by white Americans in the 1820s came from fights over the presidential electoral process. In the election of 1824, the heirs of the Democratic-Republicans (who basically were the only party in Washington after the collapse of the Federalist Party in 1815) disagreed about whom to nominate for the White House, resulting in the nomination of four men for the presidency. Part of the reason for this difficult state of affairs had to do with individual states' mistrust of the congressional caucus system (where certain insiders simply nominated candidates), instead of allowing for a more democratic process such as a state nominating convention, let alone a party nominating convention (which later generations would use). The Congressional Caucus, which was not well attended, nominated William Crawford as the Democratic-Republican candidate for the presidency, and a number of state legislative meetings nominated Andrew Jackson, John Quincy Adams, and Henry Clay. In this chaotic environment, it is perhaps not surprising that no candidate won a majority in the electoral college, but Jackson did have a clear plurality of the popular and electoral votes. Yet the supporters of the other three men were all united in their personal dislike of Jackson. Recall that Jackson appeared to be a roughneck hothead to many in the more refined East. Therefore, when the election was decided by the House of Representatives, John Quincy Adams emerged victorious, with Henry Clay becoming Adams' Secretary of State. Adams represented New England and shared in his region's belief in a strong federal government—the exact opposite philosophy as held by Crawford and Jackson (whose combined votes represented a majority in the 1824 election). Therefore, Adams was seen as an undemocratic, Federalist holdover, extremely out of touch with the small-government ideals of the South and West.

In the aftermath of the election, Jackson and his supporters vowed not to let such an undemocratic proceeding ever occur again, and went about organizing both friendly newspapers and state meetings to attempt to create an entirely new political party—the Democratic Party—in anticipation of the election of 1828. With the help of New York politician Martin Van Buren, this new grassroots organization sought not only to organize the common man of the West and South, but more importantly, hoped to submerge the divisive issue of slavery by focusing on a small government, and what some would call an anti-capitalist agenda. "Jacksonians" would therefore be composed of the odd combination of slave-owning planters, poorer farmers in both the North and the South, and immigrant workers in the free states. But the coalition assembled by Jackson and Van Buren in the 1820s would prove effective at winning most elections before the slavery issue eventually tore both the Democrats and the nation apart in 1860. The Democratic Party would for a time be a successful, trans-sectional party.

The election of 1828 constituted a landslide for Jackson, and it has been seen as a revolutionary shift in American politics toward the power of Western and Southern "common" white men. Jackson often lectured on the virtues of "democracy," even going so far as to literally invite the people to the White House on inauguration day (this proved to be quite messy). Yet, as mentioned above, Jackson clearly blurred the line between democracy and demagoguery with his repeated use of the presidential veto, and his belief that he singlehandedly represented the interests of the majority of Americans. Jackson often cast other elected officials as the ones who were hopelessly compromised or operating out of morally suspect intents. Jackson made it clear that he would veto federal spending bills, which he saw as the modern equivalent of "pork barrel" (meaning wasteful) spending, and he did indeed veto federal construction of the Maysville Road in Kentucky in 1830. But the best example of Jackson's volatile governing style came with the crisis over South Carolina's attempt to nullify the so-called "tariff of abominations" in 1832. As outlined above, South Carolinians felt that the tax on imports was an unfair aid to Northern manufacturing interests (by making foreign imports more expensive than domestic products), and they were so angry about it that they threatened to leave the Union over the tariff. When it was revealed that Jackson's own vice president, John C. Calhoun (of South Carolina), supported much of the bluster coming out of South Carolina, Jackson reputedly threatened to kill him, at which point Calhoun decided it would be best to step down. (There had also been other personal squabbles between the two men in the White House over the treatment of a cabinet member's wife, as well as over Calhoun's recently discovered lack of support for Jackson when he was being censured for military exploits in Florida in the late 1810s.) Jackson went further and issued the Force Act against South Carolina, where he then threatened to invade the state if they dared challenge federal authority. Congressional leaders worked out a compromise to defuse the whole mess, but for many, the behavior of Jackson was distressing, even if many agreed that South Carolina was in the wrong.

But the larger controversy of Jackson's presidency would come during the so-called "Bank War" of 1836. As mentioned earlier, Jackson distrusted banks, and saw the Bank of the United States as an illegal private corporation that arbitrarily controlled credit policy for subordinate banks and, by extension, most average Americans. Since the bank's charter was up for renewal in 1836—and since he won a second term in 1832—Jackson unilaterally deposited the funds of the Bank of the United States in various smaller banks, thus destroying the institution (although Congress also allowed the bank to lose its charter, it still possessed specie and could therefore generate or call in loans as needed, and this was unacceptable to Jackson). Jackson not only distrusted the Bank of the United States, but he distrusted the credit, or paper, economy based on loans and not tangible assets such as land, livestock, gold, and silver. Before he left office, he drafted the Specie Circular, which basically reduced the amount of overall credit in circulation (to stop speculation in real estate). Jackson's radical economic medicine was further practiced by his loyal successor, Martin Van Buren, aptly called President "Van Ruin," because the hard money, anti-credit policies pursued by him out of anger at the American banking system sent the country into an economic nosedive between 1837 and 1843.

This depression allowed the Whigs to gain power in the election of 1840. As a party, the Whigs primarily owed their existence to the personal enmity felt by many toward "King Andrew." The roots of the Whig Party went back to 1834, when many politicians looked for ways to thwart Jackson's power. Never as successful at electioneering as the Democrats, in some respects the Whigs represented an updated version of the Federalists. But the Whigs had learned to adapt their elitism to the modern world, so they cannot so easily be viewed as a "throwback," as it were, to the views of someone like Alexander Hamilton. In general, a large degree of Whig cohesion simply came from their hatred of Andrew Jackson, but they did share a common belief that internal improvements should be supported by the government, in addition to supporting banking and manufacturing concerns. Whigs included Northeasterners friendly to banking and industrial interests, some elite Southerners who desired internal improvement for their region, as well as those evangelical reformers who sought to bring the world into accordance with the "government of God." These reformers had also been deeply disgusted with Jackson's support for Indian removal—which culminated in the 1838 "Trail of Tears" during Martin Van Buren's term. Jackson had refused to enforce a Supreme Court ruling forbidding white Georgians from entering the Cherokee Nation, and, as a result, whites were able to expel these natives to the West. The resulting march killed thousands of natives. Out of a belief that racial and economic minorities needed supervision and aid against the kind of "survival of the fittest" mentality possessed by Jackson, the new generation of Northern evangelical reformers played an important role as "modernizers" for a rapidly changing economy and society between 1830 and 1860 in the free states.

The "reformers" who often (though not always) supported the Whig party owed much of their existence, ironically, to the lingering impact of Thomas Jefferson's assault on tax-funded religion in the 1790s and early 1800s. Jefferson believed that no one church should receive state tax funding, and this ironically led to an explosion in new churches and ministers competing for the attention of Americans, since churches were no longer receiving tax dollars by 1830. (It is important to remember that the First Amendment to the Constitution in 1790 only prevented the federal government from having an established church, and said nothing regarding state power to support an established church.) With the disestablishment of American state churches, the power of evangelical churches and reform organizations only increased from the 1820s through the 1840s. This fact can be seen with the Second Great Awakening, often said to have begun with the mesmerizing preaching of Charles Grandison Finney. This new awakening was a broad and diffuse movement of Protestants attempting to instill in other Americans a sense of a new divine purpose for their lives. In the case of those sympathetic with Finney, a new emphasis on the "perfectability" of humankind emerged, in contrast to the earlier Calvinistic emphasis on the inherent sinfulness of people. The new belief that mankind could bring about a "new heaven and a new earth" through their own efforts exerted a powerful influence on the numerous reform movements born in the early nineteenth century. To be sure, such reform efforts also existed as a response to the new economy and society in the rapidly changing free states (part of the reason why "reformers" were fewer in the slave states). It was also the case that middle-class people made wealthy by living in or near cities possessed the means to take part in philanthropic efforts, in addition to finding the subjects of that reform all around them in the new economic environment created by mechanization and urbanization.

Not all reformers owed allegiance to a specific church, yet many shared in the culture of American Protestantism and believed that individuals needed to be uplifted, or changed for their own good, as well as for the good of society. Perhaps the best known "reform" movement in this period was the temperance movement, which forever changed the drinking habits of many Americans. By establishing numerous associations where members pledged never again to drink alcohol, this movement hoped to gain support from the public to pressure lawmakers to ban alcohol. By 1851, temperance reformers managed to convince the state of Maine to ban alcohol, and by the late nineteenth and early twentieth centuries, the movement would gain even more steam. For historians, temperance advocates played an important role in speaking out against domestic violence and bringing attention to all of the new slums or communities of people left behind or otherwise taken advantage of by the new market economy. It is not surprising that many temperance advocates sought to reform Irish and German immigrants in major urban areas. These reformers believed that the nation should pay more attention to the conditions in these neighborhoods, even if the immigrants themselves rarely appreciated the intrusive, moralizing tenor of most reformers themselves. Along with the temperance movement, the other famous reform undertaken in the free states after 1820 was public schooling. Again, reformers believed that literacy should be universal, and that the survival of the republic depended upon educating new immigrants or other poor people so they would not contribute to the future degradation of American social and political life. Horace Mann, superintendent of schools for Massachusetts, believed in free, tax-supported education to end "misery and crime," not only in his state, but really throughout the country. And as with temperance, within a couple of decades several states did have mandatory education statutes on the books. Of course, these reformers also ran afoul of Catholic immigrants; since these "public" schools used the Protestant King James Bible (besides using textbooks that were often critical of Catholicism and Catholic countries), there were riots as well as other fights over the application of local tax funds away from Catholic schools, toward what immigrants essentially saw as Protestant schools. Reformers did not shy away from controversy.

The most radical "reform" undertaken by members of this evangelical culture, however, were abolition and women's rights. As mentioned in the preceding chapter, many whites and blacks in the free states were galvanized by the abolition of slavery in the British Empire in 1833, and these Americans formed the American Anti-Slavery Society with similar goals for the United States. Also, many abolitionists viewed the admission of Missouri as a slave state in 1820 as the opening wedge in attempts by Southerners to take their slaves throughout the territories, and soon abolitionists would be troubled by the ability of proslavery Americans in Texas to detach that province from Mexico. It looked to this new cadre of abolitionists that, just as Great Britain and other powers were ending slavery, the United States was becoming more attached to the institution. The Anti-Slavery Society therefore demanded that slavery be abolished immediately (though they offered no program for doing so), and the organization sent thousands of petitions to Congress demanding slavery be abolished in the nation's capital, and that no new slave territories be added to the nation. More than the petition drives, though, these abolitionists broke into churches and demanded white worshippers treat blacks as equals. Abolitionists also publicly called Southern whites sinners, and personally helped escaped slaves find freedom with the Underground Railroad. Given the sensitivity of Southerners to the prospect of "race war" after the Nat Turner uprising and the David Walker pamphlet (see Chapter 10), many abolitionists found their livelihoods or lives threatened by conservatives in both regions. But they were not deterred. In fact, abolitionists were so angered regarding the conventional prejudices of American society that many of them soon embraced another radical idea: that of a woman's right to vote.

Emboldened by the lack of respect many women received from male politicians over the vexing moral problem of slavery, by 1848 abolitionists such as Susan B. Anthony and Elizabeth Cady Stanton drafted a woman's declaration of independence (called the Declaration of Sentiments) which outlined all of the numerous ways that women were treated unequally in American society. Few took their demands seriously in 1848, but it was clear to many that a new reformist—and in some cases radical—zeal was sweeping the country for many public issues. It was still unclear in the 1840s what this new upsurge in reform would bring. But with the acquisition of new territory in the West, these reformers gained a broader audience from more Americans critical of the existence of human bondage in their republic, and "modernizing moralists" such as Stanton and Anthony would play their part in the coming sectional crisis.

Documents:

1. John C. Calhoun on the Tariff and Sectional Interests (1828)

As vice president under John Quincy Adams, Calhoun came to resent the power of Northerners and began to move toward strong support for the rights of Southern states (such as his home state of South Carolina), after he felt the rights of plantation owners were threatened by Northern advocates of higher tariffs. These same advocates had also been opposed to the recent extension of slavery into the new state of Missouri.

Those who are bound to exercise power under the Constitution [in support of high tariffs] are bound to show that it is expressly granted, or that it is necessary and proper as a means to some of the granted powers. The advocates of the Tariff have offered no such proof ... So partial are the effects of the system, that its burdens are exclusively on one side, and the benefits on the other. It imposes on the agricultural interest of the south, including South west, with that portion of our commerce and navigation engaged in foreign trade, the burden not only of sustaining the system itself, but that also of the Government ... that the manufacturing states even in their own opinion, bear no share of the burden of the Tariff in reality, we may infer with the greatest certainty from their conduct. The fact they urgently demand an increase, and consider any addition as a blessing, and a failure to obtain one a curse. ...

[In reference to the tariff] ... No system can be more efficient to rear up a monied aristocracy. Its tendency is to make the poor, poorer, and the rich, richer. Heretofore in our country this tendency has displayed itself principally in regards to the different sections, but the time will come when it will produce the same result between classes in the manufacturing States. After we are exhausted, the contest will be between the Capitalists and operatives, for into these two classes ultimately must divide society. The issue of the struggle is here, must be the same as it has been in Europe.

2. Martin Van Buren to Thomas Ritchie (January 13, 1827)

As a senator from New York, Van Buren was troubled by what he saw as the demise of the Jeffersonian Republican coalition of small farmers, workers, and plantation owners committed to limited government. In this letter to Thomas Ritchie, Van Buren is proposing a new political party, which came to be known as the Democratic Party.

You will have observed an article in the Argus upon the subject of a national convention [for a new political party, the Democrats] ... It was first suggested to me by the Vice-President [John C. Calhoun, as a way to thwart East Coast power] ... It will be an important movement and should be fully and deeply considered. ... It is the best and probably the only practicable mode of concentrating the entire vote of the opposition and of effecting what is of still greater importance, the substantial reorganization of the Old Republican Party [associated with Jefferson]. ... Its first result cannot be doubtful. Mr. Adams occupying the seat [of President] and being determined not to surrender it. ... will not submit his pretensions to this convention ... I have long been satisfied that we can only get rid of the present, and restore a better state of things, by combing General Jackson's personal popularity with the portion of old party feeling yet remaining. This sentiment is spreading and would of itself be sufficient to nominate him at the Convention. The call of such a convention, its exclusive Republican character, and the refusal of Mr. Adams and his friends to become parties to it ... would greatly improve the condition of the Republicans of the North and Middle States by substituting party principle for personal preference as one of the leading points in the context ... they would have to decide between and indulgence in sectional and personal feelings ... or acquiescence in the fairly expressed will of the party, on the other. ... [The effects of a national convention] would be highly salutary on your section [the South]. ... Political combinations between the inhabitants of the different states are unavoidable and the most natural and beneficial to the country is that between the planters of the South and the plain [Jeffersonian] Republicans of the North. The country has once flourished under a party and thus constituted, may so again. ... Geographical divisions founded on local interests or, what is worse, prejudices between free and slave holding states will inevitably take place. Party attachment in former times furnished a complete antidote for sectional prejudice ... formerly, attacks on Southern Republicans were regarded by those of the north as assaults upon their political brethren and resented accordingly.

3. Andrew Jackson's "Veto of the Maysville Road" (May 27, 1830)

As president, Jackson used his veto power more often than any of his predecessors. In this message, he lays out his reasons for opposing federal funding for internal improvements.

It is however, sufficiently definite and imperative to my mind to forbid any appropriation of any bill having the character of the one under consideration. I have given its provisions all the reflection demanded by a just regard for the interests of those of our fellow-citizens who have desired its passage, and by the respect which is due to a coordinate branch of the Government, but I am not able to view it in any other light than as a measure of purely local character; or if it can be considered national, that no further distinction between the appropriate duties of the General or State governments need be attempted, for there can be no local interest that may not with equal propriety be denominated national. This road possesses no connection with any established system of improvements; is exclusively within the limits of a State [Kentucky] starting at a point on the Ohio River and running out 60 miles to an interior town, and even as far as the State is concerned, conferring partial instead of general advantages. ...

If it be the wish of the people that the construction of roads and canals should be conducted by the Federal Government, it is not only highly expedient, but indispensably necessary, that a previous amendment of the Constitution, delegating the necessary power and defining and restricting its exercise with reference to the sovereignty of the States, should be made. Without it, nothing extensively useful can be effected. ...

4. Henry Clay's Speech in Support of the Maysville Road (1830)

The former secretary of state, and soon to be a senator from Kentucky, Clay believed in government support for projects to modernize the American economy in order to create a strong domestic market. Clay would eventually become a leading spokesman for the Whig Party, which also believed in federally supported internal improvements.

With respect to the American system ... its great object is to secure the independence of our country, to augment its wealth, and to diffuse the comforts of civilization throughout society. ... It has increased the wealth and power, and population of the nation. It has diminished the price of articles of consumption, and has placed them within the reach of a far greater number of our people than could have found means to command them, if they had been manufactured abroad instead of at home ... Its opponents opened the campaign at the last session of Congress, and, with the most obliging frankness, have since publicly exposed their plan of operations. It is to divide and conquer, to attack and subdue the system in detail. ...

If anything could be considered settled under the present Constitution of our government, I had supposed that it was [the authority of Congress] to construct such internal improvements as may be deemed by Congress necessary and proper to carry into effect the power granted to it. For nearly twenty-five years, the power has been asserted and exercised by the government.

... This power, necessary to all parts of the Union, is indispensible to the West. Without it, this section can never enjoy any part of the benefit of a regular disbursement of the vast revenues of the United States. ... Yet we are told that this power can no longer be exercised without an amendment of the Constitution. ...

The veto message proceeds to insist, that the Maysville and Lexington road is not a national but a local road, of sixty miles in length, and confined within the limits of a particular State. ... The Maysville road was undoubtedly national. It connects the largest body perhaps of fertile land in the Union, with the navigation of the Ohio and Mississippi river, and with the canals of the States of Ohio, Pennsylvania, and New York. ... The same scheme which has been devised and practiced to defeat the tariff, has been adopted to undermine internal improvements. They are to be attacked in detail. ... But is this fair? Ought each proposed road to be viewed separately and detached? Ought it not to be considered in connection with other great works which are in process of execution, or are projected? The policy of the foes indicates what ought to be the policy of the friends of the power. ...

5. Andrew Jackson's Veto Message Regarding the Bank, July 10, 1832.

This excerpt from Jackson reveals his deep distrust for the Bank of the United States. He viewed the institution as an elite, aristocratic entity that preyed on unsuspecting investors and the public.

The present corporate body, denominated the president, directors, and company of the Bank of the United States, will have existed at the time this act is intended to take effect twenty years. It enjoys an exclusive privilege of banking under the authority of the General Government, a monopoly of its favor and support, and, as a necessary consequence, almost a monopoly of the foreign and domestic exchange. ...

Every monopoly and all exclusive privileges are granted at the expense of the public, which ought to receive a fair equivalent. The many millions which this act proposes to bestow on the stockholders of the existing bank must come directly or indirectly out of the earnings of the American people. It is due to them, therefore, if their Government sell monopolies and exclusive privileges, that they should at least exact for them as much as they are worth in the open market. ... Since little stock is held in the West, it is obvious that the debt of the people in that section to the bank is principally a debt to the Eastern and foreign stockholders; that the interest they pay upon it is carried into the Eastern states and into Europe, and that it is a burden upon their industry and a drain of their currency, which no country can bear with inconvenience and occasional distress. ...

It is to be regretted that the rich and powerful too often bend the acts of government to their selfish purposes. Distinctions in society will always exist under every just government ... every man is equally entitled to protection by law; but when the laws undertake to add to these natural and just advantages artificial distinctions ... to make the rich richer and the potent more powerful ... the farmers, mechanics and laborers ... have a right to complain of the injustice of their Government. Experience should teach us wisdom. Most of the difficulties our Government now encounters and most of the dangers which impend over our Union have sprung from an abandonment of the legitimate objects of Government by our national legislation ... Many of our rich men ... have besought us to make them richer by act of Congress. By gratifying their desires we have ... arrayed section against section, interest against interest ... in a fearful commotion which threatens to shake the foundations of our Union.

6. Calvin Colton, Labour and Capital (1844)

Colton was an Anglican minister who felt it his duty to speak out on politics. He distrusted Andrew Jackson and he believed that the Whig Party, which Colton supported, had been mischaracterized as unfriendly to the interests of the common man.

"The Genius of Whig Democracy"
The Whig party of the Union is composed of men, who have been long out of power; who have been forced in the meantime to act on the conservative side, that is, as far as possible, to prevent mischief; who are of course, and necessarily, lean men, as regards the fattening effects of office; have none of the corruptions which are at least supposed to appertain to a protracted tenure of power; and if such men can anywhere be found, may fairly be regarded, as in a reasonable degree, disinterested patriots ... Nobody has ever dared to name in their ranks that wicked, corrupt, and corrupting maxim, that 'to the victors belong the spoils. ...'
"Democrats the Friends of the Labouring and Poorer Classes"
This has not only been a standing text, and there has been much effective preaching from it, by the Locofoco "Democracy." But the laboring and poorer classes have made an importance discovery in three particulars. 1. That they have been made tools of ... 2. That Whig policy and Whig measures are best for them. 3. ... [That] the tariff, a great Whig measure, is diffusing its blessings everywhere, and gladdening the hearts of the laboring and poorer classes. ... We have just received notice that a little girl in a Cotton Bag Factory at Cincinnati, earns six dollars for five and a half days' labor every week, and that there are fifty-five females and forty-five males working in the same factory with similar results. ... 'The Leaders of Industry are the Captains of the world. If there be no nobleness in them, there will never be an aristocracy more.' This is a higher toned phrase than we are addicted to employ, as they who read us well know. Nevertheless ... it plants labour where God intended it should stand, in the loftiest, most influential position.

7. Charles Grandison Finney on Sin and Redemption (1835)

As a Presbyterian revivalist working in New England and New York, Finney is said to be responsible for a growing interest among Protestants in rooting out various sins confronting people living through the intense social changes of the early nineteenth century. It is often claimed that Finney believed his listeners could bring about the perfection of the world, though Finney himself did not always go so far in his sermons.

A change of heart ... consists in changing the controlling preference of the mind in regard to the end of pursuit. The selfish heart is a preference of self-interest to the glory of God and the interests of his kingdom. A new heart consists in a preference of the glory of God and the interests of his kingdom to one's own happiness. In other words, it is a change from selfishness to benevolence, from having a supreme regard to one's own interest to an absorbing and controlling choice of the happiness and glory of God and his kingdom. In other words, it is a change from selfishness to benevolence, from having a supreme regard to one's own interest to an absorbing and controlling choice of the happiness and glory of God and his kingdom.

God has established a government, and proposed by the exhibition of his own character to produce the greatest practicable amount of happiness in the universe. He has enacted laws wisely calculated to promote this object, to which he conforms all his own conduct, and to which he requires all his subjects perfectly and undeviatingly to conform theirs.

As God requires men to make to themselves a new heart, on pain of eternal death, it is the strongest possible evidence that they are able to do it. To say that he has commanded them to do it, without telling them they are able, is consummate trifling. Their ability is implied as strongly as it can be, in the command itself.

Sinner! Instead of waiting and praying for God to change your heart, you should at once summon up your powers, put forth the effort, and change the governing preference of your mind. ...

8. Horace Mann, Report of the Massachusetts Board of Education (1848)

Mann had been the secretary of the Massachusetts State Board of Education since its founding in 1837. In this capacity, Mann is often seen as the father of the modern movement for public schooling.

Without undervaluing any other human agency, it may be surely affirmed that the common school, improved and energized as it can easily be, may become the most effective and benign of all the forces of civilization. Two reasons sustain this position. In the first place, there is a universality in its operation, which can be affirmed of no other institution whatever. If administered in the spirit of justice and conciliation, all the rising generation may be brought within the circle of its reformatory and elevating influences. ... As the child is father to the man, so may the training of the schoolroom expand into the institution and fortunes of the state .... Surely nothing but universal education can counterwork this tendency to the domination of capital and the servility of labor. If one class possesses all the wealth and the education, while the residue of society is ignorant and poor ... the latter will be the servile dependents of the formers ... A republican form of government, without intelligence in the people, must be, on a vast scale, what a mad-house without superintendent or keepers would be on a small one ... It may be an easy thing to make a republic, but it is a very laborious thing to make republicans; and woe to the republic that rests upon no better foundations than ignorance, selfishness, and passion! ...

That our public schools are not theological seminaries is admitted ... They are debarred by law from inculcating the peculiar and distinctive doctrines of any one religious denomination amongst us ... But our system earnestly inculcates all Christian morals; it founds morals on the basis of religion; it welcomes the religion of the Bible ... Such then is the Massachusetts system of common schools ... In a social and political sense, it is a free school system. It knows no distinction of rich or poor, of bond and free. ...

9. Anti-Slavery Convention of American Women—Proceedings (May 1837)

The efforts made by many abolitionist women to speak out against both slavery and racism were usually seen as highly inappropriate by more traditional men, who felt that women should not be so vocal on public issues. As a result, many women first involved in the Anti-Slavery Society soon broadened their efforts to speak out regarding the inequities they themselves faced based on gender.

... we regard the combination of interest which exists between North and South in their political, commercial, and domestic relations, as the true, but hidden cause of the unprincipled and violent efforts which have been made ... to smother free discussion, impugn the motive, and traduce the characters of abolitionists ... Resolved, that the right of petition is natural and inalienable, derived immediately from God and guaranteed by the Constitution of the U.S., and that we regard every effort in Congress to abridge this sacred right, whether it be exercised by man or woman, the bond or free, as a high-handed usurpation of power ... Resolved ... that as certain rights and duties are common to all moral beings, the time has come for woman to move in that sphere which Providence has assigned her, and no longer remain satisfied in the circumscribed limits with which corrupt custom ... has encircled her. ...

10. Women Declare Equality with Men at Seneca Falls (1848)

At a small meeting in upstate New York, several noted female abolitionists—such as Lucretia Mott and Elizabeth Cady Stanton—decided to organize a movement devoted to the rights of women. Of particular importance here is the demand for women's right to vote, something seen as extremely radical in its time.

When in the course of human events, it become necessary for one portion of the family of man to assume among the peoples of the earth a position different from that which they have hitherto occupied, but one to which the laws of nature and of nature's God entitle them, a decent respect to the opinions of mankind requires that they should declare the causes that impel them to such a course.

We hold these truths to be self-evident: that all men and women are created equal; that they are endowed by their Creator with certain inalienable rights; that among these are life, liberty, and the pursuit of happiness. ...

The history of mankind is a history of repeated injuries and usurpations on the part of man toward woman, having in direct object the establishment of an absolute tyranny over her. To prove this, let facts be submitted to a candid world.

He has never permitted her to exercise her inalienable right to the elective franchise.

He has compelled her to submit to laws, in the formation of which she has no voice.

He has withheld from her rights which are given to the most ignorant and degraded men-both natives and foreigners.

Having deprived her of this first right of a citizen, the elective franchise, thereby leaving her without representation in the halls of legislation, he has oppressed her on all sides.

He has made her, if married, in the eye of the law, civilly dead.

He has taken from her all right in property, even to the wages she earns. ...

Resolved, That such laws as conflict, in any way, with the true and substantial happiness of woman, are contrary to the great precept of nature. *Resolved,* That all laws which prevent woman from occupying such a station in society as her conscience shall dictate, or which place her in a position inferior to that of man, are contrary to the great precept of nature, and therefore of no force or authority. *Resolved,* That woman is man's equal—was intended to be so by the Creator, and the highest good of the race demands that she should be recognized as such. ...

Resolved, That it is the duty of the women of this country to secure to themselves their sacred right to the elective franchise ... [furthermore] it is demonstrably the right and duty of women, equally with men, to promote every righteous cause by every righteous means ... both in private and in public, by writing and by speaking. ...

11. Walt Whitman, *Leaves of Grass* (1855)

To many, Whitman's poems reflect a frankness and honesty that grew out of the American experiment in "democracy." It is worth noting that numerous contemporaries viewed Whitman's poetry, replete with sexually suggestive language, as offensive and pornographic.

Other states indicate themselves in their deputies ... but the genius of the United States is not best or most in its executives or legislatures, nor in its ambassadors or authors or colleges or churches or parlors, nor even in its newspapers or inventors ... but always most in the common people. Their manners speech dress friendships—the freshness and candor of their physiognomy—the picturesque looseness of their carriage ... their deathless attachment to freedom—their aversion to anything indecorous or soft or mean—the practical acknowledgement of the citizens of one state by the citizens of all other states—the fierceness of their roused resentment—their curiosity and welcome of novelty—their self-esteem and wonderful sympathy—their susceptibility to a slight—the air they have of persons who never knew how it felt to stand in the presence of superiors—the fluency of their speech—their delight in music, the sure symptom of manly tenderness and native elegance of soul ... their good temper and open-handedness—the terrible significance of their elections—the President's taking off his hat to them not they to him—these too are unrhymed poetry. It awaits the gigantic and generous treatment worthy of it.

The largeness of nature or the nation were monstrous without a corresponding largeness and generosity of the spirit of the citizen. Not nature nor swarming states nor streets and steamships nor prosperous business nor farms nor capital nor learning may suffice for the ideal of man. ... A live nation can always cut a deep mark and can have the best authority for the cheapest ... namely from its own soul. ...

As if the opening of the Western continent by discovery and what has transpired since in North and South America were less than the small theater of the antique or the aimless sleepwalking of the middle ages! The pride of the United States leaves the wealth and finesse of the cities and all returns of commerce and agriculture and all the magnitude of geography or shows the exterior victory to enjoy the breed of fullsized men or one fullsized man unconquerable and simple.

Questions to Consider:

1. How is the term "democracy" paradoxical in the context of Andrew Jackson's career, as well as in terms of the people he represented? To most Americans in the early nineteenth century, what exactly did "democracy" mean?
2. How were the reformers critical of Jackson also the product of similar social and economic changes as those who supported Jackson?
3. Was the worldview of the Whig Party that different from that of the Federalists?
4. What was the connection between the antislavery movement and the women's rights movement in the early nineteenth century?

Credits

★ CHAPTER 13
★ HURTLING TOWARD CIVIL WAR, 1844–
★ 1860

The dynamic growth of the American economy in the forty-odd years before the Civil War also led to an irresistible and powerful move to occupy land as far away as the Pacific Ocean. Individual Americans had already helped to separate Texas from Mexico in 1836. By the early 1840s, several thousand land-hungry whites, down on their luck in the East, would begin to move into the joint American-British territory of Oregon, and other whites also began to eye California. For Democrats, as the party of agrarian expansion and the Western "common man," an elaborate justification for empire building came to the fore by 1840 with several writers (most famously John L. O'Sullivan) who began to refer to a "Manifest Destiny" for American westward expansion. These expansionists believed that the United States represented a superior civilization, one that was far more robust and vital than other powers, and therefore the most able to make the "best use" of Western land. Never mind that other countries and native tribes claimed it, these entities should fall back and assent to the power of American democracy to bring schools, productive farms, and representative government to new parts of North America, according to these American imperialists. This expansionist mantra found a powerful representative in James K. Polk, the relatively obscure Democratic governor of Tennessee, who believed that the United States should strike boldly for territorial growth. Polk received the nomination in the deadlocked Democratic convention of 1844, which badly wanted to annex Texas in order get the ball rolling for the westward push (Martin Van Buren, the leading contender for the White House, did not believe in annexation, and was actually quite opposed to slavery in general. This cost him the nomination).

Polk and the Democrats therefore went to great lengths to defend their support for the annexation of Texas on the broad grounds of aiding in America's inexorable expansion to the West, and also reminded voters that Northern climes, where slavery was unlikely to flourish, would also be included in the push for westward expansion. Polk won a very tight election in 1844, arguably because antislavery forces bolted from supporting Henry Clay, the Whig Party candidate, over his more or less unknown stance on Texas. With victory, Polk got down to the business of saber rattling in order to gain all of the Oregon Territory from Great Britain: a dangerous game, given the military power of Britain. Yet Polk's daring move paid off, and Britain agreed to give the United States a large part of the Oregon Territory (present-day Oregon, Washington, and Idaho). With this win, Polk could claim that he was not simply motivated by support for slavery in his annexationist plans, and he was emboldened to take on the tougher issue of possessing what he saw as "all" of Texas from the Mexicans. He launched

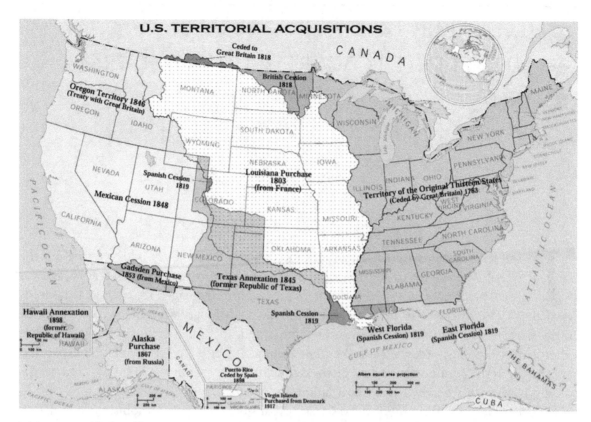

U.S. TERRITORIAL ACQUISITIONS

This map includes the Mexican Cession, which while representing a major victory for the United States in 1848, also helped to cause the Civil War.

unsuccessful diplomatic efforts to buy the territory between the Nueces and Rio Grande rivers, then stationed American troops in the disputed territory, essentially to pick a fight with Mexico. Like many expansionists, Polk felt that the Mexicans were no match for the American army.

In April 1846, the Mexicans had enough of the foreign troops on their soil: they attacked the American detachment; this, in turn, gave Democrats in Congress the pretext to support war. The Mexican-American War saw daring attempts made by young officers (such as Robert E. Lee) to scale the mountains between the Gulf of Mexico and Mexico City, eventually leading to the occupation of the Mexican capital. Meanwhile, in what is now New Mexico and California, American forces eventually overwhelmed local Mexicans and native allies. The Yankees in California briefly declared the "Bear Flag Republic" in 1846, and with the help of American military reinforcements, eventually took control of the territory from San Diego to San Francisco. For its part, Mexico would only agree to surrender to the Americans in return for $15 million in 1848, but the resulting acquisition was seen by many Americans as major victory, of course. This became clear when gold was discovered in Northern California in 1849, which must have been a bitter disappointment to Mexico.

But not unlike the paradoxical results of the Seven Years' War for Britain, this great "victory" for American expansionists over Mexico would set in motion a chain reaction of events, leading to the bloodiest, most destructive war in American history: the Civil War, which nearly destroyed the United States. For those who opposed slavery, the Mexican cession represented a poison pill. This is because by the late 1840s, the free states and the slave states had grown even further apart than where they were during the so-called Missouri Compromise of 1820. (Recall that the compromise, over the status of slavery in the Louisiana Purchase, had even in its own time revealed the sensitivity of both sections to one or the other gaining a majority in Congress.) On the one hand, a growing antislavery movement in the North, emboldened by the abolition of slavery in Great Britain and most parts of Latin America, felt that the spirit of the age demanded that no compromise be made with slavery. On the other hand, Southern cotton planters were more attached, not less, to a cotton crop, whose price continued to sky-rocket in value in the years after 1840. Such Southerners, such as James Henry Hammond, referred to "King Cotton" as the key to continued prosperity and upward mobility for millions of whites. Such men were not going to sit back and watch politicians legislate away their right to take their human beings wherever they pleased. In this way, the opening up of such a vast new territory to discussions regarding slavery's future forced slavery to the top of the agenda in national politics, even though every major politician had sought to suppress or ignore the issue for decades. In many ways, the propensity of Americans to push open new land for settle-ment, and not to be content with the land they already had, foreordained some sort of violent conflict, because slavery cannot be maintained without force, and too many Northerners—in the end—balked at Southern demands to use government, police, or military power to sustain slavery in new territories.

Sectional trouble emerged during the Mexican War itself, when an antislavery Democrat, David Wilmot, introduced his "proviso" that no territory gained from Mexico should allow slavery. This proviso outraged Southerners, even though no such prohibition went into effect. But when California voted to come into the Union as a free state in 1850, the resulting imbal-ance in Congress in favor of free states led to renewed sectional strife. If California and Oregon came in as free states (which they eventually did), there would be a solid non-slaveholding majority in Congress when it came time for presidential elections (this would prove decisive in electing Abraham Lincoln in 1860). Many Southern whites revealed how sensitive they were over losing power in the government by protesting the entire state of California being admitted as a free state. These Southerners instead wanted the old Missouri Compromise line extended to include Southern California as a pro-slave region, and threatened to secede if their rights were not respected. Meanwhile in Washington, D.C., Henry Clay cobbled together a series of bills designed to paper over the controversy caused by California's admission as a free state—the so-called "Compromise of 1850." But this compromise was nothing of the sort: using a legisla-tive technique where five separate majorities were found to pass five separate bills, Clay gained enough votes for his "compromise." However, if all aspects of the Compromise had been voted on together, the bill would have failed. And the "compromise" did nothing to assuage the growing numbers of hard-liners on each side: for example, many Southerners wanted some slavery in California and New Mexico, but did not get it, whereas many Northerners were shocked that the fugitive slave law would be strengthened, thus potentially allowing for the enslavement of thousands of Northern freed blacks. Indeed, given that there had been more Northerners (usually in the Democratic party) willing to compromise with Southerners than vice versa, the emerging story of the 1850s was that of increasing numbers of whites from free states becoming unwilling to vote with Southerners on compromise bills; soon enough the free state majority would decide that the territories would be free of slavery.

The growing furor in the North over the fugitive slave law arose because, under the terms of this new fugitive slave law passed with the "compromise" of 1850, Southern courts simply adjudicated the identity of the supposed "runaway" slave in question described by the owner, and this document was binding on the rest of the country. Northerners who defended these slaves from attempts to take them back into slavery would go to jail, and any white asked by authorities was forced to help in the efforts at re-enslavement. Resistance to the bill was, understandably, enormous in the free states. The most famous example of civil disobedience against the fugitive slave bill surrounded a former slave in Boston, Anthony Burns. When Burns was forcibly re-enslaved by federal marshals, he ignited a firestorm of protest that included rioters killing two of Burns' prison guards. In response, Democratic president Franklin Pierce decided to spend $100,000 to send in a marine regiment, simply to escort Burns out of Boston. Along the way, protesters hung American flags upside down out of a sense of disgust with their nation. The forced re-enslavement of blacks was a central theme in Harriet Beecher Stowe's *Uncle Tom's Cabin*, which popularized the horrors of slave life through the trials and selfless suffering of the Christlike slave, Uncle Tom. In conjunction with the publication of numerous slave narratives, such as the one written by Frederick Douglass in the 1840s, Northern abolitionists slowly "abolitionized" public opinion among whites who might otherwise have remained unfamiliar with slave life or black people.

Into this already testy situation, 1854 saw Senator Stephen A. Douglas' proposal to build a transcontinental railroad and his resulting proposition that slavery could be made legal in what remained of the old Louisiana Purchase. The need for the railroad was real, since the United States now stretched to the Pacific (Douglas, of course, wanted the railroad to go through his state of Illinois), and the railroad could not be built in unorganized territory. But Southerners saw little need to support an internal improvement aiding free states, in addition to their customary suspicion of both increased federal authority and federal spending projects overall. As a result, in order to get Southerners to sign onto his railroad bill, Douglas offered the possibility that the new states to be formed in anticipation of the railroad might vote for themselves to accept slavery. Douglas referred to this as "popular sovereignty." This was in direct violation of the terms of the Missouri Compromise, however, which had forbidden slavery in most of the Louisiana Purchase. It now seemed to concerned Northerners that slavery might spread north into areas where it had been previously blocked. Douglas's Kansas-Nebraska Bill was the first sign of large-scale Northern revolt against giving in to the demands of Southerners, though enough Northerners voted with the Southerners (who as always presented a far more unified front than their free-state counterparts) that the bill passed. But the damage was done. Within six months of the passage of the Kansas-Nebraska Bill, numerous meetings throughout the free states—especially in areas sympathetic to evangelical Protestant reform—coalesced behind a new party, the Republican Party, dedicated to stopping the extension of slavery in any territory. Although there had been two very minor abolitionist parties before the Republicans (the Liberty Party and Free Soil Party), this new antislavery party threatened to attain broad appeal. By 1856, the Republican Party had more or less supplanted the defunct Whig Party, though there was still lingering competition from the anti-immigrant American Party for the support of Northern Protestants. But the furor over the Kansas-Nebraska Bill created one of the quickest transitions to a new major political party in American history. To avoid breaking up the Union, politicians would have to find some way to convince Americans that slavery did not matter—that Southerners should not be afraid of losing out in the drive to spread slavery west, or that Northerners should not be concerned about national support for aspects of the slave system, such as the Fugitive Slave Act. This proved to be impossible.

The increased sectional animosity of the mid-1850s in fact led to a miniature civil war in the Kansas territory by 1855. Although Stephen Douglas hoped that American settlers in Kansas would peacefully decide the issue of slavery at the ballot box, he could not have been more wrong. Frontier settlers instead solved the issue with guns. Too many Americans

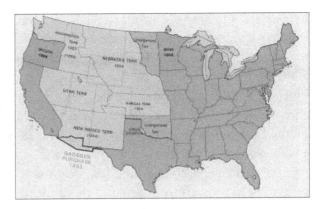

The Kansas-Nebraska Act of 1854.

had been polarized by the events of the last few years, and thousands of partisans—whether in favor of slavery or not—descended upon Kansas in an effort to influence the outcome of the state constitution and therefore the future of human bondage in that territory. Most historians blame the "border ruffians" as the instigators of the conflict. These people were proslavery Missourians who simply crossed their state's Western border and used violence to suppress the antislavery vote in Kansas. But the result of such antislavery voter suppression simply led to the existence of two separate capitals in Kansas: Lecompton for the proslavery forces, Lawrence for the antislavery ones, since neither side would accept the legitimacy of elections they felt were fraudulent. With time, the violence continued to escalate during this standoff: in May of 1856 an army of proslavery Missourians marched on the antislavery capital of Lawrence, shelling and sacking it. In response, an antislavery settler named John Brown led a raid on a proslavery settlement and butchered five men in the middle of the night. Meanwhile, on the floor of the U.S. Senate, an outraged Southern congressman, Preston Brooks, attacked and nearly killed antislavery Senator Charles Sumner for insulting the honor of his relative, Senator Andrew Butler (Sumner said Butler had "chosen" the "harlot" slavery when defending proslavery actions in Kansas). Soon enough, many members of Congress came armed with knives, guns, and more canes expecting the violence in Kansas to overtake the nation's capital. By 1859, Southerners openly threatened a mass shootout on the floor of the House, coupled with reinforcements of troops to the Capitol from South Carolina if John Sherman, a Northern antislavery Republican, was chosen as a "compromise" candidate for the speaker of the House position (no one party had a majority of the seats after the 1858 elections).

Other events further pushed the country toward warfare over the slavery issue. One, the proslavery Supreme Court's ruling in the Dred Scott case, epitomized the Southern attitude that slave owners should be able to take their human property wherever they pleased, and that the federal government should protect them when so doing. Dred Scott was a slave taken into free territory in Wisconsin, after which time he sued for his freedom. Led by Roger Taney, and with the tacit approval of Democratic president James Buchanan, the Supreme Court ruled that slaves were private property that could be taken anywhere their owner desired: Taney made the infamous quip that a "black man has no rights which a white man was bound to respect" when composing his decision. Besides the Dred Scott case, the Buchanan administration also decided to back the fraudulent "Lecompton Constitution" in Kansas, a document drafted without the support of the antislavery majority, but one which Southerners wanted to latch onto as proof that Kansas was theirs for slavery. Buchanan caved in and sent the Lecompton constitution to Congress for approval. But Northern Democrats, led by Stephen Douglas, would not go along. This was a momentous step, one that would eventually signal the breakup of the Democratic Party, which in turn led to the Republicans taking the White House in 1860. When the vote on the Lecompton constitution was finally taken in 1858, it was defeated, though it would be a while yet before Kansas would come into the Union as a free state.

And so the pendulum swung decisively toward antislavery Northerners, with the rejection of the Lecompton constitution and the impending breakup of the Democratic Party. Then, as it has been said, a meteor hit the United States in the person of John Brown. The former Kansas settler had now turned his sights on bigger battles, having organized a group of men to take over the federal arsenal of Harper's Ferry, Virginia, with the intention of leading an armed uprising of slaves throughout the South. He failed miserably in the execution of his plan in October 1859, but during his trial the damning news came out that perhaps as many as several hundred Northern abolitionists had been behind this attempted slave revolt. Although Southerners were able to execute Brown, they now lived in constant fear of slave uprisings and began organizing militias in preparation for war. And Southerners had had enough with Northerners, who they believed were basically hostile to their "way of life"—meaning the Southern economic system based squarely on chattel slavery. It is not an exaggeration to say that John Brown's attempted slave revolt was to the Civil War what the Coercive Acts were to the American Revolution—it really represented a point of no return for two sides possessing irreconcilable differences.

The election of 1860, which sent the Republican Abraham Lincoln to the White House, could almost be considered a fait accompli after Brown's raid. In this context of hyper-Southern fear, the Democratic presidential nominating convention, held in Charleston, South Carolina, saw Southerners demand a federal slave code plank for the protection of their property anywhere in the country (essentially a combination of the ideas of the Dred Scott case and Lecompton). Northern Democrats could not stand for this. The plank did not pass, and several Southerners walked out of the convention. The convention ended after 57 ballots. The Democrats reconvened in Baltimore later in the summer, where an even larger number of Southerners walked out, leading to the nomination of Buchanan's vice president, John Breckenridge. The "regular" Democrats left behind in Baltimore nominated Stephen Douglas—the man who still insisted that "popular sovereignty" (leaving the slavery issue up to territorial voters) could peacefully resolve the slavery issue in the territories (exactly how was, of course, unknown.) A third splinter group of former Southern Whigs who did not like Democrats but feared Republicans nominated John Bell of Tennessee.

By 1860, popular sovereignty had been revealed as a disaster in Kansas, and most Northerners by that time were shocked that Southerners would demand their property be defended throughout the entire country, even in free states. With Democrats and Southerners largely discredited in the free states over the policies of Senator Douglas and the Buchanan administration, the only real question would be which Republican would become the next president, since the free states possessed the majority of votes in the Electoral College. For their part, the Republicans turned to Abraham Lincoln, a once obscure Illinois congressmen who made a name for himself in 1858 running against and debating Stephen Douglas for

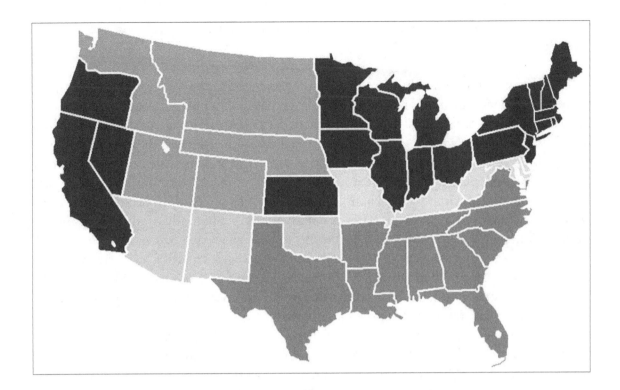

The Union, Confederacy, and Border States, in 1860. The eleven states of the Confederacy are shown in dark orange. The border states are in yellow, and free states in blue.

the Senate in Illinois. Although Lincoln lost the Senate contest in 1858, he had garnered Northern attention by criticizing Douglas' indifference to the moral issue of slavery—it was in these debates, for example, that Lincoln remarked how a "house divided against itself cannot stand," in reference to the pressing need for resolution of the slavery issue—regardless of the consequences. Most Republican leaders saw Lincoln as an ideal candidate because many found him less controversial than the better known William Seward (Seward had a reputation as a stronger abolitionist and anti-nativist than Lincoln.) Thus the party turned toward Lincoln, and without his name even on the ballot in the slave states, Lincoln won, because he carried every single free state in the Electoral College. But his popular vote total—at a mere 39.9 percent—has remained one of the lowest in U.S history for a victorious President. Southerners would not accept the outcome of this election, and many began plotting secession from the Union.

Documents:

1. "John L. O'Sullivan on Texas Annexation and Manifest Destiny" (1845)

In 1837, O'Sullivan helped to found the United States Magazine and Democratic Review, a journal dedicated not only to supporting the Democratic Party, but also devoted to publishing top-rate literature by such authors as Nathaniel Hawthorne and Walt Whitman. O'Sullivan helped to coin the term "Manifest Destiny," thus reflecting the confident nationalism and expansionist agenda of the Democratic Party.

It is wholly untrue, and unjust to ourselves, the pretence that the Annexation [of Texas] has been a measure of spoliation, unrightful and unrighteous—of military conquest under forms of peace and law—of territorial aggrandizement at the expense of justice, and justice due by a double sanctity to the weak. ... If Texas became peopled with an American population, it was by no contrivance of our government, but on the express invitation of that of Mexico herself ... [Texas] was released, rightfully and absolutely released, from all Mexican allegiance, or duty of cohesion to the Mexican political body, by the acts and fault of Mexico herself, and Mexico alone. There never was a clearer case. It was not revolution ... but rather resistance caused by the abandonment of those with whom her former federal association had existed. ...

Imbecile and distracted, Mexico never can exert any real governmental authority over such a country [as her Northern territories]. ... In the case of California this is now impossible. The Anglo-Saxon foot is already on its borders. Already the advance guard of the irresistible army of Anglo-Saxon emigration has begun to pour down upon it, armed with the plough and the rifle, and marking its trail with schools and colleges, courts and representative halls, mills and meetinghouses. ... All this without agency of our government, without responsibility of our people—in the natural flow of events, the spontaneous working of principles, and the adaptation of the tendencies and wants of the human race to the elemental circumstances in the midst of which they find themselves placed. And they will have a right to independence—to self-government ...

2. Henry David Thoreau, *Civil Disobedience* (1846)

As part of the Transcendentalist movement, Thoreau developed radical critiques of traditional sources of authority and flirted with anarchistic thinking throughout much of his life. His views on the Mexican War demonstrated how a growing number of whites in the free states began to see the U.S. government's efforts to expand to the West as defending the interests of slaveholders.

... Can there not be a government in which majorities do not virtually decide right and wrong, but conscience. ... Must the citizen ever for a moment, or in the least degree resign his conscience to the legislator? Why has every man a conscience, then? I think that we should be men first, and subjects afterward. ... There are thousands who are in opinion opposed to slavery and to the war, who yet in effect do nothing to put an end to them; who, esteeming themselves children of Washington or Franklin, sit down with their hands in their pockets, and say that they know not what to do, and do nothing; who even postpone the question of freedom to the question of free trade and quietly read the prices-current [stock prices] along with the latest news from Mexico, and, ... then fall asleep. What is the price-current of an honest man and patriot today? ... I hesitate to say, that those who call themselves Abolitionists should once effectually withdraw their support, both in person and in property, from the government of Massachusetts, and not wait till they constitute a majority ... I think that it is enough if they have God on their side. ...

3. Senator John C. Calhoun, "Proposal to Preserve the Union" (1850)

It is important to contrast Calhoun's views on slavery and westward expansion with the above quote from Thoreau. Calhoun delivered this speech during debates over the so-called "Compromise of 1850," which many historians more accurately refer to simply as the "Truce of 1850."

I have, Senators, believed from the first that the agitation of the subject of slavery would … end in disunion. … the Union is in danger. … [And one of the causes for this] is undoubtedly to be traced to the long-continued agitation of the slave question on the part of the North, and the many aggressions which they have made on the rights of the South during that time … [and now] the great equilibrium between the two sections has been destroyed. … The great increase of Senators, added to the great increase of the House of Representatives and the electoral college on the part of the North, which must take place in the next decade, will effectually and irretrievably destroy the equilibrium which existed when this Government was created. … As the North has the absolute control over the Government, it is manifest that on all questions between it and the South … that the interests of the latter will be sacrificed to the former, however oppressive the effects may be … How can the Union be saved? To this I answer there is but one way by which it can be, and that is be adopting such measures as will satisfy the States belonging to the Southern section that they can remain in the Union consistently with their honor and their safety.

4. Frederick Douglass, Fourth of July Oration (1852)

This oration was delivered by the famous former slave and abolitionist lecturer at a time when even many free blacks in the North felt unsafe in the United States, since under the terms of the strengthened Fugitive Slave Act, blacks had little ability to contest a slave owner's attempt to sell them back into slavery.

Fellow citizens, pardon me, allow me to ask, why am I called upon to speak here today? What have I, or those [black] people I represent to do with your national independence? … I am not included within the pale of glorious anniversary! Your high independence only reveals the immeasurable distance [between white and black Americans] … The rich inheritance of justice, liberty, prosperity, and independence, bequeathed by your fathers, is shared by you, not by me. The sunlight that brought light and healing to you, has brought striped and death to me. His Fourth [of] July is yours, not mine. … Go where you may, search where you will, roam through all the monarchies and despotisms of the Old World, travel through South America, search out every abuse and when you have found the last, lay your facts by the side of the everyday practices of this nation, and you will say with me, that, for revolting barbarity and shameless hypocrisy, America reigns without rival.

5. Harriet Beecher Stowe, *Uncle Tom's Cabin* (1852)

As one of the best-selling novels of the nineteenth century, Stowe's novel reached countless readers, especially in the North. The book enraged Southerners because of its portrayal of the brutality and injustice of slavery. It is not an understatement to say that Stowe's book helped to move Northern whites away from further compromise with Southerners on slavery, and therefore put the country that much closer to civil war.

"And now," said Legree, "come here, you Tom. You see, I telled ye I didn't buy ye jest for the common work. I mean to promote ye, and make a [slave] driver of ye, and tonight ye may just as well begin to get ye hand in. Now ye just take this yer gal and flog her; ye've seen enough of it to know how." "I beg Mas'r' pardon," said Tom; "hopes Mas'r won't set me at that. It's what I an't used to—never did—and can't do, no way possible."

Ye'll larn a pretty smart chance of things ye never did know, before I've done with ye!" said Legree, taking up the whip and striking Tom a heavy blow across the cheek, and following up the infliction by a shower of blows.

"There!" he said, as he stopped to rest; "now will ye tell me ye can't do it?"

"Yes, Mas'r," said Tom, putting up his hand, to wipe the blood that trickled own his face. "I'm willing to work, night and day, and work while there's life and breath in me. But this yer thing I can't feel it right to do; and Mas'r, I never shall do it—never! …

Legree looked stupefied and confounded; but at last burst forth: "What! Ye blasted black beast! Tell me ye don't think it right to do what I tell ye! What have any of you cussed cattle to do with thinking what's right? I'll put a stop to it! Why what do ye think ye are? May be ye think ye're a gentleman, master Tom, to be a telling your master what's right, and what ain't! So you pretend it's wrong to flog the gal!"

"I think so Mas'r" said Tom; "the poor crittur's sick and feeble; 'twould be downright cruel, and it's what I never will do, nor begin to. Mas'r, if you mean to kill me, kill me; but, as to my raising my hand against any one here, I never shall—I'll die first! …

"Well here's a pious dog, at last let down among us sinners—a saint, a gentlemen, and no less, to talk to us sinners about our sins! Powerful holy crittur, he must be! Here, you rascal, you make believe to be so pious—didn't you near hear, out of yer Bible, 'Servants, obey' yer masters? An't I yer master? Didn't I pay down twelve hundred dollars, cash, for all there is inside yer old cussed black shell? An't yer mine, now, body and soul?" he said giving Tom a violent kick with his heavy boot; "tell me!"

In the very depth of physical suffering, bowed by brutal oppression, this question shot a gleam of joy and triumph through Tom's soul. He suddenly stretched himself up, and, looking earnestly to heaven, while the tears and blood that flowed down his face mingled, he exclaimed, "No! no! no! my soul ain't yours, Mas'r! You haven't bought it—ye can't buy it! It's been bought and paid for by the One that is able to keep it. No matter, no matter, you can't harm me!"

6. Senator Stephen Douglas Explains the Objectives of His Bill (February 1854)

In this speech before the senate, Douglas communicates his belief that the ballot box would be able to peacefully resolve the issue of slavery in the territories. It is important to understand why Douglas was proved wrong by the events of the mid- and late 1850s.

The bill provides in words as specific and unequivocal as our language affords, that the true intent and meaning of the act is NOT to legislate slavery into any Territory or State. … "Non-intervention by Congress with slavery in the States and Territories" is expressly declared to be the principle upon which the bill is constructed. The great fundamental principle of self-government, which authorizes the people to regulate their won domestic concerns, as recognized in the Compromise measure of 1850, and affirmed by the Democratic National convention, and reaffirmed by the Whig convention at Baltimore, is declared in this bill to be the rule of action in the formation of territorial governments. The two great political parties of the country are solemnly pledged to a strict adherence to this principle as a final settlement of the slavery agitation. ...

The cry for the extension of slavery has been raised for mere party purposes by the abolition confederates and disappointed office-seekers. All candid men who understand the subject admit that the laws of climate, and production, and of physical geography ... have excluded slavery from that country. ... [A]ll candid and intelligent men make the same admission, and present the naked question as a matter of principle, whether the people shall be allowed to regulate their domestic concerns in their own way or not. In conclusion, I may be permitted to add, that the Democratic party, as well as the country, have a deep interest in this manner. Is our party to be again divided and rent asunder upon this vexed question of slavery?

7.   Letter from Axalla John Hoole, Kansas resident, to his sister (1857)

The following excerpts from a letter by proslavery settler of Kansas directly relate to the previous document from Douglas about the ability of Americans to peacefully vote slavery up or down in the West.

I fear, Sister, that coming here will do no good at last, as I begin to think that this will be made a Free State at last. 'Tis true we have elected Proslavery men to draft a state constitution, but I feel pretty certain, if it is put to the vote of the people, it will be rejected, as they have the majority here at this time. The South has ceased all efforts, while the North is redoubling her exertions. ... One of our most staunch Proslavery men was killed in Leavensworth a few days ago ... [According to some] the man who was killed (Jas Lyle) went up to the polls and asked for a ticket [to vote]. An abolitionist handed him one which he, Lyle, tore in two. The other asked him he had better not do so again, when Lyle ... [asked for another]. It was given him, and he tore it also, at which the Abolitionist drew a bowie knife and stabbed Lyle to the heart, then ran a few paces, drew a revolver, and commenced firing a the dying man. The fellow was taken prisoner ... and Governor Walker put out for Leavensworth on Friday to have the prisoner carried to the fort, in order to keep the Abolitionists from rescuing him. ...

8.   Senator Charles Sumner, Speech in the U.S. Senate on the "Crime Against Kansas," (May 1856)

Within days after delivering this speech, one of Senator Butler's relatives, Preston Brooks, assaulted Sumner with a cane while Sumner was at his desk on the floor of the Senate, and badly wounded Sumner. (In this speech. Sumner also ridiculed the speech and mannerisms of the crippled Butler). After the assault, Brooks was reprimanded by the House, resigned his seat, and most members of Congress came to the institution armed. This did not bode well for the future of sectional relations.

You are now called to redress a great transgression. Seldom in the history of nations has such a question been presented. ... It is the rape of a virgin Territory, compelling it to the hateful embrace of Slavery; and it may be clearly traced to a depraved longing for a new slave state, the hideous offspring of such a crime, in the hope of adding to the power of slavery in the National Government. ... I must say something of a general character, particularly in response to what has fallen from Senators who have raised themselves to eminence on this floor in championship of human wrongs. I mean the Senator from South Carolina [Mr. Butler], and the Senator from Illinois [Mr. Douglas]. ... The Senator from South Carolina has read many books of chivalry and believes himself a chivalrous knight, with sentiments of honor and courage. Of course he has chosen a mistress to whom he has made his vows, and who, though ugly to others, is always lovely to him; though polluted in the sight of the world, is chaste in his sight. I mean the harlot, Slavery. ... The Senator from Illinois [Douglas], is the Squire of Slavery, its very Sancho Panza, ready to do all its humiliating offices. ... Standing on this floor ... the Senator required the submission of this body to the usurped power of Kansas ... The Senator, with the slave power at his back is strong; but he is not strong enough for this purpose ... [For] against him are stronger battalions than any marshaled by mortal arm: the inborn, ineradicable, invincible sentiments of the human heart against him is nature in all her subtle forces; against him is God. Let him try to subdue these.

9. Roger Taney, Dred Scott v. Sanford (1857)

The decision in Dred Scott was written by Taney after a 7–2 vote in favor of it. At least five of the justices of the Supreme Court, like Taney, at one time had been slaveholders.

It is difficult at this day to realize the state of public opinion in relation to that unfortunate race, which prevailed in the civilized and enlightened portions of the world at the time of the Declaration of Independence, and when the Constitution of the United States was framed and adopted. But the public history of every European nation displays it in a manner too plain to be mistaken. They [African Americans] had for more than a century been regarded as being of an inferior order, and altogether unfit to associate with the white race, either in social or political relations; and so far inferior, that they had no rights which the white man was bound to respect; and that the negro might justly and lawfully be reduced to slavery for his benefit ... There are two clauses of the Constitution which point directly to the negro race as a separate class of persons, and show clearly that they were not regarded as a portion of the people or citizens of the Government then formed.

10. Excerpts from "The Lincoln–Douglas Debates" (1858)

Although the young former congressman from Illinois ultimately lost his bid for Senate, the performance of Abraham Lincoln in these debates catapulted him to national prominence and played a large role in his nomination by the Republicans in 1860.

Stephen Douglas's opening comments: Mr. Lincoln here says that our government cannot endure permanently in the same condition in which it was made by its framers. It was made divided into free States and slave States. Mr. Lincoln says it has existed for near eighty years thus divided; but he tells you that it cannot endure permanently on the same principles and in the same conditions relatively in which your fathers made it. Why can't it endure divided into free and slave States? ... Our fathers knew when they made this government that in a country as wide and broad as this with such a variety of climate, of interests, of productions ... that the people necessarily required different local laws and local institutions in certain localities from those in other localities. ... I therefore say that uniformity in the local laws and local legislations of the different states was neither possible nor desirable. ... Now, I ask you, are you in favor of conferring upon the negro the rights and privileges of citizenship? Do you desire to strike out of our State Constitution that clause which keeps slaves and free negroes *out* of the State, and allow the free negro to flow in? ... I believe that this government was made by white men for the benefit of white men and their posterity forever, and I am in favor of confirming the citizenship to white men—men of European birth and European descent, instead of conferring it upon Negroes and Indians, and other inferior races.

Abraham Lincoln's reply: Let me say I think I have no prejudice against the Southern people. They are just what we would be in their situation. If slavery did not now exist amongst them, they would not introduce it. If it did now exist amongst us, we should not instantly give it up ... When it is said that the institution of slavery exists and it is very difficult to get rid of ... I can understand and appreciate the saying. I surely will not blame them for not doing what I should not know how to do myself. My first impulse would be to free all the slaves, and send them to Liberia—to their own native land. But a moment's reflection would convince me, that whatever high hope there may be in this in the long run, its sudden execution is impossible. ...

I have no purpose to directly or indirectly interfere with the institution of slavery in the states where it exists ... I do have disposition to introduce political and social equality between the white and black races. There is a physical difference between the two, which in my judgment will probably forever forbid their living together on terms of respect, social and political equality, and ... I am in favor of the race to which I belong having the superior position. ...

But all this to my judgment furnishes no more excuse for permitting slavery to go into our own free territory, than it would for reviving the African slave trade by law. The law which forbids the bringing of slaves from Africa and that which has so long forbid the taking of them to Nebraska, can hardly be distinguished on any moral principle ... When he [Douglas] is saying that the negro has no share in the Declaration of Independence, he is going back to the year of our revolution, and, to the extent of his ability, he is muzzling the cannon that thunders its annual joyous return ... When he says that he don't care whether slavery is voted up or voted down, then, to my thinking, he is, so far as he is able to do so, perverting the human soul and eradicating the light of reason and the love of liberty on the American continent.

11. John Brown, "Last Statement to the Virginia Court" (1859)

The fact that Brown had received support from Northern abolitionists made his attempted raid at Harper's Ferry, Virginia, all the more alarming to Southerners, and increased their paranoia regarding Northern efforts to ruin their way of life.

I intended certainly to have made a clean thing of that matter, as I did last winter, when I went into Missouri and there took slaves without the snapping of a gun on either side, moving them through the country, and finally leaving them in Canada. I designed to have done the same thing again on a larger scale. That was all I intended. I never did intend murder, or treason, or the destruction of property, or to exercise or incite slaves to rebellion. ...

This Court acknowledges ... I suppose, the validity of the law of God. I see a book kissed, which I suppose to be the Bible, or at least the New Testament, which teached me that all things whatsoever I would that men should do to me, I should do even so to them. I endeavored to at up to that instruction. I say I am yet too young to understand that God is any respecter of persons. I believe that to have interfered as I have done, as I have always freely admitted I have done, in behalf of His despised poor, I did no wrong, but right. Now, if it is deemed necessary that I should forfeit my life for the furtherance of the ends of justice, and mingle my blood further with the blood of my children and with the blood of millions in this slave country whose rights are disregarded by wicked, cruel, unjust exactments, I say, let it be done. ... I feel no consciousness of guilt. I have stated from the first what was my intention, and what was not. I never had any design against the liberty of any person, nor any disposition to commit treason or incite slaves to rebel or make any general insurrection. I never encouraged any man to do so, but always discouraged any idea of that kind.

12. "Prospects of Slavery Expansion," the *Charleston Mercury* (February 1860)

It is important to compare the statements made below regarding the sanctity of Southern property held in slaves with the views of Brown and other Northerners described above.

The right to have slave property protected in the territory [of Kansas] is not a mere abstraction without application or practical value ... When the gold mines of California were discovered, slaveholders at the South saw that, with their command of labor, it would be easy at a moderate outlay of capital to make fortunes digging gold. The inducements to go there were great, and there was no lack of inclination on their part. But, to make the emigration profitable, it was necessary that the [slave] property of Southern settlers should be safe, otherwise it was plainly a hazardous enterprise ... Few were reckless enough to stake property, the accumulation of years, in a struggle with active prejudices amongst a mixed population ...

What has been the policy pursued in Kansas? Has the territory had a fair chance of becoming a Slave State? Has the principle of equal protection to slave property been carried out by the Government there in any of its departments? On the contrary, has not every appliance been used to thwart the South and expel or prohibit her sons from colonizing there? ...

New Mexico, it is asserted, is too barren and arid for Southern occupation and settlement. ... Now, New Mexico teems with mineral resources. ... There is no vocation in the world in which slavery can be more useful and profitable than in mining. ... We frequently here talk of the future glories of our republican destiny on the continent, and of the spread of our civilization and free institutions over Mexico and the Tropics. Already we have absorbed two of her States, Texas, and California. Is it expected that our onward march is to stop here? Is it not more probable and more philosophic to suppose that, as in the past, so in the future, the Anglo-Saxon race will, in the course of years occupy and absorb the whole of that splendid but ill-peopled country, and to remove by gradual process before them, the worthless mongrel races that now inhabit and curse the land? ... Our people will never sit still and see themselves excluded from all expansion, to please the North. ...

Questions to Consider:

1. How were the free states and slave states more dissimilar in 1860 than they had been in 1780?
2. At what point after 1845 did the Civil War become inevitable? Was the Civil War avoidable?
3. Do you blame politicians or their constituents for the Civil War? Is it fair to say that representative government actually led to a situation where war became unavoidable?
4. What role did civil disobedience play in creating the conditions that made war a possibility?

Credits

- "U.S. Territorial Acquisitions." 1970. Copyright in the Public Domain.
- "The Kansas-Nebraska Act of 1854."
- "The Union, Confederacy, and Border States, in 1860."
- John L. O'Sullivan, "John L. O'Sullivan on Texas Annexation and Manifest Destiny," *The United States Magazine and Democratic Review*, vol. 17, p. 6. 1845. Copyright in the Public Domain.
- Excerpt from Henry David Thoreau, *On the Duty of Civil Disobedience*. 1846. Copyright in the Public Domain.
- John C. Calhoun, "Proposal to Preserve the Union," Congressional Globe, 31st Congress, 1st Session, vol. 22, pp. 451-455. 1850. Copyright in the Public Domain.
- Excerpt from Frederick Douglass, *What to the Slave is the Fourth of July?* 1852. Copyright in the Public Domain.
- Excerpt from Harriet Beecher Stowe, *Uncle Tom's Cabin*. 1852. Copyright in the Public Domain.
- Excerpt from Stephen Douglas, Letter of Senator Douglas in Reply to the Editor of the *State Capitol Reporter*, p. 6. 1854. Copyright in the Public Domain.
- Excerpt from Axalla John Hoole, "A Letter Dated November 2, 1856," *The Kansas Historical Quarterly*, vol. 3. 1934. Copyright in the Public Domain.
- Excerpt from Charles Sumner, The Crime Against Kansas: Speech of Hon. Charles Sumner. 1856. Copyright in the Public Domain.
- Excerpt from Roger Taney, "Opinion by Chief Justice Taney," Dred Scott v. Sanford. 1857. Copyright in the Public Domain.
- Excerpts from Stephen Douglas, "The Lincoln–Douglas Debates." 1858. Copyright in the Public Domain.
- John Brown, "Last Statement to the Virginia Court," Address of John Brown to the Virginia Court. 1859. Copyright in the Public Domain.
- "Prospects of Slavery Expansion," *Charleston Mercury*. 1860. Copyright in the Public Domain.

★ CHAPTER 14
★ THE "SECOND AMERICAN REVOLUTION":
★ THE CIVIL WAR, 1861–1865

The election of Abraham Lincoln set off a firestorm of protest in many parts of the Deep South. Nowhere was this opposition stronger or more forceful than in South Carolina, where the state almost immediately seceded from the United States, in December 1860. By February, six more states followed, while Lincoln was not yet even in office (at the time, presidents were not inaugurated until March). In the meantime, President Buchanan did little to threaten war to stop the seceding states, and other politicians lamely tried to revive the same or similar compromise measures from the 1850s. Increasingly, Republicans such as Lincoln came to the realization that the Union must defend its interests and let the chips fall where they may. When Lincoln came into office, events soon focused on one of the few remaining manned federal arsenals in Confederate territory, Fort Sumter in the harbor of Charleston, South Carolina. Determined to defend Fort Sumter as a symbol of his intentions to keep the Union together, Lincoln followed through on his threat to restock the fort, after which the South Carolinians shelled it in April 1861. Able to claim that federal interests were now under attack, Lincoln responded to the shelling of Fort Sumter by calling up the Union militias. The Civil War had begun. In response, four more states, Virginia, Arkansas, Tennessee, and North Carolina seceded, bringing the total to eleven states now forming the Confederacy. In most respects, the government of the Confederacy resembled that of the United States. But the constitution of the Confederacy now recognized the legitimacy of slavery, and made several laws prohibiting higher tariffs or taxation for internal improvements—both issues Southern agrarians had long disliked in Northern tax policy.

In most economic and demographic respects, the Confederacy possessed considerable disadvantages when compared against the Union: fewer people, fewer factories, fewer banks, fewer railroads, even lower crop yields for things such as wheat, corn, and cows, since so much of Southern agriculture focused on cotton. In addition, the Civil War came to be known as the first modern war, where industrial might, coupled with new technologies such as railroads, telegraph lines, more deadly artillery, and ironclad submarines, would all play deciding roles in the eventual Union victory, since the Union overwhelmed the Confederacy in terms of industrial or manufacturing power. But the Confederacy did possess two advantages: a strong military culture, and the fact that they were fighting on home ground. That the Union Army would have to march south and make its foe surrender meant that the Confederacy was theoretically fighting a guerrilla war similar to the American Revolution. If the Confederacy could hold out long enough, wear down Northern resolve, or win enough battles, they could force a truce with the Union.

There were primarily two theaters in the Civil War: one in the East focusing on Virginia and the Confederate capital of Richmond, the other in the West concentrating on the fight for control of the Mississippi River, and therefore the easiest way to take the deep South and Atlanta, arguably the Confederacy's most important city after Richmond. In the East, the Union armies floundered for lack of effective leadership. But in the West, led by men like Ulysses S. Grant and William Tecumseh Sherman, the Union developed a pulverizing war machine that would eventually break the back of the Confederacy, while also emancipating slaves and using many of them as soldiers. The earliest, bloodiest battle occurred nearly a year into the fighting at the Battle of Shiloh in Tennessee, where Grant continued his relatively successful push south down the Tennessee, Cumberland, and then Mississippi rivers. At this battle in April 1862, both sides suffered 24,000 combined casualties (dead, missing, and wounded). This battle signaled the beginning of a process begun by the Union, where troops would simply be thrown at the Confederacy, something that became part of the "total war" strategy.

But not all of Lincoln's generals embraced this concept of total war—far from it. In Virginia, for example, General George McClellan repeatedly refused to pursue his main opponent, Robert E. Lee, or to adequately fight him during the so-called "Peninsular Campaign" during June and July of 1862. McClellan then found himself forced to retreat from taking territory south of Richmond by sea. By his actions, McClellan revealed his fundamental conservatism regarding the war in which he was engaged: he was a Democrat, he did not believe in emancipation, and he hoped to somehow bring the Confederacy back into the Union without angering them by fighting too hard. By the fall of 1862, Robert E. Lee was striking boldly to the north, within shouting distance of Washington, D.C., largely due to the bumbling and slow maneuvering of McClellan. Only when he accidentally received Lee's plans for battle around Antietam, Maryland, did McClellan begin to attack Lee with any determination, but then the Union general failed to pursue and destroy Lee's army when given the chance. For this, Lincoln removed McClellan and more importantly, signaled that the gloves were coming off, as it were, when it came to dealing with the South: now the Union would use slaves against their masters in an all-out attempt to crush the Confederacy as 1863 dawned.

The decision by Lincoln to emancipate slaves in areas still in rebellion did not end the war, but it laid the foundations for victory. Lincoln's decision to support abolition also transformed the Civil War into what has aptly been termed "the Second American Revolution." This is because by offering freedom to slaves, as well as by offering military service to African Americans, Lincoln and the Republicans both destroyed the "private property" held in other human beings, while also implying that African Americans did indeed have rights a white man was bound to respect (to paraphrase the exact opposite sentiment made in the Dred Scott case). On this last point, of course, full equality was not achieved for African Americans in many respects until the twentieth century (and in many ways still does not exist), but change was coming nonetheless. In terms of military power, the use of some 180,000 black troops likely helped end the war that much sooner, if not being a major reason for Union victory. Besides the use of former slaves, the Union military increasingly adopted the idea of waging a "total war" on the Confederacy simply by throwing thousands and thousands of troops at the enemy, besides the economic infrastructure, which enabled secession to occur.

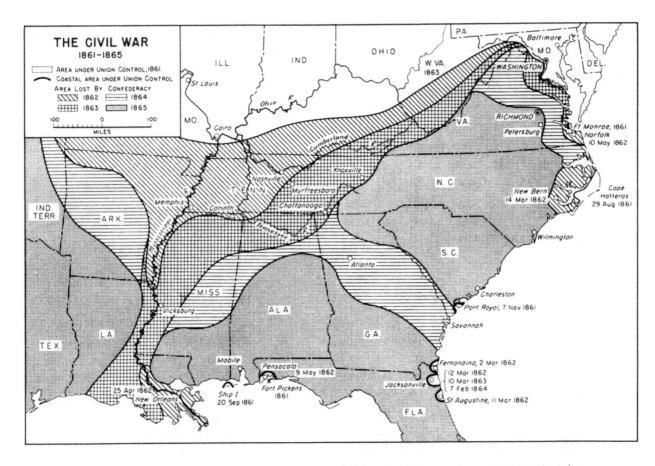

THE CIVIL WAR
1861–1865

☐ Area under Union Control, 1861
⌒ Coastal area under Union Control
Area Lost By Confederacy
▧ 1862   ▭ 1864
▦ 1863   ▤ 1865

100 0 100
MILES

This map depicts the progress of the Union occupation of the Confederacy from 1861–1865. This map reveals how much more successful Union commanders were in the western theater, than in the east.

But the Confederacy was still a force to be reckoned with in 1863, especially when one remembers that many Northerners began to get war weary as the human toll escalated with each new battle. In the Eastern theater not far from Washington, D.C., Stonewall Jackson pushed his army toward the North in May with a stunning victory at the Battle of Chancellorsville. However, Jackson was inadvertently killed by his troops in the battle, which represented a major blow to morale. But Lee's desire for risk did not lessen. By the summer of 1863, Lee decided to take the bold and daring step of invading free-state territory in Pennsylvania, in an attempt to demoralize Northerners and make them think that it would be impossible to conquer the South if they could not properly defend their own free territory. The showdown came at Gettysburg in July 1863, and Lee quite simply sacrificed his men. Lee's suicidal gamble at Pickett's Charge, where 15,000 troops marched up a hill in open sight of Union fire from an elevated position, has been called the "high watermark of the Confederacy." After this disaster, Lee offered his resignation to the president of the Confederacy, Jefferson Davis, but Davis refused. And the bad news kept coming: on July 4, 1863, just one day after Pickett's Charge, word came from Mississippi that Grant had finally taken the one last Confederate stronghold on the Mississippi River, at Vicksburg. Now the Union army was free to penetrate the Deep South, and was that much closer to taking Atlanta.

However, even after these horrible defeats, the Confederates continued to fight. Richmond and Atlanta were still in Confederate hands, and the Union did not yet occupy a majority of Confederate territory. From the Confederate view, there came signs of hope that the average Northerner was tired of the cost of the war, especially in human terms. This can be seen most clearly with the New York Draft Riots, which occurred after the Union victories at Gettysburg and Vicksburg between July 13 and July 16, 1863. The institution of the draft had been deemed necessary by Lincoln as the war went on, but by 1863 many of the men who wanted to volunteer already had done so, with the result that those left behind were likely opposed to various aspects of the Lincoln administration's agenda, particularly on the issue of civil rights for blacks. Among the Irish in New York City—many of whom competed directly with blacks for access to jobs—there was widespread resentment at being called away from home to fight a war few cared for. During the course of the melee in New York, rioters killed scores of black people, they attacked an orphanage for colored children, and forced the government to call in Union soldiers to quell the violence. The effort to suppress the riot included artillery fire, which only increased the death toll among the rioters. The Draft Riots, then, revealed a broader change in Northern public opinion from 1863 through 1864, where various aspects of Lincoln's policies came under intense criticism. As commander in chief, Lincoln had suspended habeas corpus for people he suspected of being Confederate sympathizers, and his party not only liberated slaves, but also used its power in Congress (since the Democrats lost many seats to seceding Southern states) to advance many aspects of a large-government agenda. Such long-term projects as spending for more public colleges, giving away Western land (the so-called Homestead Act), in addition to more spending on railroads, a national banking system, and the creation of a new, centralized currency (the "greenback") were all accomplishments of these activist Republican politicians. These pro-business, pro-industrial, pro-federal government policies deeply disturbed many Northern conservatives, in addition to their distaste for the costs of war. By 1864, the so-called "Peace Democrats" threatened to take control of the Union government, and it was possible (though we will never know) that the Democrats would have ended the war before the Confederacy had been defeated. (Though even by this point, one wonders how slavery would have been sustained given all of the emancipations that had taken place.)

Given the growing opposition to Lincoln, the Union war effort needed to be seen as decisively gaining ground against the Confederates if Lincoln and the Republicans were to maintain power. Throughout 1864, Union armies stalled around Richmond, even though Grant proved much more willing to throw men at the problem than McClellan; the lack of results did not help the situation on the Northern home front. Things also went slowly with the effort to move through the Deep South and take Atlanta. Particularly with the aid of John Bell Hood, the Confederates resisted Sherman as best they could from Tennessee down into Georgia through the late summer of 1864. Sherman had to settle down for a siege of Atlanta, just as the presidential election of 1864 was going into the final stretch. In that election, Lincoln faced a formidable challenge from his onetime general, George McClellan. As a centerpiece of his campaign against Lincoln, McClellan threatened a negotiated settlement with the Confederacy if he won. Luckily for Lincoln and the Republicans, word arrived in September regarding Sherman's breakthrough outside Atlanta—he had finally worn down Hood, forcing him to flee Atlanta to save his army. Through the fall, Sherman then commenced his infamous "march to the sea," where he made it clear that railroads, farms, and other nonmilitary targets would be sought out and destroyed by his army. This was part of the broader Union struggle to wear down and destroy Confederate morale.

That morale remained hard to break. Although historians speak of the Southern food riots and of the complaints against the Confederate draft made by some segments of the populace, the reality was that by the end of the war boys as young as fourteen were found in the trenches of Virginia with no shoes on, choosing to fight against impossible odds. The war destroyed the Confederate economy: all of the wealth held in slaves was gone, and the cotton crop was badly damaged. Moreover, foreigners increasingly looked elsewhere for cotton in the years after 1865, which, in addition to an overall decline in the price of cotton, only furthered the decimation of the Southern economy. It has been said that the economy of the former Confederacy did not reach 1860 levels of output until the 1930s. Thus it is difficult to blame the Confederate home front or its leadership for the loss of the war. Instead, victory in the war rested with the determination of Union generals such as Sherman and Grant to keep their war machine together and maintain the allegiance of enough voters on their home front, so as to bludgeon the Confederacy into submission. The final act in the war came in Virginia, where Ulysses S. Grant had already sacrificed as many men to Lee as were in Lee's entire army. Then, with the siege of Petersburg, Grant's superiority in men reached something near two to one over his Confederate opponent. Lee's men soon desperately fled from both Petersburg and Richmond in the spring of 1865, pursued by Grant to a little town called Appomattox. It was there that Lee finally surrendered, on April 9. Jubilant crowds received the news throughout the North, but their jubilation turned to grief when, on April 14, a Confederate named John Wilkes Booth assassinated Lincoln with a pistol at point-blank range at Ford's Theater in Washington, while Lincoln and his wife watched a play.

In some sense, this tragic ending may have been a fitting one for a war that so ravaged many parts of the United States, but the Civil War cannot be seen entirely in tragic terms. The American Civil War took a tremendous toll on the white South—but for black slaves, by gaining their freedom they achieved more than many would have hoped. For the free states, although many families lost several relatives, the war itself would lay the foundations for the triumph of an industrial order, and Northerners could go back to the more typically American endeavors of moving west, building farms, speculating in businesses, experimenting with new technologies, or a combination of all of the above. Historians have also noted the involvement of women in various humanitarian organizations during the war, and how the trend toward increasing economic opportunities for women begun before the war continued after it ended (of course women's suffrage was still fifty years away). For many in the free states, within several decades the pain of war would at least seem to be a distant memory, which is amazing considering how many people were killed by the fighting. All told, over 600,000 people lost their lives as a direct result of the war, and hundreds of thousands of others were crippled or otherwise lost their health and well-being as a result of the conflict. In present-day terms, the number of people killed or wounded would equal well over seven million people. There has never been a war in U.S. history with such a high human cost.

Documents:

1. Senator Robert Toombs of Georgia, Speech Before Constituents (November 1860)

Toombs was speaking here to Georgians debating whether or not to secede from the Union. Toombs' comparison of the Confederate cause to that of the American patriots in 1775 is a telling one regarding the Confederate mind-set during the Civil War.

We are told that secession would destroy the fairest fabric of liberty the world ever saw, and that we are the most prosperous people in the world under it. The arguments I now hear in favor of this Northern connection are identical in substance, and almost in the same words as those which were used in 1775 and 1776 to sustain the British connection. We won liberty, sovereignty, and independence by the American Revolution—we endeavored to secure and perpetuate these blessings by means of our Constitution. The very men who use these arguments admit that this Constitution, this compact, is violated, broken and trampled underfoot by the abolition party. Shall we surrender the jewels because their robbers and incendiaries have the broken the casket? Is this the way to preserve liberty? ... We are said to be a happy and prosperous people. We have been, because we have hitherto maintained our ancient rights and liberties—we will be until we surrender them. They are in danger; come, freemen, to the rescue.

2. George McClellan, Letter to Abraham Lincoln (July 7, 1862)

Although a popular general with his troops (some would say because he did not put them into battle), McClellan exasperated Lincoln by not being particularly aggressive when fighting the Confederacy. McClellan's military strategy should be compared with that of William Tecumseh Sherman, excerpted late in the chapter. Within two years of being removed from his position, McClellan would be running against Lincoln for the presidency.

This rebellion has assumed the character of a War: as such it should be regarded; and it should be conducted upon the highest principles known to Christian Civilization. It should not be a War looking to the subjugation of the people of any state, in any event. It should not be, at all, a War upon population; but against armed forces and political organizations. Neither confiscation of property, political executions of persons, territorial organizations of states or forcible abolition of slavery should be contemplated for a moment. In prosecuting the War, all private property and unarmed persons should be strictly protected; subject only to the necessities of military operations. ... Military power should not be allowed to interfere with the relations of servitude, either by supporting or impairing the authority of the master; except for repressing disorder as in other cases.

3. "General Robert E. Lee Takes the Offensive" (September 1862)

McClellan's opponent, Lee was an exact opposite in terms of temperament and military thinking. Lee's daring may have been an asset early in the war, yet by 1863 many in the Confederacy were asking whether or not Lee had taken on too many risks when his army was nearly destroyed at Gettysburg.

The army is not properly equipped for an invasion of an enemy's territory. It lacks much of the material of war, is feeble in transportation … and the men are poorly provided with clothes. … Still we cannot afford to be idle, and though weaker than our opponents in men and military equipments, must endeavor to harass, if we cannot destroy them. I am aware that the movement is attended with much risk, yet I do not consider success impossible, and shall endeavor to guard it from loss. As long as the army of the enemy are employed on this frontier I have no ears for the safety of Richmond, yet I earnestly recommend that advantage be taken of this period of comparative safety to place its defence both by land and water, in the most perfect condition.

4. Clara Barton, Memoirs (1862)

Barton was one of the most high-profile female nurses among the thousands who aided soldiers on Civil War battlefields. She is best known for helping to organize the American Red Cross in 1881. Women played an important role in various efforts at civic and political reform during the Civil War, as well as after it.

I struggled long and hard with my sense of propriety [regarding women on the battlefield] … but when our armies fought on Cedar Mountain, I broke the shackles and went to the field. … I had not yet learned to equip myself, for I was no Pallas, ready armed, but grew into my work by hard thinking and sad experience. It may serve to relieve your apprehension for the future of my labors if I assure you that I was never caught so again.

But the most fearful scene was reserved for the night. I have said that ground was littered with dry hay and that we have only two lanterns, but there were plenty of candles. The wounded were laid so close that it was impossible to move about in the dark. The slightest misstep brought a torrent of groans from some poor mangled fellow in your path.

Consequently here were seen persons of all grades from the careful man of God who walked with a prayer upon his lips to the careless driver hunting for his lost whip—each wandering about among this hay with an open flaming candle in his hands.

The slightest accident, the mere dropping of a light could have enveloped in flames this whole mass of helpless men.

How we watched and pleaded and cautioned as we worked and wept that night! How we put socks and slippers upon their cold feet, wrapped your blankets and quilts about them, and when we no longer had these to give, how we covered them in the hay and left them to their rest! …

About three o'clock in the morning I observed a surgeon with a little flickering candle in hand approaching me with cautious step up in the wood. "Lady," he said as he drew near, "will you go with me? Out on the hills is a poor distressed lad, mortally wounded, and dying. His piteous cries for his sister have touched all our hearts none of us can relieve him but rather seems to distress him by our presence."

By this time I was following him back over the bloody track, with great beseeching eyes of anguish on every side looking up into their faces, saying so plainly, "Don't step on us."

5. "Abraham Lincoln Explains His Paramount Object of Saving the Union," August (1862)

Throughout the first two years of the Civil War, Lincoln was doing a balancing act between liberals and conservatives in the country who had radically different ideas regarding the role abolition should play in the war. Even though Lincoln became the "Great Emancipator," it is worth considering to what extent abolition was simply more of a war aim (in other words, a way to break the back of the white Confederacy) than it was a humanitarian gesture.

I would save the Union. I would save it the shortest way under the Constitution. The sooner the national authority can be restored; the nearer the Union will be 'the Union as it was.' If there be those who would not save the Union, unless they could at the same time save slavery, I do not agree with them. If there be those who would not save the Union unless they could at the same time destroy slavery. If I could save the Union without freeing any slavery I would do it, and if I could it be freeing all the slaves I would do it; and if I could save it by freeing some and leaving others alone I would also do that. What I do about slavery and the colored race, I do because I believe it helps to save the Union; and what I forbear, I forbear because I do not believe it would help to save the Union.

6. Abraham Lincoln, The Gettysburg Address (November 19, 1863)

After the awful carnage of Gettysburg (where Lee's army suffered a major defeat), Lincoln traveled to the town to dedicate the Soldiers National Cemetery. This address is widely regarded as one of the best-known speeches in American history; it must be one of the shortest ones to achieve such distinction.

Fourscore and seven years ago our fathers brought forth, on this continent, a new nation, conceived in Liberty, and dedicated to the proposition that all men are created equal.

Now we are engaged in a great civil war, testing, whether that nation, or any nation so conceived, and so dedicated, can long endure. We are met on a great battlefield of war. We have some to dedicate a portion of that field, as a final resting-place for those who here gave their lives, that that nation might live. It is altogether fitting and proper than we should do this.

But in a larger sense, we can not dedicate—we can not consecrate—we can not hallow this ground. The brave men, living and dead, who struggled here, have consecrated it far above our poor power to add or detract. The world will little note, nor long remember what we say here, but it can never forget what they did here. It is for us the living, rather, to be dedicated here to the unfinished work which they who fought here thus far so nobly advanced. It is rather for us to be here dedicated to the great task remaining before us—that from these honored dead we take increased devotion to that cause for which they here gave the last full measure of devotion—that we here highly resolve that these dead shall not have died in vain- that this nation, under God, shall have a new birth of freedom—and that government of the people, by the people, for the people, shall not perish from the earth.

7. James Henry Gooding to Abraham Lincoln (September 1863)

The following letter was one of hundreds sent to Lincoln from blacks in the military who were not satisfied with the roles they had been assigned or with the prevalent racism still extant in the military ranks. But the very fact that over 100,000 blacks participated in the Union war effort went a long way toward overturning racial stereotypes in the nineteenth century.

Now, the main question is, are we Soldiers, or are we Laborers? We are fully armed, and equipped, have done all the various duties pertaining to a Soldier's life, have conducted ourselves to the complete satisfaction of General Officers, who were, if anything, prejudiced against us, but now accord us all the encouragement and honors due us. ... The patient, trusting descendent of Africa's Clime have dyed the ground with blood, in defense of the Union, and Democracy. ... Now, your Excellency, we have done a Soldier's duty. Why can't we have a Soldier's pay? You caution the Rebel's chieftain, that the United States knows no distinction in her soldiers. She insists on having all her soldiers of whatever creed or color, to be treated according to the usages of War. Now if the United States exacts uniformity of treatment of her soldiers from the insurgents, would it not be well and consistent to set the example herself by paying all her soldiers alike?

8. Clement Vallandigham, Speech before the U.S. House (January 14, 1863)

Democratic congressman Vallandigham helped to lead the effort in the Union to demand a truce with the Confederacy. His views are a reminder of how divided Northerners were regarding whether or not to continue to fight against fellow Americans. Vallandigham and the Democrats also disliked the social revolution unleashed by emancipation.

[The people] have been deceived; instead of crushing out the rebellion, the effort has been to crush out the spirit of liberty. The conspiracy of those in power is not so much for a vigorous prosecution of the war against rebels in the South as against the democracy in peace at home. Now, if in possession of the purse and the sword absolutely and unqualifiedly for two years, there be anything else wanting which describes a dictatorship [in President Lincoln's government], I beg to know what it is ... I will not consent to put the entire purse of the country and the sword of the country into the hands of the executive, giving him despotic and dictatorial power to carry out an object which I avow before my countrymen is the destruction of their liberties and the overthrow of the Union of these states. The charge has been made against us—all who are opposed to the policy of this administration and opposed to this war—that we are for "peace on any terms." It is false. I am not, but I am for an immediate stopping of the war and for honorable peace. I am for peace for the sake of the Union of these states. ...

9. William Tecumseh Sherman to James M. Calhoun (September 1864)

This letter was written just before General Sherman moved in on Atlanta, Georgia, and began his infamous "march to the sea," where Sherman carried out his threat to bring the Civil War to the Southern home front (even though the viciousness of his campaign would be dramatically overstated by Southern whites in the years to come).

You cannot qualify war in harsher terms than I will. War is cruelty, and you cannot refine it; and those who brought war into our country deserve all the curses and maledictions a people can pour out. I know that I had no hand in making this war, and I know I will make more sacrifices to-day than any of you to secure peace. But you cannot have peace and a division of our country. If the United States submits to a division now, it will not stop, but will go on until we reap the fate of Mexico, which is eternal war. The United States does and must assert its authority, wherever it once had power, for, if it relaxes one bit to pressure, it is gone, and I believe that such is the national feeling. … You might as well appeal against the thunder-storm as against these terrible hardships of war. They are inevitable, and the only way the people of Atlanta can hope once more to live in peace and quiet at home, is to stop the war, which can only be done by admitting that it began in error and is perpetuated in pride. …

10. Abraham Lincoln, Second Inaugural Address (1865)

This speech is famous for the conciliatory tone struck toward the Confederacy. An important issue to consider is how conciliatory Northern whites would be after Lincoln was assassinated by a Confederate sympathizer.

On the occasion corresponding to this four years ago, all thoughts were anxiously directed to an impending civil-war. All dreaded it—all sought to avert it. While the inaugural address was being delivered from this place, devoted altogether to saving the Union without war, insurgent agents were in the city seeking to destroy it without war … One eighth of the whole population were colored slaves, not distributed generally over the Union, but localized in the Southern part of it. These slaves constituted a peculiar and powerful interest. All knew that this interest was, somehow, the cause of the war … Neither party expected for the war, the magnitude, or the duration, which it has already attained. … Each side looked for an easy triumph. Both read the same Bible, and pray to the same God; and each invokes His aid against the other. … If we suppose that American slavery is one of those offenses which, in the providence must needs come, but which having continued through His appointed time, He now wills to remove … shall we discern therein any departure from those divine attributes which the believers in a Living God always ascribe to Him? Fondly we hope—fervently we pray—that this mighty scourge of war may speedily pass away. Yet, if God will that it continue, until all the wealth piled up by the bond-man's two-hundred and fifty years of unrequited toil shall be sunk, and until every drop of blood drawn with the lash, shall be paid by another drawn with the sword, as was said three thousand years ago, so still it must be said "the judgments of the Lord, are true and righteous altogether."

With malice towards none; with charity for all; with firmness in the right, as God gives us to see the right, let us strive on to finish the work we are in; to bind up the nation's wounds; to care for him who shall have borne the battle, and for his widow, and his orphan—to do all which may achieve and cherish a just, and a lasting peace, among ourselves, and with all nations.

11. Sidney Andrews, *The South Since the War: As Shown by Fourteen Weeks of Travel and Observation in Georgia and the Carolinas* (1866)

Although the damage done by Union general Sherman may have been overstated, there was no overstating the reality that the South was ruined after the Civil War, though in many ways this was due to the ineptitude and stubbornness of its leadership.

The "Shermanizing process," as an ex-Rebel colonel jocosely called it, has been complete everywhere. To simply say that the people hate that officer is to put a fact in very mild terms. … Certain bent rails are the first thing one sees to indicate the advent of his army. … "It passes my comprehension to tell what became of our railroads," said a travelling acquaintance; "one week we have passably good roads, on which we could reach almost any part of the State, and the next week they were all gone—not simply broken up, but gone; some of the material was burned, I know, but miles or iron have actually disappeared, gone out of existence." …

There is a great scarcity of stock of all kinds. What was left by the Rebel conscription officers was freely appropriated by Sherman's army, and the people really find considerable difficulty not less in living than in travelling. Milk, formerly an article, much in use, can only be had now in limited quantities; even at hotels we have more meals without than with it. There are more miles than horses, apparently; and the animals, whether mules or horses, are all in ill condition and give evidence of severe overwork. …

Columbia [South Carolina] was once the gem of the state. … It is now a wilderness of ruins. Its heart is but a mass of blackened chimneys and crumbling walls … Every public building was destroyed, except the new and unfinished state-house. … The poverty of this people is so deep that there is no probability that it can be finished, according to the original design, during this generation at least. … The ruin here is neither half so eloquent nor touching as that at Charlestown. This is but the work of flame … Those ghostly and crumbling walls and those long-deserted and grass-grown streets show the prostration of a community—such prostration as only war could bring. …

A man of much apparent intelligence informed me that the negroes have an organized military force in all sections of the State, and are almost certain to rise and massacre the whites about Christmas time.

Another had heard, and sincerely believed, that General Grant's brother-in-law is an Indian, and is on his staff, and that the President has issued an order permitting the general's son to marry a mulatto girl whom he found in Virginia. … The people of the central part of the State are poor, wretchedly poor, for the war not only swept away their livestock and the material resources of their plantations, but also all values—all money, stocks, and bonds—and generally left nothing that be sold for money but cotton, and only a small proportion of the landholders have any of that. …

Questions to Consider:
1. What does it mean that the Civil War was won on the Northern home front? Is this statement true, in your opinion?
2. The Civil War has been referred to as a second American Revolution. What does this mean, and is it true?

3. Many historians note that the decision made by Lincoln to emancipate the slaves did not arise entirely from humanitarian motives. Are they correct? Were there conflicting motives working on Lincoln as he decided to make abolition a war aim in late 1862?

Credits

★ CHAPTER 15
★ AMERICA'S UNFINISHED REVOLUTION:
★ RECONSTRUCTION IN THE SOUTH, 1865–1877

The question of how to readmit, or "reconstruct," the Southern states back into the Union confronted Union politicians during the Civil War itself. Before his successful reelection in 1864 and while his armies were grinding their way through the South, President Lincoln sought a conciliatory tone with the Confederacy with his so-called Ten Percent Plan. This plan offered readmission to Southern states if 10 percent of the population (excluding only the very highest former Confederates) pledged an oath of loyalty to the United States. Although the 13th Amendment finally banning slavery would not be passed until early 1865, Southern whites presumably would have had to agree to this measure as part of their loyalty oath under Lincoln's plan. Lincoln advanced his plan in 1864 because he feared a protracted guerrilla war to reclaim the Confederacy. But already in 1864, Lincoln ran into a brick wall of opposition from members of his own party, referred to as the "radicals." Led by men such as Thaddeus Stevens and Charles Sumner, the radicals put forth what was called the Wade-Davis Bill, which looked to treat the Confederacy as though it were in "the grasp of war." In other words, Southern society needed to be purged and transformed: Most Confederate officers (with the exception of lieutenants) and civil officials would be barred from voting, and a majority of white males (not merely 10 percent) had to pledge an "iron-clad oath" to the U.S. government. The Republican radicals in Congress also implied they had other ideas regarding black landownership, education, and voting rights—as well as higher taxes—which would not sit well with white Southerners (and also many conservatives in the North). Before Lincoln's death, Congress also created what would be called the Freedmen's Bureau to provide numerous services to former slaves, ranging from supplying relief goods, to education for blacks, to fighting for their rights as laborers. This bureau represented another large expansion of federal authority over aspects of Southern life, and once again signals the potential radicalism of the Congressional Republican agenda.

Before the death of Lincoln, it was unclear how the radicals would get their agenda through Congress. However, as it turned out, the assassination of Abraham Lincoln changed things—one could perversely say—in favor of the radicals' agenda. This is because Lincoln was not only killed by a Confederate sympathizer (John Wilkes Booth), but his vice president, Andrew Johnson, was a Southerner placed on the ticket to appeal to moderate Democrats in the 1864 election. Although Johnson remained loyal to the Union during the war and he hated the Southern planter class, he nonetheless revealed himself to share in the racism of Southern whites. Johnson therefore ended up extending even easier terms of readmission than proposed by Lincoln, because Johnson was prevailed upon by wealthier whites in his home state to give out large, blanket pardons to men who then quickly formed conservative state governments between Lincoln's assassination in April 1865 and the return of Congress in December of that year. These Johnson governments were not really new in any sense of the word, and they did not represent "reconstructed" states in the sense understood by most Northerners. Because Johnson was essentially a Democrat, he allowed this more lenient course of action to occur in order to position himself against the radical Republicans in the elections of 1866 and 1868. But he overreached. When Congress returned in 1865, several high-ranking Confederates (including former vice president Alexander Stephens) were returned to seats in the House and Senate, incensing most Northerners. And the state governments in the former Confederacy allowed by Johnson often simply revised the old slave codes to now apply to freed blacks, leaving many Northerners asking whether slavery had in fact been abolished or not. Republicans successfully used these facts to paint Johnson as a neo-Confederate, and this gave them the momentum they needed to drastically revise Reconstruction policy to make it consonant with the "grasp of war" theory.

Thus "Congressional Reconstruction" was born during 1866, once it became clear that Johnson would not work with Republicans in Congress, and once it was clear that Southern whites had little intention of ending racial injustice toward blacks. The Republicans began by devising the 14th Amendment to the Constitution, which explicitly prohibited states from abridging their citizens' "privileges and immunities." In other words, the amendment tried to make clear that states could not violate black people's civil rights. (As we will see, this idea would be undermined quickly in the years ahead.) The rest of the radicals' plan would have to wait for midterm Congressional elections in November 1866, but in those elections the Republicans swamped the Democrats. This was largely due to Johnson's antagonistic style on the campaign trail, in addition to the perception in the North that Johnson and the Democrats were sympathetic to the values of secession. Emboldened by a victory they saw as a mandate for black civil rights, the Republicans passed the First Reconstruction Act of 1867, which placed the former Confederacy under military rule by Union generals until the Southern states ratified the 14th Amendment. Because the Union military supervised the elections, African Americans were allowed to vote; this resulted in many black politicians being sent to Southern state capitals, as well as to Washington, D.C. Back at home, many of the state constitutions ratified under the influence of Republican government approved higher taxes for public education and also possessed some of the most liberal laws in the nation on the treatment of debtors. But the whole situation of racial progress, it seemed, depended on the threat of Union military intervention, as was obvious to most observers, including President Johnson. Throughout 1867 and 1868, Johnson tried to issue orders to generals to be lenient in enforcing civil rights acts, or to encourage Confederates to vote, in open violation of laws passed by Congress. Johnson's actions tempted Congress to try to impeach and remove him. Johnson also took aim at Secretary of War Stanton, and tried to fire him. This action only hurried the Congressional effort to remove Johnson. The House impeached Johnson in 1868, but in the resulting trial in the Senate, enough members of the Senate walked away from the measure out of fear of a popular backlash.

Indeed, by the election of 1868, growing numbers of Northerners began to grow skeptical regarding the use of troops to ensure that blacks could vote in the former Confederacy. Additionally, the radicals in Congress advanced an agenda supporting a far greater degree of racial

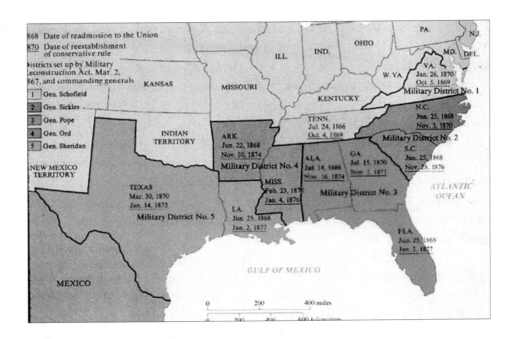

This map depicts the military districts mandated by radical Republicans in 1866, the dates of readmission to the Union, as well as of the re-establishment of conservative, Democratic rule.

equality in the South than most white Americans desired. On this last point, it became clear by 1868 that several of the most radical Republicans favored giving land owned by white landowners to blacks for free, as an attempt to make up for the tremendous injustice of slavery. Thaddeus Stevens believed that economic redistribution was badly needed to help blacks make use of their civil rights. But most Americans—even in the North—saw this as a direct attack on the private property of whites, plus many Americans feared a protracted race war with bitter whites trying violently to take back their land which had been given away. In the failure of land redistribution, historians can discern the fundamental caution animating even many Republicans in the mid-1860s. They would support the writing of new laws that theoretically gave blacks their freedom, but most Republicans would do little else in terms of concrete, material help for African Americans. As stated above, radical Reconstruction received support from whites in the North more out of a sense of "putting Confederates in their place" than out of a general concern for revolutionizing the status of blacks in the United States overall. It must be remembered that even many Northern states in the late 1860s maintained laws forbidding or curtailing black voting rights, for example, in addition to possessing varying degrees of segregation in housing and transportation.

Although Ulysses S. Grant kept the White House in the Republican ledger in the election of 1868, the tide was already turning against any effort at radically reorienting the nature of white supremacy in the former Confederacy. For one, white landowners in the South formed a new white terrorist organization, called the Ku Klux Klan, as a way of intimidating and, if need be, murdering blacks and their allies during Reconstruction. In general, this plan worked at maintaining a state of war in the South that would grind down black voting, as well as choke off black civic leadership more generally in the former Confederacy. Given what has been said above regarding the tenuous nature of Northern white commitment to a revolution in race relations, it would not take much violence to make Northerners want to stop supporting policies they were already inclined to see as futile. After all, there were more whites than blacks in the South, and many Northern whites began to wonder whether it was possible to continue to advance black rights "at the point of a bayonet," to paraphrase many observers. So, even as Congress passed and the states approved the 15th Amendment to the Constitution in 1869—which forbade using race as a grounds for limiting the right to vote—in many ways those who favored black civil rights were already losing their battle. It should also be noted that the language used in the 15th Amendment did not specifically say that black men could vote; thus, it was sufficiently vague and porous that it could be ignored once the Northern military left the South alone to do so.

As the 1870s dawned, a new force of reaction spread throughout the country aimed at ending "bayonet rule" in the former Confederacy. Even when Congress tried to enforce civil rights laws against Klan violence, they found that Southern juries would not convict Klansmen. Would this mean that the federal government would have to be perpetually involved in hunting down members of the Klan? What would this say about the relationship of the federal government to the states? Many Americans viewed the radical Republican agenda as completely obliterating state sovereignty, which they would not tolerate in their own states. Therefore, Northern whites increasingly viewed the escalating violence in the South as the fault of radicals, and not the racists. A good example can be seen in the terrorism that overtook Louisiana in 1873 and 1874. In that state, the so-called "White League" decided to start murdering Republican officials, including militia general James Longstreet (an ex-Confederate now working for the federal government). In the elections of 1874, the canvassing boards could not agree on the polling results, since federal troops were not able to stop the intimidation of blacks in all areas, thus resulting in a Democratic "victory." And when the Democrats managed to swear in a speaker of the Louisiana House of Representatives, the Republicans used the military support of General Philip Sheridan to expel five of the Democratic members of the assembly used to maintain Democratic rule. Although a compromise was later effected, the damage had been done: Carl Schurz, a moderate Republican, summed it up when he questioned, "How long before a soldier will stalk into the national House of Representatives and pointing to the Speakers mace, say, Take away that bauble!" The fact that increasing numbers of Republicans abandoned Reconstruction was not only because of their fear of protracted violence, but also because in the aftermath of the massive global banking panic of 1873 (often likened by historians to the Great Depression in the twentieth century), few Republicans wanted to expend more resources on the South. Increasingly, many Northern politicians claimed that the Republican governments in the South had been wasteful and inefficient. They disliked government intervention in the affairs of men, and wanted to rein in any revolutionary tendencies in American civil polity (whether in terms of white workers or ex-slaves.)

Northerners increasingly felt that their version of democracy was incompatible with continued support for legislative or military efforts to give black people rights in the South. For its part, the Supreme Court also increasingly agreed with those who sought to control the more radical implications of Reconstruction—though in so doing, the Court in many ways gave legal sanction to the nullification of black civil rights in the South. In the Slaughterhouse Cases

(1873), the court used a case of a company's monopoly on livestock slaughtering to maintain that the framers of the 14th Amendment had not intended to do away with the distinction between the states and the federal government, and that only such narrow things as the right of free travel were in fact supported by the 14th Amendment as a "national" right. (This appears to be a direct rejection of the spirit of the amendment, but so goes Supreme Court politics.) A similar conclusion was drawn in the Cruikshank case in 1876, which responded to a challenge from convicted whites charged with violating black civil rights in Louisiana. According to the Supreme Court, state courts, not federal, possessed sole responsibility for the protection of individual rights. Often enough, the Supreme Court would claim that intimidation, theft, or murder of blacks differed in no way from similar crimes against non-blacks, and therefore blacks did not warrant special federal attention. But in many ways, the Supreme Court's conservatism merely reflected a public mood in the North looking to forget about the war, the South, and arguably, about the former slaves themselves. This can be seen most clearly in the presidential election of 1876, where the Democrats won a majority of the popular vote, but did not win in the Electoral College, because Democrats and Republicans could not agree on the vote totals in Louisiana, South Carolina, and Florida. These disagreements stemmed from recurring complaints regarding either voter fraud or intimidation of blacks, depending on the viewpoint. Although most troops had been removed from the South by 1876, there were several thousand soldiers still there, many in the regions which produced the disputed results. Therefore, as a part of the compromise drawn up by the electoral commission chosen by Congress, the Republican Rutherford B. Hayes would win the presidential election (since the Republicans held the majority in Congress, that meant that one more Republican was on the board). But there would be a final end to any federal military presence in the South for the purpose of guaranteeing black civil rights. In addition, Southern railroads received special federal funds, as part of other money directed toward white Southerners. With the troops now gone, and with the Republicans scolded for their views on race in the former Confederacy, Reconstruction was over.

In this situation, African Americans faced an uncertain future. On the one hand, freedom enabled black families to reunite and for once-separated partners to be legally married. With the demise of slavery, blacks could also move away from the old plantation and perhaps try their luck somewhere else in the country, or move to the West. Further, a minority now owned land either in the South or elsewhere in the country. For another small minority of African Americans, military service might also prove a means toward economic advancement. Similarly, the various abolitionist-led schools could pluck young students like Booker T. Washington (who founded Tuskegee Institute) or George Washington Carver (a noted scientist and botanist) out of obscurity and into meaningful careers. Both men demonstrated that it was possible for former slaves to rise into the ranks of the middle class, but the challenges were daunting, and these men were the exceptions that proved the rule about the material poverty of former slaves in the former Confederacy. Most freed slaves became sharecroppers, which meant that they could live on land in many cases owned by their former masters, in exchange for a part of the crop produced. But most sharecroppers fell into debt, were taken advantage of by white-owned stores that sold supplies at exorbitant rates, or were otherwise subject to the vicious and insidious racism of a white South trying to reimpose culturally the economic power lost in the process of emancipation. Some of the most disgusting manifestations of Jim Crow white supremacy can be seen in the rash of lynchings of black males (who were usually innocent of any crime), besides other systemic abuses of black laborers, such as the convict leasing system. In this system, black "criminals" were essentially worked to death building various aspects of the supposedly "New South," so often trumpeted as embracing the elements of the modern industrial world.

Documents:

1. "Richard Henry Dana Presents His Grasp of War Theory" (June 1865)

This prominent Republican lawyer laid out early on a succinct description of radical Republican philosophy as it related to the former Confederacy. But Dana also revealed the constitutional limitations of any Reconstruction in an American federal system that valued some degree of individual state autonomy.

We have a right to require, my friends, that the freedmen of the South shall have the right to hold land ... We have a right to require that they shall be allowed to testify in courts ... We have a right to demand that they shall bear arms as soldiers in the militia. ... We have a right to demand that there shall be an impartial ballot. ...

The conqueror must choose between two courses—to permit the political institutions, the body politic, to go on, and treat with it, or obliterate it. We have destroyed and obliterated their central government. Its existence was treason. [But] we mean to say the states shall remain, with new constitutions, new systems. We do not mean to exercise civil jurisdiction over them in our Congress. Fellow citizens, it is not merely out of tenderness to them; it would be the most dangerous possible course for us. Our system is a planetary system; each planet revolving round its orbit ... this system is held together by a balance of powers ... let not that balance be destroyed. ... Our system is a system of states, with central power; and in that system is our safety. State rights, I maintain [support]; State sovereignty we have destroyed.

2. Thaddeus Stevens, Speech before the House *(January 1867)

Congressman Stevens was one of the most radical of the radical Republicans in the House of Representatives. He died not more than a year after this speech, and was therefore not present in Congress to continue fighting for black civil rights in the 1870s.

It is to be regretted that inconsiderate Republicans should ever have supposed that the slight amendments in the Fourteenth Amendment ... would satisfy the reforms necessary for the security of the Government. Unless the rebel states, before admission, should be made republican in spirit, and placed under the guardianship of loyal men, all our blood and treasure will have been spent in vain. ... Impartial suffrage, both in electing the delegates and ratifying their proceedings, is now the fixed rule. ... In the Southern states [black men] form the great mass of the loyal men. Possibly with their aid loyal governments may established in most of those States. Without it all are sure to be ruled by traitors; and loyal men, black and white, will be oppressed, exiled, and murdered. There are several good reasons for the passage of this bill [ensuring black men the right to vote]. In the first place, it is just. I am now confining my argument to negro suffrage in the rebel States. Have not loyal blacks quite as good a right to choose rulers and make laws as rebel whites? In the second place, it is a necessity in order to protect the loyal white men in the seceded States. The white Union men are in a great minority in each of those States [but with black suffrage] … it would ensure the ascendancy of the Union party. Do you support the party purpose?—Exclaims some horror stricken demagogue. I do. For I believe, on my conscience, that on the continued ascendancy of that party depends the safety of this great nation. If impartial suffrage is excluded in rebel States then every one of them is sure to send a solid rebel representative delegation to Congress, and cast a solid rebel electoral vote. They with their kindred Copperheads in the North will always elect the President and control Congress. … Now you must divide them … or you will be the perpetual vassals of the free trade, irritated, revengeful South. For these, among other reasons, I am for negro suffrage in every rebel State. If it be just, it should not be denied; if it be necessary is should be adopted; if it be punishment to traitors, they deserve it.

But it will be said, as it has been said, "this is negro equality!" What is negro equality, about which so much is said by knaves. … it means as understood by honest Republicans, just this much, and no more: every man, no matter what his race or color; every earthly being who has an immortal soul, has an equal right to justice, honesty, and fair play with every other man; and the law should secure him those rights.

3. Andrew Johnson, Third Annual Message (December 1867)

As president, Johnson detested the radical Republicans, but consistently lost in his attempts to curtail their power in Washington.

It is manifestly and avowedly the object of these laws to confer upon negroes the privilege of voting and to disfranchise such a number of white citizens as will give the former a clear majority at all elections in the Southern states. This, to the minds, of some persons, is so important that a violation of the Constitution is justified as a means of bringing it about. The morality is always false which excuses a wrong because it proposes to accomplish a desirable end. We are not permitted to do evil that good may come. But in this case the end itself is evil, as well as the means. The subjugation of the States to negro domination would be worse than the military despotism under which they are now suffering. It was believed beforehand the people would endure any amount of military oppression for any length of time rather than degrade themselves by subjection to the negro race. Therefore, they have been left without a choice. Negro suffrage was established by an act of Congress, and the military officers were commanded to superintend the process of clothing the negro race with the political privileges torn from the white man. … If it were practicable at this time to give them [blacks] a government of their own, under which they might manage their own affairs in their own way, it would become a grave question whether we ought to do so, or whether common humanity would not require us to save them from themselves. … It is not proposed, however, merely that they shall govern themselves, but that they shall rule the white race, make and administer State laws, elect Presidents and members of Congress and shape to a greater or less extent the future destiny of the whole country. Would such a trust and power be safe in such hands?

4. Elizabeth Cady Stanton, "Who Are Our Friends?" (1868)

With passage of the 15th Amendment looming, many Northern women's rights activists began to quibble with the fact that there was no language in the proposed amendment forbidding withholding the right to vote from women. The disappointment felt by women such as Stanton did not help radical Republicans in their future efforts to gain further support for radical Reconstruction.

To what a depth of degradation must the women of this nation have fallen to be willing to stand aside, silent and indifferent spectators in the reconstruction of the nation, while all the lower stratas of manhood are to legislate in their interests, political, religious, educational, social, and sanitary, moulding to their untutored will the institutions of a mighty continent. … Charles Sumner, Horace Greeley, Gerrit Smith and Wendell Phillips, with one consent bid women of the nation stand aside and behold the salvation of the negro. Wendell Phillips says, "one idea for a generation," to come up in the order of their importance. First negro suffrage, then temperance, then the eight hour movement, then women's suffrage … What an insult to the women who have labored thirty years for the emancipation of the slave, now when he is their political equal, to propose to lift him above their heads. Gerrit Smith, forgetting that our great American idea is "individual rights" … says this is the time to settle the rights of races; unless we do justice to the negro we shall bring down on ourselves another bloody revolution, another four years' war, but we have nothing to fear from woman, she will not avenge herself!

5. Testimony of Elias Hill Before Congress Regarding Ku Klux Klan Violence (1871)

To its credit, Congress did try to clamp down on Klan violence in the 1870s, and publicized the plight of Southern blacks such as Hill by holding hearings on the rampant white terrorism in the former Confederacy.

On the night of the 5th of last May, after I had heard a great deal of what they had done nearby, they came. It was between 12 and 1 o'clock at night when I was awakened. … Then I knew they would take me. … Then one man said: Here he is! Here he is! We have found him! And he threw the bedclothes off me and caught me by one arm, while another man took me by the other and they carried me into the yard between the houses, my brothers' and mine … [they then asked] "when did you hold a night-meeting of the Union league, and who were the officers? Who was the President?" I told them I had been the president, but that there had been no Union League meeting held at that place where they were formerly held. … Haven't you been preaching political sermons [they said]. … They went on asking me hadn't I been writing to Mr. A.S. Wallace, in Congress, to get letters from him. I told them I had. They asked what I had been writing about? … you were writing something about the Ku Klux and wasn't that what Mr. Wallace was writing to me about." "Not at all," I said. …

[Then] I said I would rather live; that I hoped they would not kill me that time. … One said "G-d damn it, hush!" He had a horsewhip, and he told me to pull up my shirt, and he hit me … I made a moan every time he cut with the horsewhip. …one [then said] not to kill me. They said, "Look here! Will you put a card in the paper next week like June Moore and Sol Hill?" They had been prevailed upon to put a card in the paper to renounce all republicanism and never to vote. I said, "if I had the money to pay the expense, I could." They said I could borrow, and gave me another lick … They said I must stop it [preaching]. …

[This man later left the community and investigated going to Liberia, in Africa.]

6. Carl Schurz, Speech in the Senate (January 1872)

As with many more libertarian-minded Republicans, Schurz had begun to tire of federal interventions in the former Confederacy. His views are important as a gauge of Northern exhaustion with Reconstruction, and go a long way toward explaining why Reconstruction failed.

[T]he stubborn fact remains that they [Southern blacks and officeholders] were ignorant and inexperienced; that the public business was an unknown world to them, and that in spite of the best intentions they were easily misled, not infrequently by the most reckless rascality that had found a way to their confidence. Thus their political rights and privileges were undoubtedly well calculated, and even necessary to protect their rights as free laborers and citizens; but they were not well calculated to secure a successful administration of other public interests. …

To the uneducated and inexperienced classes—uneducated and inexperienced, I repeat, entirely without their fault—we opened the road to power; and, at the same time, we condemned a large proportion of the intelligence of those States, of the property-holding, the industrial, the professional, the tax-paying interest, to a worse than passive attitude. We made it, as it were, easy for rascals who had gone South in quest of profitable adventure to gain the control of masses so easily misled, by permitting them to appear as the exponents and representatives of the National power and of our policy; and at the same time we branded a large number of the men of intelligence … as outcasts, telling them they ought not to be suffered to exercise any influence upon the management of public business, and that it would be unwarrantable presumption in them to attempt it.

7. James Sheppard Pike Offers a Liberal Republican View of Reconstruction (1873)

Pike's views are similar to those of Schurz. In this case, he refers to Reconstruction as a "foreign yoke," invoking the language of imperialism to condemn radical Republican policies.

[South Carolina] really bears a foreign yoke; not one imposed by its own people, or by an authority which has arisen of itself among themselves. And this is the anomaly of the situation. It is so-called democracy sustained by external force. In other words, it is a government that the intelligent public opinion of the State would overthrow if left to itself. It may be called self-government, or republican, or democratic government, but in no just sense is it either. … The only authority to which these miscreants [Reconstruction politicians] pay the least deference is the Federal government; for its power and its countenance are requisite to the success of many of their own operations … [The federal government] might do much toward repressing many corrupt practices and raising the moral tone of the State government. It has not done this. …

Why should the Republican Party ... be compelled to endure the foul stain inflicted by the robberies and outrages of these despicable wretches?

8. Representative Lucius Q. C. Lamar of Mississippi, Speech Before the House,1(874)

Lamar, an ex-Confederate who managed to win election to Congress in 1872, epitomized the reactionary turn being taken in the congressional elections in the South by the mid-1870s, once blacks had been effectively neutralized as a political force in the former Confederacy.

By persistent misrepresentation in Congress a majority came to believe that the presence of the United States Army would be necessary not merely to put these [Republican] governments in force. ... Thus with a quick, sudden, and violent hand, these men tore the two races asunder and hurled one in violent antagonism upon the other, and to this day the negro vote massed into an organization hostile to the whites is an instrument of absolute power in the hands of these men. These governments are in external form civil, but they are in their essential principle military. They are called local governments, but in reality they are Federal executive agencies. Not one of them emanates from the uncontrolled will of the people, white or black; not one which rests upon the elective principle in its purity. They have been aptly styled by a distinguished statesmen and jurist in Mississippi, State governments without States, without popular constituencies. For they are as completely insulated from the traditions, the feelings, the interests, and the free suffrages of the people, white and black, as if they were outside the limits of those States. ...

Questions to Consider:
1. Was Northern public opinion motivated simply by vindictiveness towards treasonous ex-Confederates during the process of reconstructing the South? What does this mean regarding the willingness of Northerners to defend black civil rights in the former Confederacy?
2. How did certain American ideals about private property, states' rights, and race limit the scope and power of Reconstruction's ability to overturn white supremacy in the South?
3. It has been said that former slaves possessed "nothing but freedom" when Reconstruction ended in 1877. What does this mean, and is it true? What were the range of economic, political, and social possibilities facing freed slaves in the 1870s and beyond?

Credits
- "The military districts mandated by radical Republicans in 1866."
- Richard Henry Dana, Jr., "Richard Henry Dana Presents His 'Grasp of War Theory'," *Speeches in Stirring Times and Letters to a Son*, pp. 250-259. 1910. Copyright in the Public Domain.
- Excerpt from Thaddeus Stevens, "Speech in the House, January 3, 1867," *The Congressional Globe, 39th Congress*, vol. 37, pp. 251-253. 1867. Copyright in the Public Domain.
- Excerpt from Andrew Johnson, Third Annual Message. 1867. Copyright in the Public Domain.
- Excerpt from Elizabeth Cady Stanton, "Who Are Our Friends?," *The Revolution, 15*. 1868. Copyright in the Public Domain.

- Elias Hill, "Elias Hill Testifies About the Ku Klux Klan Before a Congressional Committee." 1872. Copyright in the Public Domain.
- Excerpt from Carl Schurz, "Speech in the Senate, January 30, 1872," *Speeches, Correspondence and Poltical Papers of Carl Shurz*, ed. Frederic Bancroft, pp. 326-327. 1913. Copyright in the Public Domain.
- Excerpt from James S. Pike, "Chapter 11," *The Prostrate State: South Carolina Under Negro Government*, pp. 83-84. 1874. Copyright in the Public Domain.
- Excerpt from Lucius Q. C. Lamar, "Speech in the House, June 8, 1874," Congressional Record, 43rd Congress, vol. 2. 1874. Copyright in the Public Domain.
- "The Constitution of the United States of America." Copyright in the Public Domain.
- "U.S. Constitutional Amendments." Copyright in the Public Domain.

APPENDIX

THE CONSTITUTION OF THE UNITED STATES OF AMERICA

Article I —The Legislative Branch

Section 1— The Legislature

All legislative Powers herein granted shall be vested in a Congress of the United States, which shall consist of a Senate and House of Representatives.

Section 2—The House

The House of Representatives shall be composed of Members chosen every second Year by the People of the several States, and the Electors in each State shall have the Qualifications requisite for Electors of the most numerous Branch of the State Legislature.

No Person shall be a Representative who shall not have attained to the Age of twenty five Years, and been seven Years a Citizen of the United States, and who shall not, when elected, be an Inhabitant of that State in which he shall be chosen.

(Representatives and direct Taxes shall be apportioned among the several States which may be included within this Union, according to their respective Numbers, which shall be determined by adding to the whole Number of free Persons, including those bound to Service for a Term of Years, and excluding Indians not taxed, three fifths of all other Persons.) **(The previous sentence in parentheses was modified by the 14th Amendment, Section 2.)** The actual Enumeration shall be made within three Years after the first Meeting of the Congress of the United States,

and within every subsequent Term of ten Years, in such Manner as they shall by Law direct. The Number of Representatives shall not exceed one for every thirty Thousand, but each State shall have at Least one Representative; and until such enumeration shall be made, the State of New Hampshire shall be entitled to chuse three, Massachusetts eight, Rhode Island and Providence Plantations one, Connecticut five, New York six, New Jersey four, Pennsylvania eight, Delaware one, Maryland six, Virginia ten, North Carolina five, South Carolina five and Georgia three.

When vacancies happen in the Representation from any State, the Executive Authority thereof shall issue Writs of Election to fill such Vacancies.

The House of Representatives shall chuse their Speaker and other Officers; and shall have the sole Power of Impeachment.

Section 3—The Senate

The Senate of the United States shall be composed of two Senators from each State, *(chosen by the Legislature thereof)*. **(The preceding words in parentheses superseded by the 17th Amendment, Section 1)** for six Years; and each Senator shall have one Vote.

Immediately after they shall be assembled in Consequence of the first Election, they shall be divided as equally as may be into three Classes. The Seats of the Senators of the first Class shall be vacated at the Expiration of the second Year, of the second Class at the Expiration of the fourth Year, and of the third Class at the Expiration of the sixth Year, so that one third may be chosen every second Year; *(and if Vacancies happen by Resignation, or otherwise, during the Recess of the Legislature of any State, the Executive thereof may make temporary Appointments until the next Meeting of the Legislature, which shall then fill such Vacancies.)* **(The preceding words in parentheses were superseded by the 17th Amendment, Section 2.)**

No person shall be a Senator who shall not have attained to the Age of thirty Years, and been nine Years a Citizen of the United States, and who shall not, when elected, be an Inhabitant of that State for which he shall be chosen.

The Vice President of the United States shall be President of the Senate, but shall have no Vote, unless they be equally divided.

The Senate shall chuse their other Officers, and also a President pro tempore, in the absence of the Vice President, or when he shall exercise the Office of President of the United States.

The Senate shall have the sole Power to try all Impeachments. When sitting for that Purpose, they shall be on Oath or Affirmation. When the President of the United States is tried, the Chief Justice shall preside: And no Person shall be convicted without the Concurrence of two thirds of the Members present.

Judgment in Cases of Impeachment shall not extend further than to removal from Office, and disqualification to hold and enjoy any Office of honor, Trust or Profit under the United States: but the Party convicted shall nevertheless be liable and subject to Indictment, Trial, Judgment and Punishment, according to Law.

Section 4—Elections, Meetings

The Times, Places and Manner of holding Elections for Senators and Representatives, shall be prescribed in each State by the Legislature thereof; but the Congress may at any time by Law make or alter such Regulations, except as to the Place of Chusing Senators.

The Congress shall assemble at least once in every Year, and such Meeting shall *(be on the first Monday in December,)* **(The preceding words in parentheses were superseded by the 20th Amendment, Section 2)** unless they shall by Law appoint a different Day.

Section 5—Membership, Rules, Journals, Adjournment

Each House shall be the Judge of the Elections, Returns and Qualifications of its own Members, and a Majority of each shall constitute a Quorum to do Business; but a smaller number may adjourn from day to day, and may be authorized to compel the Attendance of absent Members, in such Manner, and under such Penalties as each House may provide.

Each House may determine the Rules of its Proceedings, punish its Members for disorderly Behavior, and, with the Concurrence of two-thirds, expel a Member.

Each House shall keep a Journal of its Proceedings, and from time to time publish the same, excepting such Parts as may in their Judgment require Secrecy; and the Yeas and Nays of the Members of either House on any question shall, at the Desire of one fifth of those Present, be entered on the Journal.

Neither House, during the Session of Congress, shall, without the Consent of the other, adjourn for more than three days, nor to any other Place than that in which the two Houses shall be sitting.

Section 6—Compensation

(The Senators and Representatives shall receive a Compensation for their Services, to be ascertained by Law, and paid out of the Treasury of the United States.) **(The preceding words in parentheses were modified by the 27th Amendment.)** They shall in all Cases, except Treason, Felony and Breach of the Peace, be privileged from Arrest during their Attendance at the Session of their respective Houses, and in going to and returning from the same; and for any Speech or Debate in either House, they shall not be questioned in any other Place.

No Senator or Representative shall, during the Time for which he was elected, be appointed to any civil Office under the Authority of the United States which shall have been created, or the Emoluments whereof shall have been increased during such time; and no Person holding any Office under the United States, shall be a Member of either House during his Continuance in Office.

Section 7— Revenue Bills, Legislative Process, Presidential Veto

All bills for raising Revenue shall originate in the House of Representatives; but the Senate may propose or concur with Amendments as on other Bills.

Every Bill which shall have passed the House of Representatives and the Senate, shall, before it become a Law, be presented to the President of the United States; If he approve he shall sign it, but if not he shall return it, with his Objections to that House in which it shall have originated, who shall enter the Objections at large on their Journal, and proceed to reconsider it. If after such Reconsideration two thirds of that House shall agree to pass the Bill, it shall be sent, together with the Objections, to the other House, by which it shall likewise be reconsidered, and if approved by two thirds of that House, it shall become a Law. But in all such Cases the Votes of both Houses shall be determined by Yeas and Nays, and the Names of the Persons voting for and against the Bill shall be entered on the Journal of each House respectively. If any Bill shall not be returned by the President within ten Days (Sundays excepted) after it shall have been presented to him, the Same shall be a Law, in like Manner as if he had signed it, unless the Congress by their Adjournment prevent its Return, in which Case it shall not be a Law.

Every Order, Resolution, or Vote to which the Concurrence of the Senate and House of Representatives may be necessary (except on a question of Adjournment) shall be presented to the President of the United States; and before the Same shall take Effect, shall be approved by him, or being disapproved by him, shall be repassed by two thirds of the Senate and House of Representatives, according to the Rules and Limitations prescribed in the Case of a Bill.

Section 8—Powers of Congress

The Congress shall have Power to lay and collect Taxes, Duties, Imposts and Excises, to pay the Debts and provide for the common Defence and general Welfare of the United States; but all Duties, Imposts and Excises shall be uniform throughout the United States;

To borrow money on the credit of the United States;

To regulate Commerce with foreign Nations, and among the several States, and with the Indian Tribes;

To establish an uniform Rule of Naturalization, and uniform Laws on the subject of Bankruptcies throughout the United States;

To coin Money, regulate the Value thereof, and of foreign Coin, and fix the Standard of Weights and Measures;

To provide for the Punishment of counterfeiting the Securities and current Coin of the United States;

To establish Post Offices and Post Roads;

To promote the Progress of Science and useful Arts, by securing for limited Times to Authors and Inventors the exclusive Right to their respective Writings and Discoveries;

To constitute Tribunals inferior to the supreme Court;

To define and punish Piracies and Felonies committed on the high Seas, and Offenses against the Law of Nations;

To declare War, grant Letters of Marque and Reprisal, and make Rules concerning Captures on Land and Water;

To raise and support Armies, but no Appropriation of Money to that Use shall be for a longer Term than two Years;

To provide and maintain a Navy;

To make Rules for the Government and Regulation of the land and naval Forces;

To provide for calling forth the Militia to execute the Laws of the Union, suppress Insurrections and repel Invasions;

To provide for organizing, arming, and disciplining, the Militia, and for governing such Part of them as may be employed in the Service of the United States, reserving to the States respectively, the Appointment of the Officers, and the Authority of training the Militia according to the discipline prescribed by Congress;

To exercise exclusive Legislation in all Cases whatsoever, over such District (not exceeding ten Miles square) as may, by Cession of particular States, and the acceptance of Congress, become the Seat of the Government of the United States, and to exercise like Authority over all Places purchased by the Consent of the Legislature of the State in which the Same shall be, for the Erection of Forts, Magazines, Arsenals, Dock-Yards, and other needful Buildings; And

To make all Laws which shall be necessary and proper for carrying into Execution the foregoing Powers, and all other Powers vested by this Constitution in the Government of the United States, or in any Department or Officer thereof.

Section 9—Limits on Congress

The Migration or Importation of such Persons as any of the States now existing shall think proper to admit, shall not be prohibited by the Congress prior to the Year one thousand eight hundred and eight, but a tax or duty may be imposed on such Importation, not exceeding ten dollars for each Person.

The privilege of the Writ of Habeas Corpus shall not be suspended, unless when in Cases of Rebellion or Invasion the public Safety may require it.

No Bill of Attainder or ex post facto Law shall be passed.

(No capitation, or other direct, Tax shall be laid, unless in Proportion to the Census or Enumeration herein before directed to be taken.) (Section in parentheses clarified by the 16th Amendment.)

No Tax or Duty shall be laid on Articles exported from any State.

No Preference shall be given by any Regulation of Commerce or Revenue to the Ports of one State over those of another: nor shall Vessels bound to, or from, one State, be obliged to enter, clear, or pay Duties in another.

No Money shall be drawn from the Treasury, but in Consequence of Appropriations made by Law; and a regular Statement and Account of the Receipts and Expenditures of all public Money shall be published from time to time.

No Title of Nobility shall be granted by the United States: And no Person holding any Office of Profit or Trust under them, shall, without the Consent of the Congress, accept of any present, Emolument, Office, or Title, of any kind whatever, from any King, Prince or foreign State.

Section 10—Powers Prohibited of States

No State shall enter into any Treaty, Alliance, or Confederation; grant Letters of Marque and Reprisal; coin Money; emit Bills of Credit; make any Thing but gold and silver Coin a Tender in Payment of Debts; pass any Bill of Attainder, ex post facto Law, or Law impairing the Obligation of Contracts, or grant any Title of Nobility.

No State shall, without the Consent of the Congress, lay any Imposts or Duties on Imports or Exports, except what may be absolutely necessary for executing it's inspection Laws: and the net Produce of all Duties and Imposts, laid by any State on Imports or Exports, shall be for the Use of the Treasury of the United States; and all such Laws shall be subject to the Revision and Controul of the Congress.

No State shall, without the Consent of Congress, lay any duty of Tonnage, keep Troops, or Ships of War in time of Peace, enter into any Agreement or Compact with another State, or with a foreign Power, or engage in War, unless actually invaded, or in such imminent Danger as will not admit of delay.

Article II—The Executive Branch

Section 1—The President

The executive Power shall be vested in a President of the United States of America. He shall hold his Office during the Term of four Years, and, together with the Vice-President chosen for the same Term, be elected, as follows:

Each State shall appoint, in such Manner as the Legislature thereof may direct, a Number of Electors, equal to the whole Number of Senators and Representatives to which the State may be entitled in the Congress: but no Senator or Representative, or Person holding an Office of Trust or Profit under the United States, shall be appointed an Elector.

(The Electors shall meet in their respective States, and vote by Ballot for two persons, of whom one at least shall not lie an Inhabitant of the same State with themselves. And they shall make a List of all the Persons voted for, and of the Number of Votes for each; which List they shall sign and certify, and transmit sealed to the Seat of the Government of the United States, directed to the President of the Senate. The President of the Senate shall, in the Presence of the Senate and House of Representatives, open all the Certificates, and the Votes shall then be counted. The Person having the greatest Number of Votes shall be the President, if such Number be a Majority of the whole Number of Electors appointed; and if there be more than one who have such Majority, and have an equal Number of Votes, then the House of Representatives shall immediately chuse by Ballot one of them for President; and if no Person have a Majority, then from the five highest on the List the said House shall in like Manner chuse the President. But in chusing the President, the Votes shall be taken by States, the Representation from each State having one Vote; a quorum for this Purpose shall consist of a Member or Members from two-thirds of the States, and a Majority of all the States shall be necessary to a Choice. In every Case, after the Choice of the President, the Person having the greatest Number of Votes of the Electors shall be the Vice President. But if there should remain two or more who have equal Votes, the Senate shall chuse from them by Ballot the Vice-President.) **(This clause in parentheses was superseded by the 12th Amendment.)**

The Congress may determine the Time of chusing the Electors, and the Day on which they shall give their Votes; which Day shall be the same throughout the United States.

No person except a natural born Citizen, or a Citizen of the United States, at the time of the Adoption of this Constitution, shall be eligible to the Office of President; neither shall any Person be eligible to that Office who shall not have attained to the Age of thirty-five Years, and been fourteen Years a Resident within the United States.

(In Case of the Removal of the President from Office, or of his Death, Resignation, or Inability to discharge the Powers and Duties of the said Office, the same shall devolve on the Vice President, and the Congress may by Law provide for the Case of Removal, Death, Resignation or Inability, both of the President and Vice President, declaring what Officer shall then act as President, and such Officer shall act accordingly, until the Disability be removed, or a President shall be elected.) **(This clause in parentheses has been modified by the 20th and 25th Amendments.)**

The President shall, at stated Times, receive for his Services, a Compensation, which shall neither be increased nor diminished during the Period for which he shall have been elected, and he shall not receive within that Period any other Emolument from the United States, or any of them.

Before he enter on the Execution of his Office, he shall take the following Oath or Affirmation:

"I do solemnly swear (or affirm) that I will faithfully execute the Office of President of the United States, and will to the best of my Ability, preserve, protect and defend the Constitution of the United States."

Section 2—Civilian Power over Military, Cabinet, Pardon Power, Appointments

The President shall be Commander in Chief of the Army and Navy of the United States, and of the Militia of the several States, when called into the actual Service of the United States; he may require the Opinion, in writing, of the principal Officer in each of the executive Departments, upon any subject relating to the Duties of their respective Offices, and he shall have Power to Grant Reprieves and Pardons for Offenses against the United States, except in Cases of Impeachment.

He shall have Power, by and with the Advice and Consent of the Senate, to make Treaties, provided two thirds of the Senators present concur; and he shall nominate, and by and with the Advice and Consent of the Senate, shall appoint Ambassadors, other public Ministers and Consuls, Judges of the supreme Court, and all other Officers of the United States, whose Appointments are not herein otherwise provided for, and which shall be established by Law: but the Congress may by Law vest the Appointment of such inferior Officers, as they think proper, in the President alone, in the Courts of Law, or in the Heads of Departments.

The President shall have Power to fill up all Vacancies that may happen during the Recess of the Senate, by granting Commissions which shall expire at the End of their next Session.

Section 3—State of the Union, Convening Congress

He shall from time to time give to the Congress Information of the State of the Union, and recommend to their Consideration such Measures as he shall judge necessary and expedient; he may, on extraordinary Occasions, convene both Houses, or either of them, and in Case of

Disagreement between them, with Respect to the Time of Adjournment, he may adjourn them to such Time as he shall think proper; he shall receive Ambassadors and other public Ministers; he shall take Care that the Laws be faithfully executed, and shall Commission all the Officers of the United States.

Section 4—Disqualification

The President, Vice President and all civil Officers of the United States, shall be removed from Office on Impeachment for, and Conviction of, Treason, Bribery, or other high Crimes and Misdemeanors.

Article III—The Judicial Branch

Section 1—Judicial powers

The judicial Power of the United States, shall be vested in one supreme Court, and in such inferior Courts as the Congress may from time to time ordain and establish. The Judges, both of the supreme and inferior Courts, shall hold their Offices during good Behavior, and shall, at stated Times, receive for their Services a Compensation which shall not be diminished during their Continuance in Office.

Section 2—Trial by Jury, Original Jurisdiction, Jury Trials

(The judicial Power shall extend to all Cases, in Law and Equity, arising under this Constitution, the Laws of the United States, and Treaties made, or which shall be made, under their Authority; to all Cases affecting Ambassadors, other public Ministers and Consuls; to all Cases of admiralty and maritime Jurisdiction; to Controversies to which the United States shall be a Party; to Controversies between two or more States; between a State and Citizens of another State; between Citizens of different States; between Citizens of the same State claiming Lands under Grants of different States, and between a State, or the Citizens thereof, and foreign States, Citizens or Subjects.) **(This section in parentheses is modified by the 11th Amendment.)**

In all Cases affecting Ambassadors, other public Ministers and Consuls, and those in which a State shall be Party, the supreme Court shall have original Jurisdiction. In all the other Cases before mentioned, the supreme Court shall have appellate Jurisdiction, both as to Law and Fact, with such Exceptions, and under such Regulations as the Congress shall make.

The Trial of all Crimes, except in Cases of Impeachment, shall be by Jury; and such Trial shall be held in the State where the said Crimes shall have been committed; but when not committed within any State, the Trial shall be at such Place or Places as the Congress may by Law have directed.

Section 3—Treason

Treason against the United States, shall consist only in levying War against them, or in adhering to their Enemies, giving them Aid and Comfort. No Person shall be convicted of Treason unless on the Testimony of two Witnesses to the same overt Act, or on Confession in open Court.

The Congress shall have power to declare the Punishment of Treason, but no Attainder of Treason shall work Corruption of Blood, or Forfeiture except during the Life of the Person attainted.

Article IV—The States

Section 1—Each State to Honor All Others

Full Faith and Credit shall be given in each State to the public Acts, Records, and judicial Proceedings of every other State. And the Congress may by general Laws prescribe the Manner in which such Acts, Records and Proceedings shall be proved, and the Effect thereof.

Section 2—State Citizens, Extradition

The Citizens of each State shall be entitled to all Privileges and Immunities of Citizens in the several States.

A Person charged in any State with Treason, Felony, or other Crime, who shall flee from Justice, and be found in another State, shall on demand of the executive Authority of the State from which he fled, be delivered up, to be removed to the State having Jurisdiction of the Crime.

(No Person held to Service or Labour in one State, under the Laws thereof, escaping into another, shall, in Consequence of any Law or Regulation therein, be discharged from such Service or Labour, But shall be delivered up on Claim of the Party to whom such Service or Labour may be due.) (This clause in parentheses is superseded by the 13th Amendment.)

Section 3—New States

New States may be admitted by the Congress into this Union; but no new States shall be formed or erected within the Jurisdiction of any other State; nor any State be formed by the Junction of two or more States, or parts of States, without the Consent of the Legislatures of the States concerned as well as of the Congress.

The Congress shall have Power to dispose of and make all needful Rules and Regulations respecting the Territory or other Property belonging to the United States; and nothing in this

Constitution shall be so construed as to Prejudice any Claims of the United States, or of any particular State.

Section 4—Republican Government

The United States shall guarantee to every State in this Union a Republican Form of Government, and shall protect each of them against Invasion; and on Application of the Legislature, or of the Executive (when the Legislature cannot be convened) against domestic Violence.

Article V—Amendment

The Congress, whenever two thirds of both Houses shall deem it necessary, shall propose Amendments to this Constitution, or, on the Application of the Legislatures of two thirds of the several States, shall call a Convention for proposing Amendments, which, in either Case, shall be valid to all Intents and Purposes, as part of this Constitution, when ratified by the Legislatures of three fourths of the several States, or by Conventions in three fourths thereof, as the one or the other Mode of Ratification may be proposed by the Congress; Provided that no Amendment which may be made prior to the Year One thousand eight hundred and eight shall in any Manner affect the first and fourth Clauses in the Ninth Section of the first Article; and that no State, without its Consent, shall be deprived of its equal Suffrage in the Senate.

Article VI—Debts, Supremacy, Oaths

All Debts contracted and Engagements entered into, before the Adoption of this Constitution, shall be as valid against the United States under this Constitution, as under the Confederation.

This Constitution, and the Laws of the United States which shall be made in Pursuance thereof; and all Treaties made, or which shall be made, under the Authority of the United States, shall be the supreme Law of the Land; and the Judges in every State shall be bound thereby, any Thing in the Constitution or Laws of any State to the Contrary notwithstanding.

The Senators and Representatives before mentioned, and the Members of the several State Legislatures, and all executive and judicial Officers, both of the United States and of the several States, shall be bound by Oath or Affirmation, to support this Constitution; but no religious Test shall ever be required as a Qualification to any Office or public Trust under the United States.

Article VII—Ratification

The Ratification of the Conventions of nine States, shall be sufficient for the Establishment of this Constitution between the States so ratifying the Same.

Done in Convention by the Unanimous Consent of the States present the Seventeenth Day of September in the Year of our Lord one thousand seven hundred and Eighty seven and of the Independence of the United States of America the Twelfth. In Witness whereof We have hereunto subscribed our Names.

Geo Washington—President and deputy from Virginia

New Hampshire— John Langdon, Nicholas Gilman

Massachusetts—Nathaniel Gorham, Rufus King

Connecticut—Wm Saml Johnson, Roger Sherman

New York—Alexander Hamilton

New Jersey—Wil Livingston, David Brearley, Wm Paterson, Jona. Dayton

Pennsylvania—B Franklin, Thomas Mifflin, Robt Morris, Geo. Clymer, Thos FitzSimons, Jared Ingersoll, James Wilson, Gouv Morris

Delaware—Geo. Read, Gunning Bedford jun, John Dickinson, Richard Bassett, Jaco. Broom

Maryland—James McHenry, Dan of St Tho Jenifer, Danl Carroll

Virginia—John Blair, James Madison Jr.

North Carolina—Wm Blount, Richd Dobbs Spaight, Hu Williamson

South Carolina—J. Rutledge, Charles Cotesworth Pinckney, Charles Pinckney, Pierce Butler

Georgia—William Few, Abr Baldwin

Attest: William Jackson, Secretary

The Amendments

The following are the Amendments to the Constitution. The first ten Amendments collectively are commonly known as the Bill of Rights.

Amendment One—Freedom of Religion, Press, Expression. Ratified 12/15/1791.

Congress shall make no law respecting an establishment of religion, or prohibiting the free exercise thereof; or abridging the freedom of speech, or of the press; or the right of the people peaceably to assemble, and to petition the Government for a redress of grievance.

Amendment Two—Right to Bear Arms. Ratified 12/15/1791.

A well regulated Militia, being necessary to the security of a free State, the right of the people to keep and bear Arms, shall not be infringed.

Amendment Three—Quartering of Soldiers. Ratified 12/15/1791.

No Soldier shall, in time of peace be quartered in any house, without the consent of the Owner, nor in time of war, but in a manner to be prescribed by law.

Amendment Four—Search and Seizure. Ratified 12/15/1791.

The right of the people to be secure in their persons, houses, papers, and effects, against unreasonable searches and seizures, shall not be violated, and no Warrants shall issue, but upon probable cause, supported by Oath or affirmation, and particularly describing the place to be searched, and the persons or things to be seized.

Amendment Five—Trial and Punishment, Compensation for Takings. Ratified 12/15/1791.

No person shall be held to answer for a capital, or otherwise infamous crime, unless on a presentment or indictment of a Grand Jury, except in cases arising in the land or naval forces, or in the Militia, when in actual service in time of War or public danger; nor shall any person be subject for the same offense to be twice put in jeopardy of life or limb; nor shall be compelled in any criminal case to be a witness against himself, nor be deprived of life, liberty, or property, without due process of law; nor shall private property be taken for public use, without just compensation.

Amendment Six—Right to Speedy Trial, Confrontation of Witnesses. Ratified 12/15/1791.

In all criminal prosecutions, the accused shall enjoy the right to a speedy and public trial, by an impartial jury of the State and district wherein the crime shall have been committed, which district shall have been previously ascertained by law, and to be informed of the nature and cause of the accusation; to be confronted with the witnesses against him; to have compulsory process for obtaining witnesses in his favor, and to have the Assistance of Counsel for his defence.

Amendment Seven—Trial by Jury in Civil Cases. Ratified 12/15/1791.

In Suits at common law, where the value in controversy shall exceed twenty dollars, the right of trial by jury shall be preserved, and no fact tried by a jury, shall be otherwise re-examined in any Court of the United States, than according to the rules of the common law.

Amendment Eight—Cruel and Unusual Punishment. Ratified 12/15/1791.

Excessive bail shall not be required, nor excessive fines imposed, nor cruel and unusual punishments inflicted.

Amendment Nine—Construction of Constitution. Ratified 12/15/1791.

The enumeration in the Constitution, of certain rights, shall not be construed to deny or disparage others retained by the people.

Amendment Ten—Powers of the States and People. Ratified 12/15/1791.

The powers not delegated to the United States by the Constitution, nor prohibited by it to the States, are reserved to the States respectively, or to the people.

Amendment 11—Judicial Limits. Ratified 2/7/1795.

The Judicial power of the United States shall not be construed to extend to any suit in law or equity, commenced or prosecuted against one of the United States by Citizens of another State, or by Citizens or Subjects of any Foreign State.

Amendment 12—Choosing the President, Vice-President. Ratified 6/15/1804.

The Electors shall meet in their respective states, and vote by ballot for President and Vice-President, one of whom, at least, shall not be an inhabitant of the same state with themselves; they shall name in their ballots the person voted for as President, and in distinct ballots the person voted for as Vice-President, and they shall make distinct lists of all persons voted for as President, and of all persons voted for as Vice-President and of the number of votes for each, which lists they shall sign and certify, and transmit sealed to the seat of the government of the United States, directed to the President of the Senate;

The President of the Senate shall, in the presence of the Senate and House of Representatives, open all the certificates and the votes shall then be counted;

The person having the greatest Number of votes for President, shall be the President, if such number be a majority of the whole number of Electors appointed; and if no person have such majority, then from the persons having the highest numbers not exceeding three on the list of those voted for as President, the House of Representatives shall choose immediately, by ballot, the President. But in choosing the President, the votes shall be taken by states, the representation from each state having one vote; a quorum for this purpose shall consist of a member or members from two-thirds of the states, and a majority of all the states shall be necessary to a choice. And if the House of Representatives shall not choose a President whenever the right of choice shall devolve upon them, before the fourth day of March next following, then the Vice-President shall act as President, as in the case of the death or other constitutional disability of the President.

The person having the greatest number of votes as Vice-President, shall be the Vice-President, if such number be a majority of the whole number of Electors appointed, and if no person have a majority, then from the two highest numbers on the list, the Senate shall choose the Vice-President; a quorum for the purpose shall consist of two-thirds of the whole number of Senators, and a majority of the whole number shall be necessary to a choice. But no person constitutionally ineligible to the office of President shall be eligible to that of Vice-President of the United States.

Amendment 13—Slavery Abolished. Ratified 12/6/1865.

1. Neither slavery nor involuntary servitude, except as a punishment for crime whereof the party shall have been duly convicted, shall exist within the United States, or any place subject to their jurisdiction.

2. Congress shall have power to enforce this article by appropriate legislation.

Amendment 14—Citizenship Rights. Ratified 7/9/1868.

1. All persons born or naturalized in the United States, and subject to the jurisdiction thereof, are citizens of the United States and of the State wherein they reside. No State shall make or enforce any law which shall abridge the privileges or immunities of citizens of the United States; nor shall any State deprive any person of life, liberty, or property, without due process of law; nor deny to any person within its jurisdiction the equal protection of the laws.

2. Representatives shall be apportioned among the several States according to their respective numbers, counting the whole number of persons in each State, excluding Indians not taxed. But when the right to vote at any election for the choice of electors for President and Vice-President of the United States, Representatives in Congress, the Executive and Judicial officers of a State, or the members of the Legislature thereof, is denied to any of the male inhabitants of such State, being twenty-one years of age, and citizens of the United States, or in any way abridged, except for participation in rebellion, or other crime, the basis of representation therein shall be reduced in the proportion which the number of such male citizens shall bear to the whole number of male citizens twenty-one years of age in such State.

3. No person shall be a Senator or Representative in Congress, or elector of President and Vice President, or hold any office, civil or military, under the United States, or under any State, who, having previously taken an oath, as a member of Congress, or as an officer of the United States, or as a member of any State legislature, or as an executive or judicial officer of any State, to support the Constitution of the United States, shall have engaged in insurrection or rebellion against the same, or given aid or comfort to the enemies thereof. But Congress may by a vote of two-thirds of each House, remove such disability.

4. The validity of the public debt of the United States, authorized by law, including debts incurred for payment of pensions and bounties for services in suppressing insurrection or rebellion, shall not be questioned. But neither the United States nor any State shall assume or pay any debt or obligation incurred in aid of insurrection or rebellion against the United States, or any claim for the loss or emancipation of any slave; but all such debts, obligations and claims shall be held illegal and void.

5. The Congress shall have power to enforce, by appropriate legislation, the provisions of this article.

Amendment 15—Race No Bar to Vote. Ratified 2/3/1870.

1. The right of citizens of the United States to vote shall not be denied or abridged by the United States or by any State on account of race, color, or previous condition of servitude.

2. The Congress shall have power to enforce this article by appropriate legislation.

Amendment 16—Status of Income Tax Clarified. Ratified 2/3/1913.

The Congress shall have power to lay and collect taxes on incomes, from whatever source derived, without apportionment among the several States, and without regard to any census or enumeration.

Amendment 17—Senators Elected by Popular Vote. Ratified 4/8/1913.

The Senate of the United States shall be composed of two Senators from each State, elected by the people thereof, for six years; and each Senator shall have one vote. The electors in each State shall have the qualifications requisite for electors of the most numerous branch of the State legislatures.

When vacancies happen in the representation of any State in the Senate, the executive authority of such State shall issue writs of election to fill such vacancies: Provided, That the legislature of any State may empower the executive thereof to make temporary appointments until the people fill the vacancies by election as the legislature may direct.

This amendment shall not be so construed as to affect the election or term of any Senator chosen before it becomes valid as part of the Constitution.

Amendment 18—Liquor Abolished. Ratified 1/16/1919. Repealed by Amendment 21, 12/5/1933.

1. After one year from the ratification of this article the manufacture, sale, or transportation of intoxicating liquors within, the importation thereof into, or the exportation thereof from the United States and all territory subject to the jurisdiction thereof for beverage purposes is hereby prohibited.

2. The Congress and the several States shall have concurrent power to enforce this article by appropriate legislation.

3. This article shall be inoperative unless it shall have been ratified as an amendment to the Constitution by the legislatures of the several States, as provided in the Constitution, within seven years from the date of the submission hereof to the States by the Congress.

Amendment 19—Women's Suffrage. Ratified 8/18/1920.

The right of citizens of the United States to vote shall not be denied or abridged by the United States or by any State on account of sex.

Congress shall have power to enforce this article by appropriate legislation.

Amendment 20—Presidential, Congressional Terms. Ratified 1/23/1933.

1. The terms of the President and Vice President shall end at noon on the 20th day of January, and the terms of Senators and Representatives at noon on the 3d day of January, of the years in which such terms would have ended if this article had not been ratified; and the terms of their successors shall then begin.

2. The Congress shall assemble at least once in every year, and such meeting shall begin at noon on the 3d day of January, unless they shall by law appoint a different day.

3. If, at the time fixed for the beginning of the term of the President, the President elect shall have died, the Vice President elect shall become President. If a President shall not have been chosen before the time fixed for the beginning of his term, or if the President elect shall have failed to qualify, then the Vice President elect shall act as President until a President shall have qualified; and the Congress may by law provide for the case wherein neither a President elect nor a Vice President elect shall have qualified, declaring who shall then act as President, or the manner in which one who is to act shall be selected, and such person shall act accordingly until a President or Vice President shall have qualified.

4. The Congress may by law provide for the case of the death of any of the persons from whom the House of Representatives may choose a President whenever the right of choice shall have devolved upon them, and for the case of the death of any of the persons from whom the Senate may choose a Vice President whenever the right of choice shall have devolved upon them.

5. Sections 1 and 2 shall take effect on the 15th day of October following the ratification of this article.

6. This article shall be inoperative unless it shall have been ratified as an amendment to the Constitution by the legislatures of three-fourths of the several States within seven years from the date of its submission.

Amendment 21—Amendment 18 Repealed. Ratified 12/5/1933.

1. The eighteenth article of amendment to the Constitution of the United States is hereby repealed.

2. The transportation or importation into any State, Territory, or possession of the United States for delivery or use therein of intoxicating liquors, in violation of the laws thereof, is hereby prohibited.

3. The article shall be inoperative unless it shall have been ratified as an amendment to the Constitution by conventions in the several States, as provided in the Constitution, within seven years from the date of the submission hereof to the States by the Congress.

Amendment 22—Presidential Term Limits. Ratified 2/27/1951.

1. No person shall be elected to the office of the President more than twice, and no person who has held the office of President, or acted as President, for more than two years of a term to which some other person was elected President shall be elected to the office of the President more than once. But this Article shall not apply to any person holding the office of President, when this Article was proposed by the Congress, and shall not prevent any person who may be holding the office of President, or acting as President, during the term within which this Article becomes operative from holding the office of President or acting as President during the remainder of such term.

2. This article shall be inoperative unless it shall have been ratified as an amendment to the Constitution by the legislatures of three-fourths of the several States within seven years from the date of its submission to the States by the Congress.

Amendment 23—Presidential Vote for District of Columbia. Ratified 3/29/1961.

1. The District constituting the seat of Government of the United States shall appoint in such manner as the Congress may direct: A number of electors of President and Vice President equal to the whole number of Senators and Representatives in Congress to which the District would be entitled if it were a State, but in no event more than the least populous State; they shall be in addition to those appointed by the States, but they shall be considered, for the purposes of the election of President and Vice President, to be electors appointed by a State; and they shall meet in the District and perform such duties as provided by the twelfth article of amendment.

2. The Congress shall have power to enforce this article by appropriate legislation.

Amendment 24—Poll Tax Barred. Ratified 1/23/1964.

1. The right of citizens of the United States to vote in any primary or other election for President or Vice President, for electors for President or Vice President, or for Senator or Representative in Congress, shall not be denied or abridged by the United States or any State by reason of failure to pay any poll tax or other tax.

2. The Congress shall have power to enforce this article by appropriate legislation.

Amendment 25—Presidential Disability and Succession. Ratified 2/10/1967.

1. In case of the removal of the President from office or of his death or resignation, the Vice President shall become President.

2. Whenever there is a vacancy in the office of the Vice President, the President shall nominate a Vice President who shall take office upon confirmation by a majority vote of both Houses of Congress.

3. Whenever the President transmits to the President pro tempore of the Senate and the Speaker of the House of Representatives his written declaration that he is unable to discharge the powers and duties of his office, and until he transmits to them a written declaration to the contrary, such powers and duties shall be discharged by the Vice President as Acting President.

4. Whenever the Vice President and a majority of either the principal officers of the executive departments or of such other body as Congress may by law provide, transmit to the President pro tempore of the Senate and the Speaker of the House of Representatives their written declaration that the President is unable to discharge the powers and duties of his office, the Vice President shall immediately assume the powers and duties of the office as Acting President.

Thereafter, when the President transmits to the President pro tempore of the Senate and the Speaker of the House of Representatives his written declaration that no inability exists, he shall resume the powers and duties of his office unless the Vice President and a majority of either the principal officers of the executive department or of such other body as Congress may by law provide, transmit within four days to the President pro tempore of the Senate and the Speaker of the House of Representatives their written declaration that the President is unable to discharge the powers and duties of his office. Thereupon Congress shall decide the issue, assembling within forty eight hours for that purpose if not in session. If the Congress, within twenty one days after receipt of the latter written declaration, or, if Congress is not in session, within twenty one days after Congress is required to assemble, determines by two thirds vote of both Houses that the President is unable to discharge the powers and duties of his office, the Vice President shall continue to discharge the same as Acting President; otherwise, the President shall resume the powers and duties of his office.

Amendment 26—Voting Age Set to 18 Years. Ratified 7/1/1971.

1. The right of citizens of the United States, who are eighteen years of age or older, to vote shall not be denied or abridged by the United States or by any State on account of age.

2. The Congress shall have power to enforce this article by appropriate legislation.

Amendment 27—Limiting Congressional Pay Increases. Ratified 5/7/1992.

No law, varying the compensation for the services of the Senators and Representatives, shall take effect, until an election of Representatives shall have intervened.